D0783374

ONLY IN
EDINBURGH

Duncan J. D. Smith

ONLY IN
EDINBURGH

A Guide to Unique Locations,
Hidden Corners and Unusual Objects

Photographs by
Duncan J. D. Smith

**The
Urban
Explorer**

For my mother and my Scottish ancestors

"Edinburgh has been happily compared to a flag –
a thing of history, worn and stained with old deeds and great days,
and starred with burning names."

Alanson B. Haughton, US Ambassador to Britain (1863–1941)

Above: The Heart of Midlothian outside St. Giles' Cathedral on the High Street (Royal Mile)
(see no. 13)

Page 2: Russell Dempster's mural of Leith-born artist Sir Eduardo Paolozzi (1924–2005) on
Henderson Street (see nos. 50, 65 & 76)

Contents

APPENDICES

Introduction

> "It seems like a city built on precipices, a perilous city.
> Great roads rush down hill like rivers in spate.
> Great buildings rush up like rockets."
>
> G. K. Chesterton, *Illustrated London News*, 1905

Edinburgh, Scotland's capital since the 15th century, has long divided opinion. English author G. K. Chesterton (1874–1936)* was clearly taken by the city's striking volcanic geography and architectural modernism. Conversely Glaswegian journalist James Bone (1872–1962) alluded to something more sinister: "Below you lies Auld Reekie, blackened and dried, an immortal herring, 'smeeked' for hundreds of years and cured in the sun".

Like Robert Louis Stevenson's Dr. Jekyll, Edinburgh displays a split personality. This is hardly surprising when one considers the history of the place. In the words of UNESCO, which lists Edinburgh as one of its World Heritage Sites, it comprises "an old city dominated by a medieval fortress and a new neoclassical city, whose development from the 18th century onward exerted a far-reaching influence on European urban planning". It is the juxtaposition of these disparate areas that gives the city its unique character.

Spread out over a series of hills and valleys, Edinburgh has for centuries been at the heart of Scottish history. Dubbed the Athens of the North for its elegant architecture and central role in the Scottish Enlightenment, it is a seat of learning with a dark side. A beautiful city of vice and virtue, world famous for its literature, learning and festivals but with a violent past that includes war, witchcraft and bodysnatching.

This book is for both the carefree stroller and the city explorer. A few minutes' planning with a street map** will get the reader quickly off the beaten track and under the city's skin. This is the Edinburgh of secret gardens and haunted theatres, mysterious monuments and unexpected underworlds, industrial relics and unusual places of worship.

The journeys detailed represent the author's own odysseys through the city – from the Firth of Forth south to the Edinburgh City Bypass (A720) and from Corstorphine east to Craigmillar. The hundred or so locations described will enable readers to experience the treasures of Edinburgh old and new.

Many locations lie within the Old Town, Edinburgh's labyrinthine medieval heart. This area encompasses two formerly distinct *burghs* (towns licensed to trade), Edinburgh and the Canongate, connected by the Royal Mile and merged in 1856. Around 80 narrow 'closes' (alleys) branch off this busy thoroughfare, each containing towering 'lands' (tenement buildings), the whole, when seen from above, appearing like a herringbone. At its head is the rocky fastness of Edinburgh Castle, where the city's story began in the 12th century.

Immediately south of the Old Town is Southside, Edinburgh's first real suburb. The construction of George Square here in 1766 was the first major development *outside* the Old Town. It was also here in the 19th century that the University of Edinburgh expanded when it outgrew its original campus on South Bridge.

West of the Old Town is the West End, the city's cultural heart. Here can be found Edinburgh's oldest working cinema and swimming pool, as well as industrial-era features, including the Union Canal in Fountainbridge and Dean Village on the Water of Leith.

The architectural counterpoint to the Old Town is the Georgian New Town, which lies north of the Castle Rock. Laid out on a gridiron and designed to cultivate social stratification, this area includes gardens and galleries, writers' homes and elegant squares. To the east rises Calton Hill, with its extraordinary monument-topped acropolis.

Many equally intriguing locations await discovery in Edinburgh's suburbs. Comprising former villages absorbed into the metropolis, those to the north and west include the Port of Leith, now in the throes of reinvention, and pretty Cramond, with its Roman remains at the mouth of the River Almond. Also here are historic green spaces, including the Royal Botanic Garden and several important golf courses.

A final selection of locations is to be found in the city's south and east suburbs. These encompass Holyrood Park, with its palace and ruined abbey at the tail end of the Canongate, the wild delights of Arthur's Seat and Duddingston Loch, and the lost seaside resort of Portobello.

Whilst walking is undeniably the best way to explore Edinburgh, the suburbs are quickly accessed using the extensive Lothian Bus network and the new tramway out to Edinburgh Airport***.

Whether frequenting the café where *Harry Potter* was penned, taking a *Trainspotting* tour of Leith or unearthing the secrets of Gilmerton Cove, *Only in Edinburgh* will I hope encourage readers to set out on their own expedition through the Scottish capital. Happy Exploring!

Duncan J. D. Smith, Edinburgh & Vienna

---

* Dates given after the names of Scotland's rulers are regnal years.

** Recommended is the *Edinburgh A–Z Premier Map* published by the Geographer's A–Z Map Co. Ltd. Smartphone users will find postcodes at the start of each chapter.

*** Visit www.lothianbuses.com and www.travelinescotland.com.

1 Secrets of Edinburgh Castle

EH1 2NG (Old Town), Edinburgh Castle on Castlehill
Bus 23, 27, 41, 42, 67 to Victoria Street

The story of Edinburgh begins on the Castle Rock, where archaeologists have found evidence of human activity during the Bronze Age (972–830 BC). This makes it the longest continuously occupied site in Scotland. According to a Welsh epic poem, the Iron Age Votadini tribe had a hill fort here called *Din Eidyn*, whence the name Edinburgh is most likely derived. The first record of a royal castle, however, dates to the reign of David I (1124–1153). Attacked no less than 26 times thereafter – from the 14th century Wars of Scottish Independence to the Jacobite Rising of 1745 – it is on record as the most besieged castle in Britain. The most apt superlative for the castle these days is Scotland's most popular visitor attraction. Despite the crowds, however, especially in July and August, the old walls still retain some secrets.

The English art critic John Ruskin (1819–1900) described Edinburgh Castle as "simply the noblest in Scotland conveniently unapproachable by any creatures but seagulls". He was referring to the fact that it sits atop an extinct volcanic flue rendered near impregnable by subsequent glaciation. The movement of ice, however, left a ramp of softer sedimentary rock to the east along which the Old Town was subsequently laid out. It is up this ramp that visitors approach the castle today.

The first castle secret concerns the Gatehouse. Despite looking old, it only dates back to 1888 and is a decorative feature built when the castle's tourist potential was first being exploited. Even more recent is the tunnel to the right of it, added in the 1980s for military vehicles to enter the castle without disturbing the tourists. By contrast, the Portcullis Gate beyond is genuinely defensive. It was built in the wake of the Lang Siege of 1571–1573, during which the castle was held (and eventually surrendered) by the Catholic supporters of the exiled Mary, Queen of Scots (1542–1567) against the Protestant regency representing the infant James VI/I (1567–1625).

The gate gives access to the castle's Middle Ward, which contains a series of military buildings installed after the castle became a garrison in the early 18th century. These include a munitions depot (now the National War Museum) and the New Barracks (now a museum illustrating the history of Scotland's only cavalry regiment, the Royal Scots Dragoon Guards). Don't be surprised when the nearby One o'clock

Gun is fired. The tradition dating back to 1861 originally enabled ships in the Firth of Forth to set their maritime clocks accurately.

To discover the castle's best-kept secrets one must penetrate the castle's Upper Ward by means of the late 17th century Foog's Gate. The origin of this curious name is unknown but it might relate to the dense sea fogs, or *haars*, which sometimes envelop the city's highpoints.

First to be encountered is the tiny St. Margaret's Chapel on the left-hand side. Dating from around 1100, it was commissioned by David I as a royal chapel and named in honour of his Hungarian-born mother, who died in the castle in 1093. Since most of the medieval castle was destroyed during the Lang Siege, this rare survival is now considered the oldest intact building in Edinburgh.

On a rampart just beyond the chapel is the cannon *Mons Meg*, which fired a cannonball as far as what is now the Royal Botanic Garden to celebrate the marriage in 1558 of Mary, Queen of Scots to the French dauphin. On a ledge beneath the rampart is an easily-missed 19th century Cemetery for Soldiers' Dogs, where regimental mascots have been laid to rest since Victorian times.

Walk along the Forewall Battery now to reach the huge Half Moon Battery, which was completed in 1588 to protect the castle's main approach. During maintenance work here in 1912, the ruins of an earlier structure were revealed. This was David's Tower, the royal palace built for David II (1329–1371) in the late 14th century and destroyed by cannon fire during the Lang Siege. At the time it would have been the most prominent of at least five towers dominating Edinburgh's skyline. Today a narrow staircase leads down through the Battery to the enigmatic remains.

Now enter Crown Square and what is today the heart of the castle. Three buildings flanking the square each hold a secret. First is the Royal Palace built in the 15th century as the Stewart dynasty's official residence. In a small chamber here in 1566 Mary, Queen of Scots gave birth to a son, the future James VI. Or did she? It is recorded that the birth was difficult and an attendee attempted to transfer the queen's pain to a servant using magic. There is even a tenacious rumour that the baby was still-born and substituted with another (the tiny skeleton allegedly being sealed up in the castle walls wrapped in a shawl bearing the letter 'J'). Whilst this has now been debunked, there's no denying the chamber's magnificent painted ceiling undertaken for James' sole return visit from London in 1617. It is no secret of course that the Scottish Crown Jewels, known as the Honours of Scotland, are also displayed in the palace, together with the Stone of Scone on which the early monarchs of Scotland were crowned (captured by Edward I in 1296 and removed to West-minster Abbey, the stone was installed in the castle in 1996).

Next is the Great Hall completed in the early 16th century as the castle's main place of assembly. Despite being converted into a barracks in 1650 following Oliver Cromwell's seizure of the castle, the hall retains its original hammerbeam roof. The tiny barred window above the fireplace is a 'Laird's Lug', where the king could eavesdrop on conversation. In preparation for a visit by Mikhail Gorbachev to the castle in 1984, the window was blocked at the request of the KGB!

The third building in the square is the National War Memorial completed in 1927 in a reworked barrack block. The altar,

Edinburgh Castle seen from the Vennel, with the Half Moon Battery on the right

which occupies the highest point of the volcanic Castle Rock, supports a casket containing the names of Scottish soldiers killed in the First World War. High up in one of the stained glass windows by Douglas Strachan (1875–1950) is a horseman with a swastika on his cloak. But don't be alarmed: it dates from the time just prior to Nazi rule, when the swastika still retained its original meaning as an ancient symbol of good fortune.

One final secret lurks beneath Crown Square. The stone vaults constructed to level the ground here in the 15th century were used to hold military prisoners. The first to be incarcerated were French privateers captured after the outbreak of the Seven Years War (1756–1763). Others arrived during the American War of Independence (1775–1783), when privateers harried Leith, and during the Napoleonic Wars (1803–1815), including a five-year-old drummer boy captured at the Battle of Trafalgar. Their graffiti on the wooden cell doors, which includes an early version of the American flag, adds poignancy to the scene.

Other locations nearby: 2, 3, 4, 5, 6, 7, 8, 9

2   Witches, Warriors and Wells

EH1 2NG (Old Town), a selection of curiosities on the Esplanade
in front of Edinburgh Castle
Bus 23, 27, 41, 42, 67 to Victoria Street

In front of Edinburgh Castle is a broad paved area called the Esplanade. Laid out in 1753, it was originally a parade ground for resident troops. Those days are remembered each August when the boisterous Royal Edinburgh Military Tattoo is staged here (the name is a corruption of the Dutch "tap toe", a request issued in Flanders in the 18th century for tavern owners to turn off their ale taps so troops would turn in). When the Tattoo's grandstand is dismantled some interesting memorials can be found here.

On the right hand side immediately upon entry is a wall-mounted drinking fountain installed in 1912. Known as the Witches' Well, it recalls the 300 supposed witches who were strangled and burned hereabouts between 1492 and 1722. King James VI/I (1567–1625) fuelled popular paranoia about witches in his book *Daemonologie* (1597) claiming they had summoned a storm during his sea journey back to Scotland from Denmark. The fountain's ambiguous iconography, including a serpent (deadly yet also representative of Aesculapius, the god of medicine) and a foxglove (both a cure and a poison), serves as a reminder that not all witches were evil.

Between here and the top of the Esplanade are three traditional monuments. First is a granite cross commemorating Ensign Charles Ewart (1769–1846) of the North British Dragoons (more commonly known as the Scots Greys), who captured the eagle standard of the French 45th Regiment at Waterloo. Next is a statue of Frederick, Duke of York and Albany (1763–1827) holding a field marshal's baton as Commander of the British Army. Third is a Peterhead granite obelisk commemorating the men of the 72nd Duke of Albany's Own Highlanders, who died during the 1878–1880 campaign in Afghanistan.

Now peer over the railings onto Castle Bank below. Those with good eyesight will make out a rough-hewn grey granite stone. This is the Ramsingarde rune stone and it is older than the castle itself! Carved in Sweden in 1040 it was shipped to Edinburgh in 1787 by Sir Alexander Seton, who had trade links with a Stockholm merchant, and given to the Society of Antiquaries of Scotland. On one side are engraved the words "Ari engraved this stone in memory of Hialm his father. God help his soul."

The Witches' Fountain on the Esplanade

A plaque attached to the wall overlooking the nearby castle moat recalls the curious practice of territorial *sasine* (a Scots legal term for 'possession'). In order to encourage the colonisation of Nova Scotia, Charles I (1625–1649) sold 64 baronetcies as a means of raising funds. Each of these baronets then paid others to do the emigrating and colonising. In 1943 a sack of earth from the castle was sent to Nova Scotia to mark the tercentenary of the episode and a decade later the Premier of Nova Scotia deposited a handful of Nova Scotia earth into the moat and unveiled the plaque.

Returning to the entrance of the Esplanade, look up at gable end of the Contini Cannonball Restaurant and notice two rusted iron balls embedded in it. Some say they are cannonballs fired in 1745 by government troops from the castle towards the Palace of Holyroodhouse, when Bonnie Prince Charlie was in residence during the Jacobite Rebellion. More likely they were deliberately placed here by engineers to mark the precise height above sea level of the springs at Comiston seven miles to the south, which in the 17th century provided Edinburgh with its first piped supply of fresh water. The Castlehill Reservoir, which stood opposite on the site of the Tartan Weaving Mill, once fed ten Old Town wells, two of which can still be seen in the High Street.

Other locations nearby: 1, 3, 4, 5, 6, 7, 8, 9

3 Lady Short's Camera Obscura

EH1 2ND (Old Town), the Camera Obscura on Castlehill (Royal Mile)
Bus 23, 27, 41, 42, 67 to Mound Place or Victoria Street (note: the
last Camera Obscura presentation begins one hour before closing
and sometimes earlier in winter)

Outside the entrance to Edinburgh Castle stands a sturdy stone tower. Although it appears defensive in origin it is actually a converted tenement block. At the top is a small octagonal turret containing a *camera obscura*. Used to project a real-time panoramic image of the city onto a screen inside, it is Edinburgh's oldest purpose-built visitor attraction.

The convoluted story of the tower and its camera is always worth re-telling. It begins in 1777, when Leith optician Thomas Short (1711–1788) inherited a telescope made by his brother for the King of Denmark, who went mad and never accepted it. Thomas planned to install it in a custom-built observatory on Calton Hill but died before its completion (see no. 64). The telescope then passed out of the family until 1827, when Short's daughter Maria returning from abroad claimed it. Unable to sell it she instead made it the centrepiece of Short's Popular Observatory, which opened alongside the National Monument in 1835.

Despite its popularity, the observatory was closed in 1850 when Maria fell foul of the Town Council. She and her husband then relocated to Castlehill, where they purchased the former 17th century townhouse of the Ramsays of Dalhousie (Lairds of Cockpen), which had been converted into tenements in the 18th century. By adding two storeys they created Short's Observatory, Museum of Science and Art, which opened for business in 1853. The main attraction was the turret containing the *camera obscura*. A mirror on the roof reflected a 'live' outside image down through a lens and onto a round viewing table. This changed as the mirror was tilted and rotated, so that the whole city could be seen, with colour and perspective preserved.

The new observatory proved a great success until Maria's death in 1869. Her husband continued but his debts grew and in 1892 the observatory was taken over by the pioneering Scottish environmental town planner Sir Patrick Geddes (1854–1932) (see no. 5). Geddes used scientific methods to identify relationships between place, people and work. To enable the public to observe these relationships he reinvented the observatory as a sociological laboratory. Called the Outlook Tower he installed a series of geographical exhibits, which grew more specialised as the visitor ascended. The world came first on the ground floor, then Europe, Scotland and finally Edinburgh. The *camera obscura* at the top provided an opportunity for people to observe their own landscape and the interconnected units of society it contained. In this way Geddes encouraged visitors from all walks of life to learn about their city and to understand its place in the world. Not surprisingly he is credited with coining the phrase 'Think global, act local'.

Enjoying the view from the Camera Obscura on Castlehill

After Geddes died in 1932 the building was sold to a private owner. These days Geddes's and Short's contributions are recalled on the top floor, where the *camera obscura* still operates. Geddes said "The child's desire of seeing and hearing, touching and handling...are all true and healthy hungers, and it can hardly be too strongly insisted that good teaching begins neither with knowledge nor discipline, but through delight." To that end, the lower five floors now contain the World of Illusions, with an array of exciting hands-on exhibits, including a mirror maze and vortex tunnel.

Sandwiched between the Camera Obscura and Edinburgh Castle are two further attractions popular with visitors: the Scotch Whisky Experience at 354 Castlehill and the Tartan Weaving Mill & Exhibition at number 555. The whisky experience continues at the recently-opened Whiski Rooms at 4–7 North Bank Street (EH1), where tastings are available by appointment in an elegant suite of rooms overlooking The Mound (www.whiskirooms.co.uk).

Other locations nearby: 2, 4, 5, 6, 7, 8, 9, 10

4   A World Famous Festival

EH1 2NE (Old Town), the Hub on Castlehill
Bus 23, 27, 41, 42, 67 to Mound Place or Victoria Street

Edinburgh is one of the world's great festival cities. A dozen major annual events attract talent from over a third of the world's countries, with two and a half million visitors to appreciate them. The performances range from the traditional to the experimental. The venues vary, too, from theatres, cinemas and churches to gardens, cafés and even converted police boxes.

First to be founded was the Edinburgh International Festival, the result of a meeting in a London restaurant between Harvey Wood (1903–1977), the Scottish representative of the British Council, and the Austrian-born opera impresario Rudolf Bing (1902–1997). Keen to create "a flowering of the human spirit" in the wake of the horrors of the Second World War, the festival was inaugurated in 1947 and featured the Vienna Philharmonic Orchestra.

It would be wrong, however, to think this was the first ever festival in Edinburgh. An inscribed cornerstone at 84 Great King Street (EH3) records the involvement of a Polish musician, Felix Yaniewicz (1762–1848), in the first of three 19th century music festivals. Organised by

Theatrical masks adorn the Fringe headquarters on the High Street

a group of enterprising Edinburgh citizens, they were staged in 1815, 1819 and 1824, with all profits going to the town's poor.

Today the Edinburgh International Festival is spread over three weeks each August. A celebration of the finest classical music, theatre, opera and dance, it is orchestrated from its headquarters, the Hub on Castlehill (EH1). No ordinary office, the Hub occupies the former Tolbooth St. John's Church built in the 1840s as the Victoria Hall to house the General Assembly of the Church of Scotland. It became empty in 1979 after its congregation merged with Greyfriars Kirk.

The Victorian church architecture certainly lends grandeur to the activities conducted here but it is the modern flourishes that really catch the eye. It's worth calling by – the Café Hub is open all year round – just to witness the pulsating colour schemes now in place, including the boldest red staircase imaginable (see Front Cover). The 200 plaster sculptures by Edinburgh sculptor Jill Watson (b. 1957) represent past festival performances, with the names of important sponsors beneath (note the cheering audience at ceiling level). The Hub's main performance space is the cavernous hall on the first floor, which is painted red, purple and gold, with matching curtains. The offices themselves are in the attic beneath a series of huge, blue-painted roof trusses. Above them towers the neo-Gothic spire, which at 164 feet is the highest built structure in central Edinburgh.

Edinburgh's other festivals include the Fringe for performing arts, with its suitably zany headquarters at 180 High Street, as well as others dedicated to film, food, art, television, jazz, world music, and storytelling. Those wishing to escape the frenzy should try the Book Festival, the world's biggest, which takes place in the relative calm of New Town's Charlotte Square (EH2).

In recent decades, Edinburgh's festival spirit has been extended throughout the year by various theatres, clubs and cabarets. Chief amongst them is the Traverse at 10 Cambridge Street (EH1), a writers' theatre established in 1963.

The tiny roundabout in front of the Hub marks the former site of the medieval Butter Tron (from the Old French *tronel* or *troneau* meaning 'balance'), a public weigh house where butter and cheese were accurately weighed and sold. Rebuilt several times, it was finally demolished in 1822, when the road was widened for the visit of George IV (1820–1830). A Salt Tron was located farther down the Royal Mile outside the Tron Kirk, another abandoned Old Town church, which closed in 1952. Built in 1647, it originally served Presbyterians ousted from St. Giles' when that church became Episcopalian under Charles I (1625–1649).

Other locations nearby: 2, 3, 5, 6, 7, 8, 9, 10

5 By Living We Learn

EH1 2PG (Old Town), the Patrick Geddes Centre in Riddle's Court
at 322 Lawnmarket
Bus 23, 27, 41, 42, 67 to Mound Place or Victoria Street (note: the
Patrick Geddes Centre is scheduled to open in Summer 2017)

Trunk's Close at 55 High Street (EH1) is one of many alleys running off
the Royal Mile (see nos. 11 & 18). Part of what makes this one special is
Hope's Court garden, which contains a bust of the pioneering Scottish
environmental town planner, Sir Patrick Geddes (1854–1932). Despite
its modern makeover, the garden was originally one of over 70 created
by Geddes as a means of bringing light and nature into the gloomy Old
Town. The bust sits atop a beehive reflecting the importance of bees in
pollinating such gardens and the dissemination of Geddes' eco-friendly
ideas around the world.

Ballater-born Geddes was a man of diverse interests, whose con-
cern for how people lived led to pioneering work in the fields of urban
planning, conservation, education and social science. He spent half
his professional life in Edinburgh's Old Town, where between 1880
and 1900 he undertook an ambitious urban renewal programme. By
applying what he termed "conservative surgery", Geddes overhauled
the crumbling fabric of the Old Town while preserving its historic
character.

The creation of green spaces, where children could play and adults
could experience nature through gardening, was just one aspect of his
work (see no. 27). Geddes also renovated slum tenements, notably on
the Lawnmarket (EH1), including Brodie's Close, Lady Stair's Close,
Mylne's Court and James' Court, where Geddes lived so as to be near
his work. In 1887 he transformed a former slum at 1 Mound Place into
the world's first purpose-built student accommodation.

Riddle's Court, a former 16th century merchant's house at 322
Lawnmarket, is of particular interest to the Geddes story. Chiselled
over the entrance into the courtyard is Geddes' favourite motto, *Viv-
endo Discimus* (By Living We Learn). It recalls the fact that in the late
19th century he founded a university hall here, from where he ran
summer schools. Before him James VI/I (1567–1625) courted foreign
nobles to ensure his succession to the English crown and David Hume
wrote his seminal *History of England*.

With such history in mind (and some superb historic interiors
still intact) work began in 2014 to transform Riddle's Court into the

A Latin inscription marks the entrance to Riddle's Court

Patrick Geddes Centre. A superb restoration by the Scottish Historic Buildings Trust will see this become a world-class centre for learning, where Geddes' educational philosophy will continue to be espoused. The historic fabric has been adapted to make the building as versatile as possible, where everything from seminars and weddings to community and corporate events can be staged. This will help pay for the building's upkeep making it the sort of project that Geddes would have supported were he still alive.

With an eye on community development, Geddes also encouraged the return of the affluent and educated to the Old Town. This he achieved with Ramsay Garden at the top of the Royal Mile (EH1), an extraordinary turreted apartment block constructed around Ramsay Lodge, the octagonal former home of wigmaker-turned-poet Allan Ramsay the Elder (1684–1758) (see no. 13). Geddes was also responsible for the Outlook Tower on Castlehill, a visitor attraction containing geographical exhibits used to illustrate his famous "Think global, act local" philosophy (the tower today contains the Camera Obscura) (see no. 3).

When not in Edinburgh, Geddes was working abroad in India, Columbo and Haiti. With his son-in-law architect Sir Frank Mears (1880–1953), he also worked on several projects in the Middle East, including the drawing up of master plans for Jerusalem and Tel Aviv. Even in his later years the ever-busy Geddes managed to found the Collège des Écossais, an international teaching school in Montpellier.

Other locations nearby: 3, 4, 6, 7, 8, 9, 10, 35

6 The Land that Time Forgot

EH1 2NT (Old Town), Gladstone's Land at 477b Lawnmarket
(Royal Mile)
Bus 23, 27, 41, 42, 67 to Mound Place or Queen Victoria Street

"What a wonderful city Edinburgh is! What alternation of height and depth! A city looked at in the polish'd back of a Brobdignag Spoon, held lengthways, so enormously stretched-up are the houses!" With these excited words the English poet Samuel Taylor Coleridge (1772–1834) described the towering tenement buildings (or 'lands') of Edinburgh's Old Town, which together with the alleys ('closes') used to access them are the area's defining architectural features.

The Old Town's distinctive layout is a result of geology. Millions of years ago a volcanic flue pushed up through the surrounding sedimentary rocks (see no. 96). When this cooled it formed a hard dolerite plug, which not only resisted the scouring effects of subsequent glacial erosion but also shielded a tapering, steep-sided ramp of softer rock to the east, resulting in what geologists call a crag-and-tail formation. Edinburgh Castle, the oldest part of the city, was built on the crag: the Old Town was laid out along the tail.

The main thoroughfare of the Old Town was the *Kingis Hie Street* (today Castlehill, the Lawnmarket and the High Street), which was built along the ridge of the tail from the Castle down to the Netherbow Port. With building space at a premium, the architects could only build upwards resulting in lands up to 15 storeys high (see nos. 11 & 18). Before the well-to-do relocated to the New Town in the late 18th century, all classes lived here albeit on different floors: the wealthiest on the first floor, the professionals, merchants, and working class above, and the poorest in the cellars and the attics (see no. 53). The Old Town lands were some of the world's earliest high rise residences and for a while Edinburgh was the most densely populated place in Europe.

Many Old Town lands were destroyed during the Great Fire of Edinburgh in 1824 and subsequently redeveloped. A remarkable survival therefore is Gladstone's Land at 477b Lawnmarket (EH1). Built in the late 1500s, it is named after the merchant Thomas Gledstanes, who purchased the property in 1617. Like other property owners he increased the size of his building by replacing the original wooden façade with a new stone frontage in front of it.

By the 1930s Gladstone's Land was a slum scheduled for demolition.

Fortunately the National Trust for Scotland stepped in and restored the building to how it appeared in Gledstanes' day. The front of the building rises six storeys (and many more to the rear), with a forestair leading to the first floor and then a spiral turnpike. The windows are typically half closed with shutters. The arcade at ground level provided cover to pedestrians and livestock, and provided a luckenbooth (lockable retail premise) for a cloth merchant (see no. 13).

The gilded kite hanging outside is a play on the owner's name, 'Gled' being an old Scottish word for the bird.

Inside the building a series of recreated rooms include a grand bedroom, with its original painted decoration, the main living area known as the Green Room, and a more modest kitchen, with a servant's fold-out bed.

Gladstone's Land on the Lawnmarket is a rare survival

Lands were also built beyond the Netherbow Port in the Canongate *burgh* but never so densely. Three of them adorned with interesting house signs were restored in the 1950s, when much of the area was replaced with council housing. They are Morocco Land at number 267 (a sculpture of the Emperor of Morocco), Shoemakers' Land at 197 (a cordiner's knife and the crown of St. Crispin), and Bible Land at 187 (biblical quotations) (see no. 14).

Other locations nearby: 3, 4, 5, 7, 8, 9, 10, 11

7 Tellers of Tales

EH1 2PA (Old Town), the Writers' Museum in Lady Stair's Close off
the Lawnmarket
Bus 23, 27, 41, 42, 67 to Mound Place or Queen Victoria Street

When UNESCO made Edinburgh the world's first City of Literature in 2004 it was acknowledging glories both past and present. Hugely popular authors such as J. K. Rowling and Ian Rankin have helped put Edinburgh squarely on today's literary map. But their successes have built on the city's writers of old and none moreso than Sir Walter Scott (1771–1832), Robert Burns (1759–1796) and Robert Louis Stevenson (1850–1894). The Writers' Museum in Lady Stair's Close (EH1) celebrates the life and works of all three.

Lady Stair's Close can be accessed either from the Lawnmarket or North Bank Street. Either way it's a surprise to emerge suddenly in front of Lady Stair's House, which contains the museum. The sturdy building is named after Elizabeth Dalrymple, Dowager Countess of Stair, who bought the building in 1719. It was built by her grandfather, the merchant Sir William Gray of Pittendrum, in 1622 and its restoration in the 1890s for use as a museum returned it to its original appearance. Rendered in the Scottish Baronial style inspired by medieval castles, its entrance and spiral staircase are inside a corner turret.

Although neither Burns, Scott nor Stevenson had any direct links with the house, Burns lived in nearby Baxter's Close on his arrival in Edinburgh in 1786, and both Scott and Stevenson were born in the city. Burns is celebrated in the rooms on the ground floor, where his likeness is rendered in various media, as is that of his wife, Jean Armour, whose tiny gloves are displayed in one of the cabinets. Also here can be seen his desk, his swordstick from his time as an excise officer, and the chair he used whilst correcting proofs at William Smellie's printing office in Anchor Close (EH1).

The first floor rooms are devoted to Scott. Amongst the items displayed here are his walking stick and cap, wallet, chess set, and extravagant meerschaum pipe. Also here is the rocking horse he rode as a child growing up at 25 George Street (EH2). It is touching to see that the foot rests are set at different heights because of the polio he suffered. There is also the dining table from his home at 39 North Castle Street (EH2), where he lived in the 1790s. In an upstairs room can be seen a reconstruction of the Canongate printing press, on which his famous *Waverley* novels were printed by James Ballantyne (1772–1833).

The Writer's Museum celebrates the lives of three literary giants

The basement rooms, which are reached by descending the spiral staircase from the entrance, deal with Stevenson. Here can be found the fishing rod, pipe, riding boots and hat he used while living in Samoa, as well as the tortoiseshell ring he was wearing when he died there (it is inscribed *Tusitala* meaning 'teller of tales'). Also on display is his wardrobe made by the infamous Deacon Brodie, whose double life inspired Stevenson's *Strange Case of Dr. Jekyll and Mr. Hyde* (1886) reflecting the light and shade in Edinburgh society at the time (see no. 91).

Lady Stair's Close also contains Makars' Court, which is paved with flagstones inscribed with literary quotations. They range from the 14th century (John Barbour's "A! Fredome is a noble thing") to more recent times (Dame Muriel Spark's "The transfiguration of the commonplace"). The first Makars were court poets and bards skilled in the use of diction. The post of Edinburgh Makar was created in 2002 followed two years later by that of Scots Makar (National Poet). Both are tasked with representing and promoting Scottish poetry.

Other locations nearby: 3, 4, 5, 6, 7, 10, 11, 57

8   Where to Find a Million Pounds

EH1 1YZ (Old Town), the Museum on the Mound
on North Bank Street
Bus 23, 27, 41, 42, 67 to Mound Place

Between 1781 and 1830 an estimated two million cartloads of earth and rubble were removed during the construction of Edinburgh's New Town (see no. 61). This material was used to build The Mound, a ramp-like thoroughfare connecting the Old Town with Princes Street. At the top is North Bank Street (EH1), where the Bank of Scotland opened in 1806. Now the Scottish headquarters of the Lloyds TSB Group, the imposing building is also home to the Museum on the Mound, which tells the story of Scottish money.

Far more interesting than it sounds, the Museum on the Mound takes a fresh and innovative look at the world of Scottish banking. This is immediately evident to visitors who upon arrival are confronted by a million pounds in cancelled notes! Thereafter they embark on a journey through six display zones, with plenty of hands-on activities that will appeal to all ages.

The first zone (A Bank for Scotland) explores the origins of the Bank of Scotland, Scotland's oldest bank, which was established by

A few of the million pounds in the Museum on the Mound

an Act of the Scottish Parliament in 1695. The original document is on display alongside a ledger signed by the first investors, who were known as 'Adventurers'.

The second zone (The Bank on the Mound) illustrates the changing architectural face of Edinburgh and how the original bank building of 1806 was later reworked by the Edinburgh architect David Bryce (1803–1876). Known for his work in the Gothic variant known as Scottish Baronial style, the result shows him to have been proficient in the Italianate classical style, too. There are interactive maps here and children can have a go at building a model bank for themselves.

The third zone (Money Matters) looks not just at coins and banknotes but also other currency forms, such as seashells, tea and exotic feathers. Visitors can try their hand at safe-cracking and there is another million pounds' worth of cancelled banknotes, this time displayed alongside the plate used to print them. The Bank of Scotland was one of the first European banks to issue paper currency redeemable for cash on demand and it has continued to do so despite opposition from the Bank of England.

The next two zones (Building Societies/Life Assurance) have a social angle. The first illustrates housing conditions during the Industrial Revolution and how people clubbed together to build better homes. The second is a stark reminder of how early 19th century health insurance premiums were linked to illness and disease.

The final zone (Making it Work) illustrates banking as a career and includes everything from how much teenage apprentices earned in the 19th century and the first female employees to how early computers changed the workplace.

Visitors wishing to take away a piece of banking history can do so in the gift shop, which offers limited edition banknote 'pulls' hand-printed using the museum's antique plates. All the profits go to Lloyds' Charity of the Year.

The Bank of Scotland should not be confused with the Royal Bank of Scotland, which was formed by royal charter in 1727. That the former was suspected of Jacobite sympathies only added to the initial rivalry between the two. Today the Royal Bank of Scotland occupies the former mansion of Edinburgh MP Sir Lawrence Dundas (1710–1781) at 36 St. Andrew Square (EH2). Acquired by the Bank in the 1820s, the building was extended to include one of Britain's finest banking halls. Now restored to its original Victorian colour scheme, it is illuminated by a magnificent dome pierced by 120 glazed stars (see no. 61).

Other locations nearby: 3, 4, 5, 6, 7, 10, 11, 57

9 Twenty Four Million Pieces of Print

EH1 1EW (Old Town), the National Library of Scotland on George IV Bridge
Bus 3, 5, 7, 8, 14, 29, 30, 31, 33, 35, 37, 45, 49 to South Bridge
(the Visitor Centre is open to all but to use the reading rooms and order items requires registration)

That the citizens of Edinburgh enjoy reading is evident from their public libraries. From Gilmerton to Granton there are 28 of them – and they are no longer just places for reading. In the suburbs they have become an integral part of community life by offering internet access, printing facilities, councillors' surgeries, activity groups and all manner of creative projects.

Two of Edinburgh's greatest libraries – the National Library of Scotland and the Central Library – face each other where George IV Bridge crosses the Cowgate. It was on the Cowgate in 1507 that Walter Chepman and Androw Myllor were authorised by James IV (1488–1513) to print Scotland's first book, *The Aberdeen Breviary*. At the king's request it detailed prevailing Catholic Church ritual but with a distinctive Scottish twist.

A copy of *The Aberdeen Breviary* is today one of many rare books, manuscripts and letters held in the National Library of Scotland. Constituted by Act of Parliament in 1925, this is Scotland's largest reference library and as a legal deposit library it is entitled to a copy of all works printed in the United Kingdom. This explains its massive holdings of 24 million items across multiple printed formats, including a Gutenberg Bible, a Shakespeare First Folio, the last letter written by Mary, Queen of Scots, and the letter submitted by Charles Darwin with the manuscript of his *Origin of Species* (see no. 34). Such items are sometimes featured in the library's regular free exhibitions.

The role of national library had originally been fulfilled by the privately-funded Advocates Library opened in 1689 by the Faculty of Advocates, a body of lawyers governing the Scottish Bar. By the 1920s, however, the upkeep of such a collection was too great and so the non-legal books were removed to form the core of the new National Library. This left the Advocates Library to collect only legal texts in its Victorian premises on Parliament Square (EH1), which it still does today. It can be visited during Edinburgh Doors Open Day, when buildings not normally accessible to the public are opened (www.doorsopen-days.org.uk).

The cost of acquiring the non-legal books and presenting them to the nation was borne by Alexander Grant (1864–1937), proprietor of Scottish biscuit manufacturer McVitie & Price. Initially the books were stored in Sheriff Court until a further bequest from Grant made the building of the present National Library possible. Built to a design by Reginald Fairlie (1883–1952), with sculptural decoration by Fairlie's friend Hew Lorimer (1907–1993), the building was completed in 1956. A more recent building at 159 Causewayside (EH9) contains the Bartholomew Map Archive reflecting the

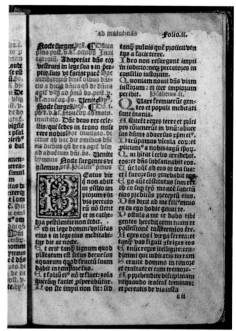

Scotland's first book was the Aberdeen Breviary

importance of the Edinburgh cartographic firm of John Bartholomew & Son, which until 1995 was based in a Palladian mansion around the corner on Duncan Street.

Directly opposite the National Library is the Central Library, which opened in 1890. Edinburgh's first public library, it was financed by the Scottish-American industrialist and philanthropist, Andrew Carnegie (1835–1919), who laid the foundation stone of the French Renaissance-styled building. Although the galleried reference library on the top floor retains its Victorian atmosphere, all the other departments have now been modernised.

When Edinburgh became the world's first UNESCO City of Literature in 2004 several worthwhile literary projects resulted. One of them is the City of Literature Trust's Literary Salon, a networking event for librarians, authors, publishers and booksellers, which takes place at 6pm on the last Tuesday of each month (except August and December) in the Wash Bar at 11–13 North Bank Street (EH1).

Other locations nearby: 4, 5, 10, 14, 35, 36, 37, 38

10   The Last Public Execution

EH1 1RN (Old Town), the site of Edinburgh's last public
execution outside Lothian Chambers at the junction
of the Lawnmarket (Royal Mile) and George IV Bridge
Bus 23, 27, 41, 42, 67 to Victoria Street

Set into the pavement at the junction of the Lawnmarket and George IV
Bridge are three brass plates in the shape of an 'H'. They are easy to
miss and their significance would be lost without the plaque on the
wall of Lothian Chambers. This informs passers-by that it was here
on 21st June 1864 that George Bryce became the last person to be executed publically in Edinburgh. What it doesn't say is why.

Bryce grew up in the village of Ratho west of Edinburgh, where
he was a carter. In 1863 he took a job at a nearby large house, where
he met and began courting a young cook called Isabelle. The relationship was frowned upon, especially by the nursery maid, Jane Seton,
who told Isabelle that Bryce was a drunkard and recommended she
break off the relationship. This Isabelle did, informing Bryce of Seton's
disapproval in the process. Enraged Bryce broke into the house and
attacked Seton. Hearing the commotion, the lady of the house awoke
and restrained Bryce temporarily. Seton escaped but Bryce was soon
in pursuit and caught up with her in the doorway of a neighbouring
cottage. There he slashed her throat with a razor and left her to die.

Bryce was apprehended the next morning and gave himself up
without a fight. With so many witnesses to his crime he could only
plead guilty, whereupon the court sentenced him to hang. In those
days public executions were becoming less frequent, with many cases
commuted to deportation. As a result, where once there had been a
dozen or so public gallows in Edinburgh, now there was only one
on the Lawnmarket near the former site of the Old Tolbooth jail (see
no. 13). This had been demolished in 1817 and replaced by a new
jail on Calton Hill, where Bryce was incarcerated until the day of his
execution.

The rarity of public executions and the grisly nature of Bryce's
crime inevitably drew a large crowd. As Bryce was escorted to the scaffold he was jeered and pelted with stones. The scaffold itself consisted
of a crossbeam supported on two vertical posts, positioned so that the
victim would be facing the castle (the brass plates in the pavement illustrate this arrangement). Only when the attending minister said his
final prayers did the noise abate.

At this point the crowd knew what to expect. Bryce would be dropped out of sight through a trapdoor and the noose would break his neck. On this occasion, however, the execution did not go to plan. Since the permanent post of hangman had been scrapped, one Thomas Askern, a retired hangman from York, was employed instead. For whatever reason, Askern failed to measure the rope correctly causing Bryce to fall barely two feet before being slowly strangulated in full view. The crowd's animosity turned quickly against the authorities and Askern only just escaped with his life. This explains why the

Brass plates embedded in the Lawnmarket pavement

botched execution of George Bryce was the last public execution in Edinburgh. Henceforth all executions were carried out behind closed doors in Calton Jail.

All that remains of Calton Jail, once the largest prison in Scotland, is the castellated Governor's House on Calton Crags. The rest of the site was cleared after the jail's closure in 1925, when the last inmate was transferred to Saughton Prison in Stenhouse. Since 1938 the area has been occupied by the Scottish Government's sprawling *Art Deco* St. Andrew's House, although several murderers remain buried in the car park. The door from the condemned cell is now in the Beehive Inn at 18–20 Grassmarket (EH1).

Other locations nearby: 5, 6, 7, 9, 11, 12, 13, 14

11 Close Encounters on the Royal Mile

EH1 1PW (Old Town), a tour of Old Town closes beginning with
Byre's Close at 375 High Street (Royal Mile)
Bus 23, 27, 41, 42, 67 to Victoria Street; 35 to South Bridge

The distinctive layout of Edinburgh's Old Town is a result of geology.
Millions of years ago a volcanic flue pushed up through the surrounding sedimentary rocks (see no. 96). When this cooled it formed a hard
dolerite plug, which resisted the scouring effects of subsequent glacial
erosion and shielded a tapering, steep-sided ramp of softer rocks to
the east, resulting in what geologists call a crag-and-tail formation.
Edinburgh Castle, the oldest part of the city, was built on the crag; the
main street of the Old Town, the Royal Mile, was laid out along the tail.

The Royal Mile, which runs downhill for approximately one Scots
mile between the Castle and the Palace of Holyroodhouse, is really four
streets: Castlehill, the Lawnmarket, the High Street and the Canongate.
Daniel Defoe in 1723 described it as "the largest, longest and finest
street for buildings and number of inhabitants…in the World".

Branching off the Royal Mile at right angles are 82 narrow alley-
ways giving the impression of a herringbone when viewed from above.
Known as 'closes' (or sometimes entries, courts, pends or wynds) these
were originally lined with tall tenement buildings ('lands'), wherein
hundreds of people once lived (see no. 6). What follows is a tour of
closes located on the High Street between St. Giles Street and North
Bridge (for those between North Bridge and Jeffrey Street see no. 18).

1) Byre's Close: Old Town closes were usually named after a prominent occupant or a trade carried on there. The steep Byre's Close,
which dates from the 16th century, is typical in that it was originally
known as Malcolme's Close, then Lauder's Close and is today named
after John Byres (1569–1629), a wealthy merchant who was variously
a magistrate, City Treasurer and Old Provost.

2) Advocate's Close: this close is named after Sir James Stewart
(1635–1713), who as an opponent of the Stewarts was appointed Lord
Advocate after the Glorious Revolution and introduced legal reforms
in Scotland. The view of the Scott Memorial and the New Town beyond is a favourite with photographers. Visible from the close is the
tall, wedge-shaped house of Adam Bothwell (1530–1593), the Com-
mendator (lay administrator) of Holyrood Abbey. A Roman Catholic

priest with a talent for survival, he married Mary, Queen of Scots (1542–1567) to her third husband, the Earl of Bothwell, in 1567 and two months later as a Protestant crowned James VI/I (1567–1625) at Stirling. Cromwell once sat in the north window observing his fleet in the Firth of Forth.

3) Writers' Court/Warriston's Close: pass Roxburgh's Close to reach Writers' Court, the name of which recalls a library for the Society of Writers to Her Majesty's Signet established here before relocating to Parliament Square (see no. 14). The literary connection was later reinforced by the presence of the publisher W. & R. Chambers. The court was built in

Mary King's Close is today hidden underground

the late 17th century on the site of a mansion occupied in the 1560s by the church reformer John Knox (c. 1513–1572).

4) Mary King's Close: this 17th century close is remarkable in that it lies *beneath* the City Chambers, which were built over it in the 1750s (as the Royal Exchange) to a design by John Adam (1721–1792). As such the close retains much of its original cramped and gloomy aspect. It is also remarkable in being named after a woman, Mary King, who was a burgess and a fabric merchant. In 1645 plague struck the close and a colourful legend recounts how it was bricked up with the residents still inside (in reality the victims were either quarantined on the Burgh Muir or treated in situ). Such tales have since 2003 drawn ghost hunters to the close, when it opened to the public as the Real Mary King's Close. It should be stressed, however, that the guided tours here are all about real social history and not alleged hauntings. The City Chambers themselves can be visited during Edinburgh Doors Open Day (www.doorsopendays.org.uk).

5) Anchor Close: created in 1521, this close is named after the Anchor Tavern, where the Crochallan Fencibles met to discuss volunteer arming against foreign invasion. Club founder William Smellie had his printing house here, where Robert Burns came to proof his works.

6) Geddes Entry: named after an Edinburgh surgeon, this 17th century close once contained a tavern, where members of the Cape Club

met, including tragic poet Robert Fergusson (1750–1774) (see no. 26).

7) North Foulis' Close: named after an apothecary, this is where tobacco merchant James Gillespie (1726–1797) had his shop. He bequeathed money to found a girls' school, where novelist Muriel Spark (1918–2006) gained inspiration for *The Prime of Miss Jean Brodie*.

8) Old Stamp Office Close: the Government Stamp Office and the New (now Royal) Bank of Scotland once stood here. Susanna, Countess of Eglinton (1690–1780) and her seven daughters proceeded from here in sedan chairs to dancing lessons in Old Assembly Close opposite.

9) Fleshmarket Close: this lies beyond Lyon's Close and Jackson's Close and is named after a former meat market, which lead to a slaughterhouse on the banks of the Nor' Loch. The close provided the title for one of Ian Rankin's popular Inspector Rebus novels.

Cross now to the opposite side of the High Street.

10) Stevenlaw's Close: this close is named after Steven Law, a supporter of Mary, Queen of Scots during the civil war of 1571 and is where Bonnie Prince Charlie worshipped in a Roman Catholic chapel.

11) New Assembly Close: this gated close gives access to New Assemblies Hall, a handsome Georgian building used from 1736 onwards for society dances and get-togethers, and later as a masonic lodge, bank, children's home and wax museum.

12) Burnet's Close: beyond Bell's Wynd, named after a brewer, is Burnet's Close, where *The Scots Magazine*, the world's oldest magazine still in production, was first published in 1739.

13) Covenant Close: so-named because a copy of the National Covenant was signed here, this was once home to Lord Braxfield (1722–1799), a judge known for his severity, who inspired a character in Robert Louis Stevenson's unfinished novel, *Weir of Hermiston*.

14) Old Assembly Close: the predecessor to New Assembly Close, it was here that Edinburgh's most destructive fire broke out in 1824 destroying everything between here and Parliament Square, including the Tron Kirk. Note the old stencilled sign to Smith, Fletcher & Co. Wireworks. Previously George Heriot's School, this building was later reworked as a store for the Faculty of Advocates (see no. 9).

15) Old Fishmarket Close: beyond Borthwick's Close is Old Fishmarket Close, where this tour finishes. Leading down to the Cowgate, this once notoriously pungent close was variously home to the city hangman, wealthy jeweller and school benefactor George Heriot, and possibly Daniel Defoe, who may have acted as a secret agent for the English at the time of the Act of Union (1707).

Other locations nearby: 6, 7, 8, 10, 12, 13, 14, 15

12 Edinburgh's Unusual Cathedral

EH1 1RE (Old Town), St. Giles' Cathedral on the High Street (Royal Mile)
Bus 23, 27, 41, 42, 67 to Victoria Street; 35 to South Bridge

St. Giles' Cathedral on the High Street (EH1) should really be called the High Kirk of Edinburgh. Only for two short periods during the 17th century (1634–1638 and 1662–1689) was it actually a cathedral (i.e. the seat of a bishop), when episcopalianism backed by the Crown briefly gained ascendancy in Scotland. Prior to the Scottish Reformation of 1560 Edinburgh had no cathedral, as it fell under the jurisdiction of the Catholic Bishop of St. Andrew's in Fife. And for most of its post-Reformation history, the Protestant Church of Scotland has rejected bishops and cathedrals.

The story of St. Giles' begins in 1130, when a parish church was built on the only level piece of ground between the castle and Holyrood. Comprising a simple nave and tower, it was granted to the Lazarites and dedicated to St. Giles, the patron saint of cripples and lepers. Rebuilt sometime during the 14th century, the church was burned in 1385 when English troops sacked Edinburgh. Repairs followed and by 1400 the addition of transepts and a choir formed the cruciform plan seen today. Various aisles (chapels) were then installed, which were serviced by a college of canons, whose job it was to

The spectacular vaulted ceiling of the Thistle Chapel

pray for the souls of rich patrons. The main external change came around 1490, when the distinctive Gothic crown steeple was added.

Dramatic changes inside the church occurred during the Reformation, which was ignited by a sermon given here in 1559 by firebrand cleric John Knox (c.1513–1572). The medieval altars were swept away and by 1561 St. Giles' was serving three different Reformed congregations, with internal walls erected to separate them. The church was also used for secular purposes, including as an annexe to the nearby Old Tolbooth jail, and as a storeroom for a guillotine used for executions!

A defining moment for St. Giles' came in 1637 during the first period of Episcopalianism. A streetseller called Jenny Geddes hurled a chair at the Dean, when he tried to use the Book of Common Prayer imposed on Scotland by Charles I (1625–1649). The disturbance led to the National Covenant and the Bishops' Wars, the first conflicts of the Wars of the Three Kingdoms, which included the English Civil War.

During the 19th century attempts were made to make St. Giles' more like a real cathedral. The clutter of lock-up shops known as the Luckenbooths, which had long obscured its façade, were demolished and the interior was opened up again (see no. 13). In 1911 a medieval-style chapel for the chivalric Order of the Thistle (an honour bestowed by the monarch on 16 notable Scots since the Middle Ages) was installed, replete with intricate ceiling vaults and carved bagpipe-playing angels. Finally in the late 19th century the focus of worship was shifted from the traditional east end of the chancel to directly beneath the tower, and a magnificent 4,000-pipe organ was installed in the south transept.

Notable monuments at St. Giles' include recumbent alabaster effigies of James Graham, Marquess of Montrose (1612–50), who supported Charles I, and his arch-enemy the Covenanter Archibald Campbell, Marquess of Argyll (1607–61). A statue and a stained glass window in the Moray Aisle of John Knox are reminders that the Protestant reformer became minister here in 1559. He was buried here, too, although his grave now lies beneath the tarmac of Parliament Square, where a stone in bay 23 marks the spot! There is also a bronze relief to Robert Louis Stevenson in the Moray Aisle and a West Window to Robert Burns.

Guided rooftop tours of St. Giles' are conducted daily by appointment from 10am (email stgilestower@gmail.com).

Other locations nearby: 7, 9, 10, 11, 13, 14, 15, 35

13 What's Left of the Luckenbooths?

EH1 1RE (Old Town), a series of brass pavement plates outside St. Giles' Cathedral on the High Street (Royal Mile) marking the former site of the Luckenbooths
Bus 23, 27, 41, 42, 67 to Victoria Street; 35 to South Bridge

Embedded in the High Street (EH1) immediately north of St. Giles' Cathedral are several brass plates. They mark where the Luckenbooths once stood, a row of medieval tenements containing Edinburgh's first permanent shops. Shortly before their demolition they were colourfully described by Walter Scott in his novel *The Heart of Midlothian*.

The Luckenbooths originated with a two-storey timber-framed tenement built in the middle of the High Street in 1440. This was gradually extended to form a row of seven tenements, each between four and six storeys high, which stretched the full length of St. Giles' Cathedral. At street level each tenement had a luckenbooth, or lockable booth, for the sale of goods. Folding wooden boards were used to form a stock counter by day and to shutter them at night (examples can still be seen at the John Knox House at 43–45 High Street and Gladstone's Land at

This model in the Museum of Edinburgh shows clearly where the Luckenbooths once stood

477b Lawnmarket). Between the Luckenbooths and the cathedral was a narrow alley occupied by temporary stalls of trinket and toy sellers known as *krames* (from an old German word for 'pedlar').

Originally the Luckenbooths were used exclusively by goldsmiths, silversmiths and jewellers. It was they who invented the Luckenbooth Brooch, a Scottish love token typically made of silver in the form of a crown above a heart, or two entwined hearts. These were often given as a betrothal or wedding brooch and also worn on babies' shawls to ward off evil spirits and encourage the mother's milk. Legend has it that one was given by Mary, Queen of Scots to Lord Darnley as a symbol of love, and that another was given to her as an engagement brooch by the Dauphin of France. The Luckenbooths were later used by a variety of retailers, including a baker, milliner, hairdresser and a "chymist and druggist".

Whilst the westernmost tenement of the Luckenbooths was built up against the Old Tolbooth jail, the easternmost and last to be built in the late 17th century was of fine stone. This is where the wigmaker-turned-poet Allan Ramsay the Elder (1684–1758) had his shop and where in 1752 he established Scotland's first circulating library, which became a focus for the city's literati. Visitors included the poet John Gay (1685–1732), who is best remembered for *The Beggar's Opera*, and the novelist Tobias Smollet (1721–1771). Later in 1786 the publisher William Creech (1745–1815) took over the premises attracting his own clientelle, including Robert Burns (1759–1796), Dugald Stewart (1753–1828) and Adam Smith (1723–1790).

Inevitably with the increase in wheeled traffic, the Luckenbooths caused congestion in the High Street. Accordingly they were demolished by order of the Town Council between 1802 and 1817 leaving only the brass pavement plates and their namesake brooches to tell the tale.

Brass plates also mark where the Old Tolbooth jail once stood. Built in 1386, it doubled as a meeting place for the Scottish Parliament and Town Council, and as a tax collection office. The former exit is marked with a mosaic heart made of granite setts – the Heart of Midlothian – where it was customary for prisoners to spit if they gained their freedom. Those less fortunate were publically executed here, including the infamous Deacon William Brodie (1741–1788), whose double life inspired Robert Louis Stevenson to write his *Strange Case of Dr. Jekyll and Mr. Hyde*. Although the Old Tolbooth was demolished in 1817 and replaced by a new jail on Calton Hill, public executions continued nearby until 1864 (see no. 10).

Other locations nearby: 6, 7, 9, 10, 11, 12, 14, 15

14   Sustenance in Strange Places

EH1 1RF (Old Town), a tour of unusual restaurants including the Signet Library Colonnades in Parliament Square
Bus 23, 27, 41, 42, 67 to Victoria Street; 35 to South Bridge
(note: lunch and Afternoon Tea by appointment only)

Some of Edinburgh's cultural institutions offer restaurants that are attractions in their own right. They include the Tower Restaurant of the National Museum of Scotland on Chambers Street (EH1) and the Scottish Café & Restaurant of the Scottish National Gallery on the Mound, both of which offer fine views of the city. There are others, however, that revel in their comparative obscurity.

The Signet Library in Parliament Square (EH1) is a Georgian masterpiece designed by Robert Reid (1774–1856) and completed in 1822 for the Society of Writers to Her Majesty's Signet. Its members belonged to the College of Justice established in 1532 by James V (1513–1542), which recognised judges and lawyers as being distinct from the state. As such they were allowed to generate royal manuscripts bearing the monarch's seal. The Society still comprises respected practising solicitors, who admit the public to their magnificent Lower Library for lunch and Afternoon Tea. The venue is called the Colonnades because of the Corinthian columns supporting the ceiling.

Across the High Street is something quite different. The Devil's Advocate at 9 Advocate's Close is a modern restaurant and bar with a pared-back industrial feel. This is because the building originally

The Signet Library Colonnades are hidden in Parliament Square

served as a Victorian pump house that transported water up to Castlehill. There it was stored in the Castlehill Reservoir (now the Tartan Weaving Mill) opposite the Contini Cannonball Restaurant. The latter is named after two iron balls embedded in its gable wall in the 17th century to mark the precise height above sea level of the springs at Comiston, whence Edinburgh's first piped supply of fresh water came (see no. 2). The restaurant door allegedly sports Edinburgh's oldest door knocker!

Outside the Wedgwood Restaurant at 267 Canongate (EH8) is a sculpture said to represent the Emperor of Morocco. In the 1600s a man called Andrew Gray fled after assaulting an unpopular Provost of Edinburgh. He ended up a slave at the court of the Emperor of Morocco but rose through the ranks and returned a rich man. Forgiven after curing the Provost's daughter of plague, Gray married her and set up home here – hence the sculpture.

On George Street (EH2) in the New Town are two restaurants in magnificent former banks: the Dome at number 14 and the Contini Ristorante at number 103. In a similar vein, the Amarone at 13 St. Andrew Square (EH2) occupies the former Caledonian Insurance Company, with private dining in its vault. Far more modest is the Songkran Thai restaurant at 8 Gloucester Street (EH3), a house built in the 1790s from Old Town salvage. It was the birthplace of the Orientalist painter David Roberts (1796–1864), known affectionately as the 'Scottish Canaletto'.

This tour finishes with the Gardener's Cottage at 1 Royal Terrace Gardens on London Road (EH7). The charming Georgian building of 1837 was designed by William Playfair (1790–1857) for a tenant gardener, who rented out keys to locals wishing to grow vegetables here. The current owners still grow produce, which is consumed at communal tables.

An alternative to conventional dining is Charlie and Evelyn's Table, Edinburgh's original secret supper club (bookings and address by emailing rachelandchrisrowley@gmail.com). Supper clubs can also be staged at the Library of Mistakes at 4a Wemyss Place Mews (EH4), an intimate members-only library established to promote the study of financial history. Different again is Edinburgh College's Apprentice Training Restaurant on the Granton Campus at 350 West Granton Road (EH5), where diners watch their meal prepared on-screen before being served by hospitality students. The same happens at the EH15 Training Restaurant on the Milton Road Campus at 24 Milton Road East (EH15).

Other locations nearby: 7, 9, 10, 11, 12, 13, 15, 36

15 The Moving History of the Mercat Cross

EH1 1RF (Old Town), the Mercat Cross in Parliament Square off
the High Street (Royal Mile)
Bus 23, 27, 41, 42, 67 to Victoria Street; 35 to South Bridge

In Parliament Square off the High Street (EH1) stands the Mercat Cross. Scots for 'market cross', this is traditionally where the right to hold a market or fair was granted by the monarch. A feature of many towns and villages in Scotland, a mercat cross acted not only as a symbol of a *burgh's* prosperity but also of its authority, where state and civic proclamations could be read out, public events marked and punishments dispensed. The earliest reference to a mercat cross dates from the reign of William the Lion (1165–1214) and there are still over 120 extant.

Edinburgh's Mercat Cross is first mentioned in a charter of 1365, which indicates that it stood in the middle of the High

The Mercat Cross with St. Giles' Cathedral behind

Street immediately north of its current position. It consisted of a stepped octagonal base topped with a stone column. Since then it has moved around a fair bit. In 1617 it was relocated several yards east to the head of Fishmarket Close, where an octagonal arrangement of setts marks the spot. Then in 1756 it was demolished in readiness for the opening of the new Royal Exchange, which had been built to a design by John Adam (1721–1792). In 1811 when the city's merchants continued to congregate where the Cross had once stood, the new building was taken over by the Council instead and renamed the City Chambers (see nos. 11 & 18).

For a while the broken column of the Cross was reconstituted in the grounds of the Drum, a country house in Gilmerton (EH17), although what prompted this is unclear. Perhaps it was to deny the Jacobites a shrine, since it was at the Cross on 18th September 1745 that the Young Pretender Bonnie Prince Charlie had his father proclaimed King James VIII of Scotland and himself Regent. Whatever the reason, in 1866 the column was returned to Edinburgh and placed on a new stepped pedestal outside the north door of St. Giles. Because the column had been damaged during the demolition of 1756 its height was now reduced from 20 to 14 feet. At the top of the column was placed a royal unicorn, symbol of the Scottish monarchy, based on one on the original Cross.

In 1885 the column was moved again to its current location, where it would not hinder traffic. There it formed part of a new Mercat Cross designed by the Scottish architect Sydney Mitchell (1856–1930) and paid for by William Gladstone MP (1809–1898), whose father and grandfather hailed from Edinburgh. It consists of an octagonal stepped base, an arcaded superstructure concealing a staircase, a parapet with eight corner turrets, and the original stone column. In the spaces between the turrets are royal, *burgh* and university coats of arms, which on the original Cross were human heads (five of these were acquired by Sir Walter Scott and incorporated into his garden wall at Abbotsford). When the column was replaced in the 1970s, the original fragments were placed in the Museum of Edinburgh on the Canongate (EH8).

For many years the Mercat Cross had a bloody reputation since state criminals were executed here. They included the Royalists George Gordon, 2nd Marquis of Huntly in 1649 and James Graham, 1st Marquis of Montrose in 1650, and after the Restoration, Archibald Campbell, 1st Marquis of Argyll, and Archibald Johnston, Lord Warriston. Following Bonnie Prince Charlie's defeat at Culloden in 1746, the Jacobite colours were ceremoniously burned here, too. These days, royal proclamations are read out at the Mercat Cross, including the calling of a general election and the succession of a new monarch.

Other locations nearby: 9, 10, 11, 12, 13, 14, 16, 18

16 A Warehouse Full of Scottish Art

EH1 1DE (Old Town), the City Art Centre at 2 Market Street
Bus 6 to Jeffrey Street, 1, 3, 4, 19, 22, 25, 29, 30, 31, 33, 34, 37
to Princes Street Waverley, 100 to Waverley Station; Tram T50
to St. Andrew Square

Edinburgh is a city that has not shied away from adapting its old buildings to new uses. Examples include a church now used as the headquarters of the Edinburgh International Festival and a café in a converted police box (see nos. 4 & 91). Another bold example is the City Art Centre (CAC) at 2 Market Street (EH1), a magnificent public gallery of Scottish art housed in a nine storey former warehouse.

Constructed between 1899 and 1902, the warehouse was built originally as an extension to the *Scotsman* newspaper offices. Erected using an iron frame with internal supporting columns, it was clad in stone to create a restrained *Beaux Arts* façade. The warehouse later became part of the city's wholesale fruit, flower and

The columns in the City Art Centre are a reminder it was once a warehouse

vegetable market and was converted for use as a gallery in 1980. At this time the floors were adapted to create light, airy and flexible exhibition spaces in a conversion that garnered a RIBA Award for Architecture.

The origin of the CAC's collection also dates from the 19th century and it has been growing ever since through purchases, donations and bequests. The gallery's holdings currently consist of more than

4,500 pieces of work across a wide range of genres – oil paintings and watercolours, drawings and prints, photographs, sculpture, and installation art – providing a rich and varied overview of Scottish art. It is worth noting that while the sculptural tradition in Scotland is relatively young having only really developed in the 19th century, the Scots were among the pioneers of photography and they are still leading the way in weaving. Most of the tapestries displayed in the CAC were made at Edinburgh's Dovecot Studios (see no. 31).

Not surprisingly the CAC's Fine Art collection includes works by all Scotland's leading artists from the 17th century onwards. Many of those from the last century arrived in the early 1960s, when the Scottish Modern Arts Association donated over 300 works. They include Lothian landscapes by William McTaggart (1835–1910) and portraits of Glasgow street children by Joan Eardley (1921–1963).

As well as a collection of civic portraits and a large collection of Edinburgh views, the CAC is well known for its representative collections covering Scotland's major art movements. The Edinburgh School, for example, comprised a group of mid-20th century artists such as Gillies, Maxwell and Redpath, who attended the Edinburgh School of Art and shared a love of vibrant colours and bold brushstrokes. The Glasgow Boys strove for realism by painting outdoors and their number included Henry, Hornel, Lavery and Crawhall. A third group, the Scottish Colourists, were united in their love of French painting and they included Fergusson, Peploe, Cadell and Hunter (see no. 50).

The CAC is justifiably proud of its rolling exhibition programme, showcasing a wide range of vintage and contemporary Scottish and international artists. Past events have included works by Henri de Toulouse-Lautrec and *The Art of Star Wars*, which attracted more than 100,000 visitors. Running alongside such exhibitions are free talks and family workshops, which can be booked in advance (school and community groups are especially welcome). Also free but without the need for booking is the CAC's ArtSpace, where attendeess can create their own artworks.

Directly opposite the CAC at 45 Market Street is the Fruitmarket Gallery. Built in 1938 as a fruit and vegetable market, it has been used to display world class contemporary art since 1974. Don't miss the nearby Scotsman Steps connecting Market Street with North Bridge, comprising 104 spiral steps each clad in a different marble by artist Martin Creed (b. 1968).

Other locations nearby: 15, 17, 18, 58

17 All Change at Waverley

EH1 1BB (Old Town), Edinburgh Waverley railway station on
Waverley Bridge
Bus 1, 3, 4, 19, 22, 25, 29, 30, 31, 33, 34, 37 to Princes Street
Waverley; Bus 10, 11, 16 to Princes Street Scott Monument;
Tram T50 to St. Andrew Square

Waverley is Edinburgh's main railway station and covers an impressive 25 acres in the heart of the city. With 18 platforms servicing 20 million passengers annually it is Britain's second largest mainline station after London Waterloo.

Edinburgh Waverley railway station spanned by the North Bridge

The Waverley story begins in the 1750s, when overcrowding in Edinburgh's Old Town prompted plans to expand the city northwards. The major obstacle was the Nor' Loch, an unhygienic bog created in the 15th century by the damming of a river valley for defensive purposes. By 1766, when the plan for the New Town was approved, the loch had been drained and traversed by the North Bridge (see no. 61). At this time an early physic garden on the shore of the loch was relocated to Leith Walk as recorded by a plaque on platform 11 (see no. 82).

The former site of the loch became the Princes Street Gardens and in the 1830s a railway from Glasgow was proposed, running through the gardens to a station at North Bridge. Despite opposition from property owners, the Edinburgh and Glasgow Railway opened in 1842, initially with a terminus at Haymarket. It was extended two years later through a concealed cutting to North Bridge, where a station was installed in 1847. Around the same time the Edinburgh, Leith and Newhaven Railway opened their own station, as did the North British Railway as a terminus for their line from Berwick-upon-Tweed. To avoid confusion the three stations were connected in 1854 and collectively named Waverley after the novels of Sir Walter Scott (this explains the literary quotations around the station today). In 1868 the North British Railway acquired all three stations, demolished them and built the single station seen today.

There are several impressive engineering feats at Waverley. When the North Bridge was rebuilt in 1897 one of the huge stone piers used to convey it over the station's roof was cleverly concealed within the magnificent skylit booking hall (today's Travel Centre), which contains a memorial plaque to Edinburgh-born railway engineer Sir Nigel Gresley (1876–1941). The enormous glazed roof itself covers an area of 111,000 square feet. The imposing North British Station Hotel built on Princes Street is now called the Balmoral and retains its reputation for luxury. Of the Waverley Market that once stood outside the hotel only the Victorian cast-ron railings remain, incorporated into Princes Mall.

Waverley's best kept secret is a half mile-long rail tunnel constructed in 1847 by the Edinburgh, Leith and Newhaven Railway. It was used to transport freight northwards to the docks, where the world's first train ferry continued the journey across the Firth of Forth. The blocked entrance can still be seen on platform 20 from where the tunnel ran beneath St. Andrew Square, Dublin Street and Scotland Street before exiting in King George V Park. Despite the effort and expense to dig the tunnel, which required the use of a stationary steam engine to haul the wagons, it was abandoned in 1868, when Waverley was rebuilt. Since then it has served as a coal depot, a Second World War air raid shelter and most recently to grow mushrooms. This was discontinued in the 1970s after thieves used the tunnel as a getaway route!

On 30th September 1940 word reached Edinburgh that three German spies had put ashore in a dinghy. Two were quickly apprehended but the third, one Werner Wälti, made his way to Waverley. Upon arrival he deposited a heavy case later found to contain a radio transmitter. When Wälti returned to collect it he was arrested by Detective Superintendant Willie Merrilees, who had disguised himself as a railway porter.

Other locations nearby: 15, 16, 58

18 More Close Encounters on the Royal Mile

EH1 1SG (Old Town), a tour of Old Town closes beginning with
Carruber's Close at 135 High Street (Royal Mile)
Bus 6 to Jeffrey Street or St. Mary's Street; 35 to Royal Mile;
3, 5, 7, 8, 14, 29, 30, 31, 33, 37, 45, 49 to South Bridge

This is a tour of Old Town closes located along the High Street between North Bridge and Jeffrey Street (for those between North Bridge and St. Giles Street see no. 11).

1) Carruber's Close: this close is probably named after the merchant William de Carriberis, who lived hereabouts in the 1450s. The presence of Old St. Paul's Scottish Episcopal Church is a reminder that the former Bishop of St. Giles' Cathedral brought his congregation here after the Catholic James VII/II (1685–1688) was deposed by William and Mary (1689–1702). The wigmaker-turned-poet Allan Ramsay the Elder (1684–1758), a Jacobite sympathiser, opened a short-lived theatre here in 1736. This eventually became the Carruber's Close Mission containing the dispensary of James Young Simpson (1811–1870), who discovered the anaesthetic properties of chloroform. It operates today as the Carrubers Christian Centre at 65 High Street.

2) Bishop's Close: renamed half a dozen times, this close is currently named after Thomas Sydeserf (1581–1663), who was a minister at St. Giles' and later became Bishop of Brechin, Galloway, and Orkney. Henry Dundas, 1st Viscount Melville (1742–1811) was born here and nicknamed King Harry the Ninth for his control over Scottish politics at a time when no monarch visited the country. Robert Burns visited the close in 1786 to receive French lessons from Louis Cauvin (1754–1825), whose estate financed the Dean Orphan Hospital, which today houses the Scottish National Gallery of Modern Art (see no. 50).

Paisley Close on the High Street collapsed in 1861

3) North Gray's Close: named after the burgess Alexander Gray, this close is inter-

esting for its ancient bricked-up windows and doorways, one of which is inscribed '1581'.

4) Morrison's Close: named after a merchant who lived here in the 18th century, this locked close is where Victorian art critic John Ruskin's grandfather once lived.

5) Bailie Fyfe's Close: dating back to 1572, when it was known as Trotter's Close and then Barrie's Close, this became Fyfe's Close in 1686 in deference to Gilbert Fyfe, a merchant and magistrate (or 'bailie'), who lived here at that time.

6) Paisley Close: named after Henry Paisley, who bought this close in 1711. The head carved over the entrance is that of Joseph McIver, who was pulled to safety after the tenement collapsed in 1861 killing 35 people. Rescuers responded to McIver's call of "Heave awa chaps, I'm no' dead yet". The wealthy wine and tea merchant William Fettes (1750–1836), founder of Fettes College, also had his shop here.

7) Chalmers' Close: another oft-renamed close, this one recalls the belt maker Patrick Chalmers and leads to the remains of the medieval Trinity College Kirk (see no. 20).

8) Trunk's Close: pass Monteith's Close, once possibly the site of a royal tennis court, to reach Trunk's Close. The name is thought to be a corruption of Turing's Close, named after the Aberdeenshire family that built Moubray House here in the 15th century. The corbels on the right-hand side of the close contain the stairs of the house, one of the oldest occupied residential buildings in Edinburgh, which today has a 17th century façade. Daniel Defoe edited the *Edinburgh Courant* newspaper here in 1710 and until 1822 the shopfront belonged to the publisher and bookseller Archibald Constable (1774–1827). Today the building is home to the Cockburn Association, which restored the property in 1910 as part of its mission to preserve Edinburgh's built heritage, and can be visited during Doors Open Day, when buildings not normally accessible to the public are opened (www.doorsopendays. org.uk). At the end of the close is Sandeman House, which houses the Scottish Book Trust, and Hope's Court garden containing a bust of pioneering Scottish environmental town planner Sir Patrick Geddes (1854–1932) (see no. 5). Outside the close is the Netherbow Well, one of several that formerly supplied the Old Town with water

Cross now to the opposite side of the High Street.

9) World's End Close: this aptly-named close is a reminder that near here once stood the Netherbow Port, which marked the boundary between Edinburgh and the independent *burgh* of the Canongate until the two were merged in 1856 (brass plates at the road junction show the gate's outline). For many of Edinburgh's poor this really was the

end of the world because if they left they might never be able to afford to get back through the gate.

10) Tweedale Court: the unusually decorative entrance to this close reflects its history having first housed the 16th century mansion of the daughter of the 1st Earl of Lothian's daughter, which was modernised by Robert Adam (1728–1792) to become the head office of the British Linen Bank. Note the old wrought iron gates and the last remaining shelter for sedan chairs, which were used to ferry the well-to-do through the filthy streets. The sturdy stone wall down the middle of the close is thought to be the remains of the long-lost King's Wall (see no. 39).

Old Town tenements inside Tweedale Court

11) Fountain Close: named after a nearby well, this close is where in 1576 the King's Printer Thomas Bassendyne printed Scotland's earliest translation of the New Testament. The close is today home to the Saltire Society, which promotes the uniqueness of Scottish culture and heritage.

12) Hyndford's Close: once the site of the 3rd Earl of Hyndford's 17th century mansion, this close was home to the Scottish chemist Daniel Rutherford (1749–1819), who discovered nitrogen in 1772. He was the uncle of novelist Sir Walter Scott (1771–1832), who became a freemason in the nearby St. David Lodge.

13) South Gray's Close: named after merchant John Gray, this close was also known as Mint Close because it housed the Scottish Royal Mint from 1574 until 1877.

14) Toddrick's Wynd: this unassuming close on the High Street dates back to 1466 and is perhaps the most historic of them all. It was here on 9th February 1567 that Mary, Queen of Scots and her entourage coming up the wynd after visiting her second husband, Lord Darnley (1565–1567), at Kirk o' Field passed James Hepburn, 4th Earl of Bothwell (1534–1578) coming down, with explosives for Darnley's assassination.

Other locations nearby: 12, 13, 15, 19, 20, 22, 32, 33

19 Growing Up through the Ages

EH1 1TG (Old Town), the Museum of Childhood at 42 High Street (Royal Mile)
Bus 6 to Jeffrey Street or St. Mary's Street; 35 to Royal Mile; 3, 5, 7, 8, 14, 29, 30, 31, 33, 37, 45, 49 to South Bridge

The Museum of Childhood at 42 High Street on the Royal Mile (EH1) is a magical world. Beyond its modest portal is a collection of artefacts that illustrate the growing up process across the generations, from toys and schooldays to clothing, health and holidays. Whilst younger visitors will enjoy learning about their historical counterparts, adults will enjoy a nostalgic trip down memory lane.

The story of the founding of the museum is worth mentioning. In 1955 local man Patrick Murray (1908–1981), Chairman of Edinburgh Council's Libraries and Museums Committee, read of two toy dolls, which had previously belonged to Queen Victoria. He was disappointed that such historic artefacts were being sent down to London because nowhere suitable could be found to display them in Scotland. After raising the issue with his colleagues, Murray found a home for the dolls in what is now the Writers' Museum in Lady Stair's Close.

The dolls were quickly joined by some of Murray's own childhood toys, which he modestly described as "a pitiful handful of soldiers, building blocks and railway stuff". As word spread others did likewise and soon the donation of objects outstripped the space allocated to display them. As a result in 1957 the collection was relocated to a restored 18th century tenement building in Hyndford's Close on the High Street, where it became the world's first museum devoted to the social history of childhood.

In 1962 Patrick Murray gave up his job at the council and became the museum's full time curator until his retirement a decade later. Surprisingly Murray expressed a dislike for children and promoted the museum as being about them but not for them. Always looking for ways to generate publicity, he even proposed a memorial window in the museum entrance celebrating the infamous biblical King Herod!

In 1986 the museum again expanded, this time westwards into South Gray's Close, where the museum's entrance can be found today. Immediately inside is a gallery containing large exhibits such as a working model of a haunted house and various slot machines. Upstairs is a wonderful collection of dolls' houses – one contains over 2,000

A display of dolls in the Museum of Childhood

items from tiny towels in the bathroom to skittles in the nursery – as well as toy trains, cars and aeroplanes.

The original museum building next door contains three floors, each given over to a single gallery. The first contains a vast display of dolls, soft toys and various forms of automata. On the floor above are educational items ranging from indoor and outdoor games, hobbies and construction sets to arts and crafts, reading and writing. It's impossible to miss the huge Meccano Ferris wheel and the Lego washstand! The final gallery on the top floor covers a variety of themes, including clothing and fancy dress, street life, the nursery and the classroom.

The museum today certainly differs from the time of Patrick Murray. The galleries now feature small chairs for small visitors, with a hands-on puppet theatre and dressing-up area, and the sound of children's voices and nursery rhymes throughout the building. At times it seems to be the noisiest museum in the world and it is difficult not to get caught up in all the fun.

Those with a special interest in schooling should visit the History of Education Centre in the grounds of Leith Walk Primary School at 9 Brunswick Road (EH7). Here can be found a fully-functioning Victorian schoolroom, replete with wooden desks, blackboards and items of corporal punishment, including the leather strap (tawse) and finger-stocks. Visits by appointment only (www.histedcentre.org.uk).

Other locations nearby: 18, 20, 22, 32, 33

20   A Hidden Medieval Relic

EH1 1SS (Old Town), Trinity Apse in Chalmers Close off the
High Street
Bus 6 to Jeffrey Street/St. Mary's Street; 35 to Chalmers
Close (note: visits inside by appointment only)

The draining of the Nor' Loch in the 18th century and the construction
of the North Bridge allowed Edinburgh to expand northwards. Princes
Street Gardens and Waverley Station now occupy the loch's former
footprint but there was a cultural cost. To build the station a magnificent Gothic building, Trinity College Kirk, was removed. The story of
what became of it is a little-known chapter in Edinburgh's history.

Trinity College Kirk, with its adjacent hospital (almshouse), was
founded in 1460 by Queen Mary of Gueldres in memory of her husband James II (1430–1460). Its purpose was to provide divine worship
under a provost and ten priests, and to care for 14 impoverished pensioners. Whenever one of the priests celebrated Mass he was obliged to
process to the founder's tomb clutching a sprig of hyssop and reciting
the *De Profundis*.

Although only the choir and transepts were ever completed, the
church was a sumptuous affair, with vaulted ceilings, silver chalices
and silk-fringed curtains draped around a statue of the Virgin. A highlight was the magnificent Trinity Altarpiece, a painted triptych attributed to the Flemish artist Hugo van der Goes (c.1430–1482), which is
displayed today in the Scottish National Gallery on The Mound (EH2).
It is a rare example of Scottish religious art that survived the iconoclasm of the Reformation.

The Kirk continued to be used after the Reformation as the North
East Quarter Church of Edinburgh, and during the 1590s it hosted the
graduation of university students in the presence of the Queen con-
sort. By 1726, however, the almshouse had become dilapidated, with
tumbling roof slates a danger to passers-by, and the fetid waters of the
Nor' Loch lapping at its walls. With the draining of the loch and the
arrival of the railways there were inevitably calls to demolish the crumbling edifice and to rebuild it elsewhere. The Society of Antiquaries of
Scotland was up in arms describing the threat as "an outrage by sordid
traders (who) would remove Pompeii for a railway"!

Eventually in 1848 the Kirk was taken down and a search conducted
for the body of Queen Mary. Two skeletons were found and reburied
in the royal vault at Holyrood. The demolition was carefully super-

vised and each precious piece of masonry carefully numbered and stored. The North British Railway provided sufficient funds for the Kirk to be rebuilt on another site but unfortunately many stones ended up lost or stolen (some fragments are allegedly embedded in the courtyard wall at 14 Springvalley Gardens (EH10) in far-away Morningside). Eventually in 1872 only the apse was reconstructed, as part of a new church in Chalmers Close (EH1), off the High Street. When the new church itself was demolished in the 1960s only the medieval fabric was left standing.

Trinity Apse is hidden away in Chalmers Close

To safeguard the Trinity Apse from further threat it has been given a Category A listing by Historic Environment Scotland. Considered one of Edinburgh's hidden architectural gems, it is visible from the outside, with visits inside by appointment (www. Edinburghmuseums.org.uk). A community and storytelling garden created as part of Edinburgh's Green Heritage project to reduce carbon emissions in the Old Town helps tell its story.

Equally well-concealed in nearby Carrubber's Close is Old St. Paul's Scottish Episcopal Church. Completed in 1883 it replaced an earlier church of 1689 founded by Alexander Rose (1647-1720), the former Bishop of St. Giles' Cathedral, who had been ousted when the Catholic James VII/II (1685-1688) was deposed by William and Mary (1689-1702). Whilst the Church of Scotland then became fully Presbyterian, Rose's congregation continued to support James and inevitably became part of the 1745 Jacobite Uprising.

Other locations nearby: 16, 18, 19, 20, 22, 32, 33

21 Martyrs, Soldiers and Shoemakers

EH1 3BQ (Old Town), Old Calton Burial Ground
at 27 Waterloo Place
Bus 34, 113 to Regent Bridge; 1, 4, 19, 22, 25 to Leith Street

Old Calton Burial Ground sits atop crags at the western end of Calton Hill. It was established in 1718 by the Society of the Incorporated Trades of Calton for use as a non-denominational burial ground by the inhabitants of Calton Village, which once stood nearby. The present-day street called Calton Hill was the original access road from the village up to the cemetery.

From afar the cemetery's obvious focal point is the Political Martyrs' Monument. This soaring obelisk commemorates five men, who in 1793 were deported to Australia for treason. In reality their only 'crime' was to fight for universal suffrage. Not until the passing of the Scottish Reform Act in 1832 were the men eventually pardoned. Since none of them had any connection with Calton, it is assumed the obelisk was placed here purely for dramatic effect.

Another historically important monument is the American Civil War Memorial, which was erected at American expense in 1893 to five Scots, who died fighting for the union of North and South. It depicts a standing figure of Abraham Lincoln, with a freed slave at his feet, a reminder that Lincoln abolished slavery. It is notable as being not only the first statue of an American President outside the United States but also the only monument to the conflict beyond American shores.

Alongside it is the cylindrical tower tomb of the philosopher David Hume (1711–1776), who was a key figure in the Scottish Enlightenment. Designed by the neo-Classical architect Robert Adam (1728–1792), the tomb was initially guarded against vandalism due to Hume's professed atheism. Because of this it is said that Hume's friends jokingly nicknamed the street where he lived 'St. David Street', which it retains to this day.

Several graves reflect the shoemaking trade, which was once prevalent in Calton. That of "Margrat Thomson, spous to James Forsyth, shoemecker" is remarkable for its carvings, which include a skull and cross-bones, crossed spades and a winged hourglass signifying the transience of life. Another remarkable headstone is that erected by Captain John Gray in memory of his parents. It is carved beautifully

with a skull, a three-masted ship and an inscription flanked by the skeletons of his mother and father, intertwined with funerary symbols, including a scythe and a coffin.

Also worth finding is the mausoleum of architect Robert Burn (1752–1815), who designed the Nelson Monument on Calton Hill, and the grave of Archibald Constable (1774–1827), who published Walter Scott's novels (see no. 64). His publishing company founded in Edinburgh in 1795 remains the oldest independent publisher still operating under its founder's name.

The construction of Regent Bridge and Waterloo Place in 1815 dissected the Calton Burial Ground. This necessitated the relocation of many graves to the New Calton Burial Ground, which opened in 1820 half a mile east on Regent Road. Highlights here include several imposing family vaults and the graves of members of the family of Robert Louis Stevenson. A watch-tower built near the entrance was designed to deter graverobbers. Despite only being only around 16 feet in diameter it is said to have accommodated a family of ten!

Overlooking the cemetery is the Robert Burns Monument designed by Thomas Hamilton (1784–1858). Based on the Choragic Monument of Lysicrates in Athens, it originally contained a marble statue of Burns by the sculptor John Flaxman (1755–1826) but this has been removed to the Scottish National Portrait Gallery due to environmental pollution. The surrounding garden contains plants mentioned in Burns' poetry.

Other locations nearby: 62, 63, 64

22 Scotland's Religious Revolutionary

EH1 1SR (Old Town), the John Knox House and Scottish
Storytelling Centre at 43–45 High Street
Bus 6 to Jeffrey Street or St. Mary's Street; 35 to Royal Mile,
3, 5, 7, 8, 14, 29, 30, 31, 33, 37, 45, 49 to South Bridge

As a leader of the Protestant Reformation, the firebrand cleric and theologian John Knox (c.1513–1572) is considered the founder of Scottish Presbyterianism. As a supporter of the ousting of the Catholic Queen Regent, Mary of Guise (1554–1560), who governed Scotland in the name of her young daughter, Mary, Queen of Scots (1542–1567), he is also remembered as Scotland's religious revolutionary.

Knox was born in East Lothian and was probably educated at the University of St. Andrews. It was a time when the priesthood was the only career path for those with academic leanings and by 1540 he is documented as having become a Catholic priest. The execution in 1546 of the early church reformer George Wishart, however, at the hands of Cardinal David Beaton, forced a change of heart. Following the revenge killing of Beaton the same year at St. Andrew's Castle, Knox signed up to help reform the Scottish church and began developing his oratory skills there.

These were tumultuous times in Scotland and the intervention in 1547 of Mary of Guise supported by the French navy saw the castle besieged and Knox taken prisoner. After his release in 1549 he was exiled to England, where he took an active part in the ongoing English Reformation. Knox was again forced into exile in 1553, when the Catholic Mary Tudor ascended the English throne. His best known pamphlet, *The First Blast of the Trumpet Against the Monstruous Regiment of Women*, was written with her in mind!

Knox returned to Scotland in 1559, where Mary of Guise had been ousted from Edinburgh by a group of Protestant nobles known as the Lords of the Congregation (see no. 72). The town council elected him minister at St. Giles' on the High Street from where he helped organise the newly-reformed non-episcopal church known as the Kirk (see no. 12). Following Mary's unexpected death a year later Knox continued his work by admonishing Mary, Queen of Scots for supporting Catholic practices.

During the 1560s Knox occupied a house in Warriston's Close (EH1) marked today by a wall plaque. He then relocated to England for a while before returning to Edinburgh a year before his death. At this time he reputedly lived in a house at 43–45 High Street (EH1) but there are doubts since it is known to have been occupied at the time by James Mossman (1519–1573), a jeweller and goldsmith to Mary, Queen of Scots. Before his execution, Mossman was one of the Queen's Men, who seized Edinburgh Castle in an attempt to restore Mary after her forced abdication in favour of her Protestant son, James VI/I (1567–1625).

Whatever the truth, the building known today as the John Knox House was built in the late 15th century and is one of the last intact medieval buildings on the Royal Mile. Thanks to the association with Knox, the building escaped demolition enabling today's visitors to learn not only about Knox but also about one of the most turbulent chapters in Scottish history.

Religious reformer John Knox in a St. Giles' Cathedral window

Attached to the John Knox House is the award-wining Scottish Storytelling Centre, the world's first modern purpose-built centre for live storytelling. Designed by Edinburgh's Malcolm Fraser Architects, it contains an intimate 99-seat auditorium, library and interactive Storywall. The annual Scottish Storytelling Festival takes place here in October. The centre's bookshop is located in the former Luckenbooth of the John Knox House, the only remaining example of the medieval lockable retail booths that once lined the High Street (see no. 13).

Other locations nearby: 18, 19, 20, 23, 30, 32

23 The Modern Knights of St. John

EH8 8DG (Old Town), the Chancery of the Order of St. John
Scotland at 21 St. John Street
Bus 35 to Canongate Kirk (note: visits by appointment only)

At the top of St. John Street (EH8) amongst buildings of the University of Edinburgh's Holyrood Campus is an 18th century house. It wouldn't warrant attention were it not for the Maltese Cross hanging over the door. This identifies it as the Chancery (headquarters) of the Order of St. John Scotland.

The Order's origins stretch back to the mid-11th century and the founding of the Hospital of St. John in Jerusalem, which provided weary pilgrims to the Holy Land with accommodation and medical assistance. Following the conquest of Jerusalem in 1099, the hospital staff formed a Catholic military order to protect Christians, which became known as the Knights of St. John or the Knights Hospitallers.

The Order still exists today as the Rome-based Catholic lay Order of Malta. Down the centuries it has recruited members and acquired property throughout Western Europe. Its first property in Scotland was acquired at Torpichen in West Lothian during the reign of David I (1124–1153). This was the Order's administrative centre in Scotland until its forced closure during the Reformation.

Fast forward now to the 19th century, when the Order of Malta was revived in Britain through a new organisation called the Order of St. John, which Queen Victoria made a Royal Order of Chivalry, with the monarch as its Head. Out of this in 1877 grew the St. John Ambulance Association, whose purpose was to provide training in first aid. A decade later the St. John Ambulance Brigade was established as a uniformed body of trained volunteers providing first aid to the public.

In 1908 it was decided that the St. Andrew's Ambulance Association, which in 1882 had operated Scotland's first ambulance, would take over ambulance and first aid training in Scotland. By the 1940s, however, the Order of St. John saw further potential to undertake charitable public services in Scotland and so in 1947 the Chancery on St. John Street was opened. Since then it has supported mountain rescue projects in Scotland and emergency health projects around the world.

On the Chancery gates is a coat of arms featuring the crowned thistle of Torpichen, the Royal Crest of England and the Order's motto *Pro Fide, Pro Utilate Hominum* (For the Faith, In the Service of Humanity). Interested parties can visit the Chancery by appointment (tel. 0131556 8711).

Of related interest is St. Vincent's Chapel on St. Vincent Street (EH3), a Victorian Gothic gem, which was used during the 1970s and 80s by a briefly revived Military and Hospitaller Order of St. Lazarus, whose impressive armorial embellishments still adorn the interior.

Heraldic devices identify the Chancery of the Order of St. John Scotland

The Canongate is reached from St. John Street through St. John's Pend. Embedded in the road is a Maltese Cross, marking where the Canongate (or Burgh) Mercat Cross (now removed to Canongate Kirkyard) once denoted the ancient boundary between the *burgh* of Edinburgh and that of the Canongate. The Knights of the Order of St. John owned property here in the Middle Ages hence the cross also being called St. John's Cross. Nearby is Old Moray House, one of the few remaining aristocratic homes built here in the 17th century. Unmissable for its obelisk-flanked gateway, it retains a room with an ornate plaster ceiling where Cromwell stayed. In the car park to the rear (best accessed from the top of Viewcraig Street) is a pantiled former summerhouse, where allegedly the Act of Union with England was signed in 1707. The tenant of Old Moray House at the time was James Ogilvie (1664–1730), Lord Chancellor of Scotland, whose job it was to secure the controversial union with England.

Other locations nearby: 20, 22, 24, 25, 26

24 Edinburgh in Eight Objects

**EH8 8DD (Old Town), the Museum of Edinburgh at
142 Canongate
Bus 35 to Canongate Kirk**

Anyone interested in the story of Edinburgh should visit the Museum of Edinburgh at 142 Canongate (EH8). The building itself is one of the exhibits, comprising several 16th century tenements arranged around a typical Old Town close. The writer and publisher Robert Chambers (1802–1871) called it "the speaking house" on account of the Latin proverbs adorning the façade. The most recent – *Antiqua Tamen Juvenseco* (I am old but renew my youth) – was added in 1932, when the building became a museum.

The rooms inside, which in 1851 housed 323 tenants, are now filled instead with historic artefacts. Here are just eight of them:

1) The most important exhibit is an original copy of the National Covenant. Made from deerskin, it was signed in 1638 in Greyfriars Kirk by around 4,000 members of the Presbyterian Church in Scotland. In so doing they rejected the attempt by Charles I (1625–1649) to force the Scottish church to conform to English liturgical practice and church governance. The confrontations that ensued between the Covenanters and the House of Stuart led to the English Civil War.

2) Also from the 17th century is the 'Stingmen Stane'. This remarkable carving depicts the wine porters (Stingmen) of Leith unloading barrels from ships and transporting them to warehouses before transhipment up to Edinburgh (see no. 76).

3) The late 18th century is represented by copies of the plan for Edinburgh's First New Town drafted by architect James Craig (1739–1795) (see no. 61). A sedan chair illustrates how life in the elegant Georgian New Town was a world away from the squalid tenements of the Old Town.

4) A less well-known chapter is the city's involvement with the transatlantic slave trade. Imports into Edinburgh in the 1770s included cotton, coffee, sugar, rum and tobacco. On display is a tobacconist's trade sign in the form of a highlander taking a pinch of snuff. Nearby Sugarhouse Close recalls the refining of sugar harvested by slaves and it is a sobering thought that in 1817 a third of slaves in Jamaica were owned by Scots.

5) A significant date for Edinburgh was 15th August 1822, when George IV (1820–1830) became the first British monarch to visit Scot-

land for 171 years. The spectacular event was orchestrated by Sir Walter Scott (1771–1832), who encouraged Clan members to revive the wearing of Highland dress, as depicted in a lively oil painting of Princes Street at the time.

6) Firm favourites in the museum are the objects relating to Greyfriars Bobby. The story of how this loyal Skye terrier attended the grave of his master in Greyfriars Kirkyard still touches hearts despite recently being debunked (see no. 38). Bobby's feeding bowl and inscribed collar are displayed.

7) From the early 20th century are personal effects relating to Edinburgh-born Field Marshall Douglas Haig (1861–1928), Commander

A tobacconist's trade sign in the Museum of Edinburgh

of the British Forces during the First World War. A divisive figure because of his tactics, he helped promote the wearing of poppies on Remembrance Day (see nos. 53 & 81).

8) Industries connected with the Canongate are represented by silverware produced by the Hammermen's Guild, which once owned part of the museum building. Representing the industrialisation of Edinburgh is a reconstruction of William Christie's clay pipe workshop in Leith, which closed in 1962. It is in the Courtyard Gallery in Bakehouse Close alongside other pieces of historic stonework, including several craft incorporation stones.

Those objects not displayed including everything from cannonballs to early televisions are stored in the Museums Collection Centre at 10 Broughton Market (EH3). Guided tours are available on the first Tuesday of the month at 2pm.

Other locations nearby: 23, 25, 26, 27, 28

25　A Slice of Edinburgh Life

EH8 8BN (Old Town), the People's Story Museum at
163 Canongate (Royal Mile)
Bus 35 to Canongate Kirk

The name of the Canongate, which forms the lower half of Edinburgh's Royal Mile, means the Canons' Way. It is a reminder that this area was originally an autonomous *burgh* distinct from that of Edinburgh, given to the canons of Holyrood Abbey after its foundation by David I (1124–1153). Until its incorporation into Edinburgh in 1886, the Canongate *burgh* stretched from the Canongate (or Burgh) Mercat Cross outside Edinburgh's Netherbow Port down to the Girth Cross (marked by a circle of setts outside the Scottish Parliament), which in turn marked the limit of the Holyrood Sanctuary (see nos. 39, 23 & 94).

Although it was never surrounded by a wall, the Canongate was like Edinburgh in that it consisted of a series of 'closes' (alleys) running off the main street, in which 'lands' (tenement buildings) were built. It was also like Edinburgh in that it had its own jail-cum-council chamber, the Canongate Tolbooth, built in 1591 (see no. 13). Still standing and displaying the Canongate arms in the form of a stag's head with a cross between its antlers, it is home to the fascinating People's Story Museum.

The People's Story Museum focusses squarely on the human face of Edinburgh from the 1780s until the present day. As such it complements nicely the displays in the Museum of Edinburgh opposite (see no. 24). The use of sounds and life-like mannequins really brings the past to life here and the experience begins at the front door, where visitors are greeted by members of the Ross family, who represent the residents of the squalid, overcrowded Old Town of the 1700s. How times have changed!

More mannequins follow including a couple preparing for the annual St. Crispin's Day procession. They are a reminder that the Hall of the Incorporation of Cordiners (Shoemakers) was at 197 Canongate, where a cordiner's knife and the crown of St. Crispin, patron saint of cobblers, are carved on the façade. Other mannequins include a town crier, a soldier of the Town Guard and a prisoner occupying what was once the jail of the Canongate Tolbooth.

Up on the first floor there are displays illustrating how various crafts and industries have developed in Edinburgh. Particularly interesting are those relating to shipbuilding and harbour life on the Firth

Fergusson's Tea Room reconstructed in the People's Story Museum

of Forth, coopering, brewing and distilling. It is easy to forget that until as recently as the 1980s, the Canongate had several breweries, including one in Thomson's Land behind Sugarhouse Close (now student accommodation). Other displays cover baking, tailoring, printing and bookbinding, with another mannequin dressed as a First World War tram conductress.

The second floor of the museum illustrates the development of housing in Edinburgh and begins with a scene from a typical Old Town tenement slum. Thereafter are reconstructions of a sleeping booth in a Grove Street lodging house for homeless men, a World War Two working class kitchen, and a scene from the Murdoch Terrace public washhouse in Dalry (a solitary extant washhouse can be found at 23 Union Street (EH1), its red brick chimney still standing). On a lighter note are scenes showing how the people of Edinburgh spent their leisure time. A 1930s reconstruction shows two ladies taking tea in Fergusson's Tea Room, while their husbands enjoy a pint in the Empire Bar next door. Also here are cabinets illustrating faith, festivals and friendly societies, with some fascinating artefacts and photos.

The third and final floor of the museum is currently used as a temporary exhibition space.

Other locations nearby: 23, 24, 26, 27, 28

26 The Coachman's Stone and Other Burials

EH8 8BN (Old Town), Canongate Kirk and Kirkyard
at 153 Canongate (Royal Mile)
Bus 35 to Canongate Kirk

When the Canongate Kirk (EH8) was completed in 1691 it was architecturally unusual for the time. Outside it features a Dutch-style gable and a Doric entrance portico. Inside it has a cruciform layout, which is highly irregular for a post-Reformation, pre-Victorian church. An inscription over the doorway records how the building was commissioned by James VII/II (1685–1688) using money bequeathed by a local merchant. Previously the Protestant congregation had worshipped at Holyrood Abbey, which the king now converted into a Royal Chapel for the Order of the Thistle (see no. 94).

The Kirkyard, which was used for burials until the mid-20th century, is also of great interest since it contains many Edinburgh worthies and a wide variety of funerary monuments. The oldest date from the 18th century and include the so-called Coachman's Stone. Erected around 1770, it is adorned with a depiction of a coach and horses thundering over a stone bridge. The accompanying inscription explains that it commemorates the Canongate Society of Coachdrivers, which once operated the eight day Edinburgh-to-London route from nearby White Horse Close, one of the most picturesque yet easily missed closes on the Royal Mile (the five archways that once led to the stables can still be seen on Calton Road behind the close).

The most important grave from this period is that of the philosopher and economist Adam Smith (1723–1790), who founded the study of political economics and wrote *The Wealth of Nations*. He lived on nearby Panmure Close from the 1770s until his death. Simple by comparison is the headstone of the poet Robert Fergusson (1750–1774). His career was cut tragically short by a head injury that saw him placed in the Edinburgh lunatic asylum. Robert Burns (1759–1796) was inspired to become a poet after reading Fergusson's work and physician Andrew Duncan (1744–1828) was compelled to establish the more humane Royal Edinburgh Hospital (see no. 87). Burns arranged for Fergusson's headstone to be erected and penned the epitaph himself. A life-sized bronze of Fergusson was erected in 2004 just outside the Kirkyard.

Other 18th century graves include those of John Frederick Lampe (1703–1751), who composed hymns for Charles Wesley, George Drummond (1688–1766), six times Lord Provost and instigator of the New Town, and James Gregory (1753–1821), the inventor of Gregory's Powder, a once-popular stomach medicine.

Amongst the 19th century burials is the sturdy barrel-vaulted mausoleum of philosopher and Adam Smith biographer, Dugald Stewart (1753–1828). A similarly imposing mausoleum is that of wealthy merchant and philanthropist William Fettes (1750–1836) at the bottom of which is a plaque marking where the Ballantyne brothers, publishers and friends of Sir Walter Scott, were buried in poverty.

The Coachmen's Stone in the Canongate Kirkyard

Also worth tracking down is the grave of the surgeon Joseph Bell, (1787–1848), tutor to Arthur Conan Doyle and inspiration for Sherlock Holmes (see no. 66).

Other monuments in the Kirkyard include the Canongate (or Burgh) Mercat Cross of 1128, which originally stood further up the Canongate, where it denoted the ancient boundary with Edinburgh, and a cross erected in 1880 to dead soldiers from Edinburgh Castle. An ancient connection between the Augustinian canons of Holyrood Abbey and their Church of St. Mary at the Castle meant the latter was considered part of the Canongate parish despite being physically detached.

A tomb down one side of the Kirk has been claimed to be that of David Rizzio (1533–1566), the murdered private secretary of Mary, Queen of Scots (1542–1567), although it seems unlikely that an Italian Catholic would be reinterred in a Protestant graveyard 120 years after his death.

Other locations nearby: 23, 24, 25, 27, 28

27 Old Town Secret Gardens

EH8 8BW (Old Town), Dunbar's Close Garden at
137 Canongate and other Old Town secret gardens
Bus 35 to Canongate Kirk

Despite demolition, destruction and rebuilding along Edinburgh's Royal Mile, there are still more than 80 ancient 'closes' (alleys) running off it, like the bones on the spine of a fish (see nos. 11 & 18). All have a story to tell and a few contain secret gardens. Some of these are reconstructions of ancient gardens once attached to well-to-do 'lands' (tenement buildings); others are modern ones designed to bring more green into the Old Town.

The most secretive is Dunbar's Close Garden at 137 Canongate (EH8). Despite claims that it was created by pioneering Scottish environmental town planner Sir Patrick Geddes (1854–1932) as part of his vision to bring light and space into the overcrowded Old Town, it actually dates from the 1970s, when swathes of the run-down Canongate were cleared for housing. Geddes would have approved though because the space was acquired by the Mushroom Trust, a charity that supports urban greening. They gifted it to the City, which in turn commissioned Scottish landscape architect Seamus Filor to create a garden. His response was to show how a garden here might have looked in the 17th century, when the Canongate was a well-to-do place to live. Upon completion in 1978 it was named after David Dunbar, who owned tenements that stood here in the 1770s.

Typically for the Old Town, the plot is long, narrow and walled. On one side is Canongate Kirkyard and on the other Panmure House, where the philosopher and economist Adam Smith (1723–1790) lived from the 1770s until his death. The garden is divided into eight square and rectangular parterres defined by trimmed box hedging and planted with period species, including the Tulip Tree brought back in the 1660s as seed from North America and Florentine Irises once prized as a fixative for perfumes. All that's missing are the fashionable ladies who frequented the area in Robert Burns' day to wash down oyster suppers with ale and punch!

Across the road in Bakehouse Close stands Acheson House, a splendid example of a 17th century Scottish townhouse. It was built in 1633 for Sir Archibald Acheson of Glencairn (1583–1634), then Secretary of State for Scotland, and his initials appear over the windows. The long-abandoned walled garden has recently been revived by a voluntary group of Old Town residents, the Patrick Geddes Gardening Club, for growing their own vegetables. Currently, however, their efforts are only visible through the keyhole.

Walk up the Canongate now passing Chessel's Court, where a series of well-tended modern cottage gardens front several 18th century tenements. Another modern green space is peaceful Hope's Court in Trunk's Close at 55 High Street. Designed by landscape architects Mark Turnbull Jeffrey, it contains a pocket handkerchief tree, which produces papery white blooms in late May, and a bust of Geddes (see no. 5).

Away from the Royal Mile, another of Geddes' Old Town gardens is the Johnston Terrace Garden

Not everyone is aware of Dunbar's Close Garden

off the Patrick Geddes Steps (EH1), which is today the Scottish Wildlife Trust's smallest nature reserve (although it is normally kept locked). Nearby Grannie's Green, a former washing and bleaching slope, is a recent garden commemorating Geddes' achievements and the West Port Garden down on the Grassmarket (EH1) was created in 1910 by Geddes' daughter (open Sunday afternoons).

Although New Town's secret gardens are mostly private, they can be accessed on a tour with garden expert Jean Bareham (www.greenyondertours.com). She takes visitors to East Queen Street Garden (EH3), with its graceful trees and Greek temple, and Central Queen Street Garden, with its pond where the young Robert Louis Stevenson first imagined his *Treasure Island*.

Other locations nearby: 23, 24, 25, 26, 28

28   A Poem in Glass and Stone

EH8 8DT (Old Town), the Scottish Poetry Library at
5 Crichton's Close
Bus 6 to Holyrood Road then walk up Gentle's Entry; 35 to
Canongate Kirk

Between March 2011 and November 2012, ten intricate sculptures made from the pages of books were found in libraries and cultural institutions across Edinburgh. The first appeared in the Scottish Poetry Library at 5 Crichton's Close (EH8), with a gift tag that read "for you in support of libraries, books, words, ideas". Although the sculptor has never been identified, the sculpture has helped draw attention to one of Edinburgh's unique literary landmarks.

The Scottish Poetry Library (SPL) was founded in 1984 by poet Tessa Ransford (1938–2015). Her goal was not only to create a national poetry resource but also to expose as wide an audience as possible to its benefits. With poet Tom Hubbard (b. 1950) on board as librarian and grants from the Scottish Arts Council and Gulbenkian Foundation, the SPL was initially a modest affair. With a part-time staff of two, it boasted just 300 books in cramped quarters in Tweedale Court (EH1).

Ransford's determination that the SPL should one day occupy a building of its own reached fruition in 1997, when she secured a National Lottery Capital Grant. The new building, which opened in 1999 in Crichton's Close, was designed by Edinburgh's Malcolm Fraser Architects. Described as "a poem in glass and stone", the visually arresting structure has won several awards for its distinctive modern style that blends happily with its Old Town surroundings.

Although the SPL is not the only poetry library in the world it is the only purpose-built, independent one with a lending library. Now containing over 45,000 works, it is also the world's largest open-access collection of Scottish poetry, with works in all three of Scotland's indigenous languages (Scottish Gaelic, Lowland Scots, and English), as well as poetry from 200 other countries. Here Scottish poetry greats such as Don Paterson (b. 1963), Kathleen Jamie (b. 1962) and Norman McCaig (1910–1996) rub shoulders with new bloods such as Miriam Gamble, William Letford and Richie McCaffery. Also here (and viewable on request) is the full published archive of Edwin Morgan (1920–2010), who in 2004 was made the first Scots Makar (National Poet). It was a line from his poem *A Trace of Wings* that was included in the book sculpture deposited at the SPL in 2011.

The Scottish Poetry Library in Crichton's Close

In 2015 the SPL underwent a refurbishment courtesy of Nicoll Russell Studios. Reopened later the same year by the second Scots Makar, Liz Lochhead (b. 1947), there is now even more space for books, as well as a soundproofed area so that recording and performance can take place alongside quiet reading and writing. As Lochhead said at the time, the SPL now contains "space for the sounds, as well as the texts, of poetry".

The SPL was always meant to be a social space and it is even moreso now. A garage rendered redundant when the mobile library service was withdrawn has been repurposed as an events and meeting space. There is also a sheltered terrace area for conversation and outdoor performance, and a welcoming new entrance that has increased the visibility of what goes on inside. An ongoing programme of literary events, exhibitions, workshops and reading groups means that the SPL is today a place of both calm and energy.

A map detailing where to find all the mysterious book sculptures is available at the SPL (www.scottishpoetrylibrary.org.uk). It includes the Edinburgh Central Library, Scottish Storytelling Centre, Writers' Museum, National Museum of Scotland and Edinburgh Filmhouse. That belonging to the National Library of Scotland is stored away for safekeeping but several newly-commissioned sculptures are displayed in the foyer. Another has recently been made for the new Patrick Geddes Centre (see no. 5).

Other locations nearby: 23, 24, 25, 26, 27, 28, 29

29   Parliaments Old and New

EH99 1SP (Old Town), the Scottish Parliament on Horse Wynd
at the foot of the Canongate
Bus 6, 35 to Holyrood Parliament (note: reduced visiting
hours when Parliament is in recess)

Scotland's rulers have long discussed matters of state with their subjects albeit at times with only a chosen few. A number of locations have provided the venue where such Parliaments – from the French *Parlement* meaning 'discussion' – have convened. These have included Edinburgh Castle, Holyrood Abbey and the Old Tolbooth (see nos. 1, 13 & 94). Prior to Scotland's controversial Union with England in 1707, Parliament met in the custom-built Parliament Hall off the High Street, which is where this tour begins.

Considering the fact that visits to Parliament Hall are rarely advertised, it is not surprising that most visitors bypass this historic building altogether. Those interested will find it inside Parliament House at 11 Parliament Square (EH1), which lies partially concealed behind St. Giles' Cathedral. The historic 17th century debating chamber, where the notorious Deacon Brodie was tried in 1788, remains gloriously intact. The hammer-beam roof of Danish oak is an architectural marvel and the walls are hung with portraits of Edinburgh's parliamentary grandees.

That there are portraits of legal personalities here too is a reminder that after the Union with England, when the building lost its legislative role, it became the legal heart of Scotland instead. The German-made stained glass window installed in 1868 depicts the inauguration in 1532 of the Court of Session (civil court) and the College of Justice (criminal court), which originally met with the Scottish Parliament here. Courts were summoned through the tiny Macer's Window still visible at the top of one of the walls. These days Parliament Hall is just one of a complex of buildings associated with the Scottish Supreme Courts and is used as a meeting place for lawyers and their clients.

On 30th March 1989 a call for the creation of a new Scottish Parliament was made in the General Assembly Hall of the Church of Scotland on Mound Place (EH1). Organised by the Campaign for a Scottish Assembly, it was signed by 58 out of 72 Scottish Members of Parliament. A tented vigil was manned around the clock on Calton Hill to promote the cause and in 1997 a national Devolution Referendum confirmed overwhelmingly that Scotland would again have its own parliament, the first since 1707 (the tent is now displayed in the National Museum of Scotland on Chambers Street (EH1)).

It was decided to base the new Scottish Parliament at the foot of the Canongate, where the clearance of a brewery had created a brownfield site ripe for development. Built to a radical design by the Catalan architect Enric Miralles (1955–2000) and opened by Her Majesty the Queen on 9th October 2004, the building is unmissable. From the outside it comprises an organic complex of low-lying structures resembling rocky crags and upturned fishing boats representing the connection of the Scottish people with their natural surroundings. This is reinforced by the use of Scottish materials in the construction. To the north-

The new Scottish Parliament was designed by Enric Miralles

west the complex includes the 17th century Queensberry House and integrates with the pre-existing medieval street plan: to the south-east it blends more loosely into the natural landscape. Free guided and self-guided tours of the interior are available six days a week and take in the public gallery of the debating chamber (www.parliament.scot).

The second anniversary of the opening of the Scottish Parliament was marked by the creation of a stone circle at the east end of Regents Park Road (EH8). Each of the 32 stones comes from a different region of Scotland and all are joined by a unifying steel ring. It is one of several stops on the Scotland Democracy Trail, a walk illustrating Scotland's 500 year-long quest for democracy (www.greenyondertours.com).

Other locations nearby: 26, 27, 28, 94, 95

30 From High School to Low Carbon

EH1 1LZ (Old Town), the Edinburgh Centre for Carbon
Innovation in High School Yards
Bus 3, 5, 7, 8, 14, 29, 30, 31, 33, 35, 37, 45, 49 to South Bridge
(note: guided tours by appointment only)

Many European cities have made attempts at reducing the carbon footprint of their public buildings but few have found success without
controversy. London's City Hall in Southwark is a case in point. In
Edinburgh, however, there is one building that has not only had its
energy consumption significantly reduced but has also become a hub
for low carbon learning. What makes the Edinburgh Centre for Carbon
Innovation (ECCI) in High School Yards (EH1) really special is that it is
housed inside the city's 18th century Old High School.

High School Yards has witnessed a lot of history. In 1230 Blackfriars
Monastery was founded here by Alexander II (1214–1249), which explains the discovery of a medieval knight's grave in the car park. Fragments of the Flodden Wall at the corner of nearby Drummond Street
and the Pleasance show that the monastery was protected during the
16th century (see no. 39). After the monastery was destroyed in 1558
during the Scottish Reformation, Mary, Queen of Scots (1542–1567)
was persuaded to hand over the land so that the Royal High School
could be built. This was replaced in 1777 by the present larger building, which was regarded as Edinburgh's top educational establishment.
Its pupils included the novelist Sir Walter Scott (1771–1832), whose
initials may be those carved on the doorway, and the educational reformer James Pillans (1778–1864), inventor of the modern blackboard.

In 1829 the school relocated to Regent Road (EH7) and the building was occupied by the Edinburgh Royal Infirmary, with antiseptic
pioneer Joseph Lister (1827–1912) in charge of the wards. Later it was
used by the University of Edinburgh to house various departments,
including Science & Engineering, Geography, Dentistry, and Archaeology, until its abandonment in 2011.

In the years that followed, Edinburgh's Malcolm Fraser Architects
set about simultaneously preserving the heritage of the Old High School
whilst installing sustainable modern structures inside it. At design stage
it became the first refurbished historic building in the UK to be ranked
outstanding by BREEAM, the world's leading sustainability rating sys-

The Edinburgh Centre for Carbon Innovation combines old and new architecture

tem for the built environment, which takes into account factors such as waste and pollution, land use and ecology, materials, management, health and well-being, energy and transport. The building was also named Building of the Year at the Edinburgh Architectural Awards 2014.

Numerous factors are behind the ECCI's sustainable design. They include the careful consideration of building fabric, prioritising natural, local and recycled materials, and a specialised 'vapour open' system of insulation to limit energy loss whilst ensuring good indoor air quality. Other features include recovering heat from the upper levels of the central atrium to pre-heat the air serving occupied spaces, solar controlled glazing in the windows to reduce the need for cooling, energy efficient lighting controls, a rooftop rainwater harvesting system for flusing the WCs, and under-floor heating connected to a nearby Combined Heat and Power plant. It should also be noted that reusing an existing building like the Old High School rather than demolishing it and building anew is also a part of sustainability, as is improving the building's integration into the surrounding area. All these factors help contribute to an impressive 30% saving in energy consumption over the building's former performance and a 38% decrease in CO_2 emissions.

Today the ECCI attracts experts from business, government and academia to help solve problems associated with climate change and the transition to a low carbon way of life. Members of the public are welcome to visit, too, with guided tours available on request (www. Edinburghcentre.org).

Other locations nearby: 31, 32, 33, 34, 42, 43

31 The Dovecot Tapestry Weavers

EH1 1LT (Old Town), the Dovecot Tapestry Studio
at 10 Infirmary Street
Bus 3, 5, 7, 8, 14, 29, 30, 31, 33, 35, 37, 45, 49 to South Bridge
(note: the Weaving Floor can only be observed on Thursday,
Friday and Saturday at appointed times)

Old Town's Infirmary Street (EH1) has quite a story to tell. It is named after the Edinburgh Royal Infirmary, which was established in 1736 with just four beds in a small house on the corner with South Bridge. In 1741 after outgrowing these premises it moved down the street to a 228-bed building designed for the purpose by renowned architect William Adam (1689–1748). Here it remained until 1832, when it relocated to the disused Royal High School in nearby High School Yards, then moved again in 1853 to a new building on nearby Drummond Street (thereafter the Infirmary moved in 1879 to Lauriston Place (EH3) and finally in 2003 to Little France (EH16) in Liberton).

In 1884 the William Adam-designed building was demolished and replaced by the Infirmary Street Baths. Designed by City Architect Robert Morham (1839–1912), these were Edinburgh's first public baths, built as part of an ongoing plan to avoid cholera outbreaks by improving public sanitation. It is worth noting that one of Scottish medicine's unsung heroes is Leith-born Thomas Latta (1796–1833), who pioneered the saline drip to rehydrate cholera patients during the 1832 epidemic. When the Baths eventually closed in 1995, the building stood empty for a decade and was threatened with demolition. Fortunately in 2006 it was sold to the Dovecot Tapestry Studio and transformed into the landmark workshop and gallery seen today.

The Studio had been founded in Corstorphine in 1912 by John Crichton-Stuart, 4th Marquess of Bute (1881–1947). The original weavers came from William Morris' furnishings and decorative arts workshops in London and their first commission was for a series of large tapestries for the Marquess's home, Mount Stuart House, on the Isle of Bute. Rebranded the Edinburgh Tapestry Company after the Second World War, the Studio evolved constantly. It embraced modernism in the fifties, for example, utilising designs supplied by Henry Moore and Cecil Beaton, and in the sixties associated with artists such as David Hockney and Leith's Eduardo Paolozzi. In the 1990s the studio wove Britain's largest ever tapestry, which now hangs in the British Library.

New funding in 2001 saw the Dovecot Tapestry Studio name re-established and in 2008 it moved into the former Infirmary Street Baths, which had undergone a sensitive and award-winning refurbishment at the hands of Edinburgh's Malcolm Fraser Architects, re-nowned for their work at Edin-burgh's Scottish Poetry Library and Scottish Storytelling Centre (see nos. 22 & 28). The weav-ers and tufters of the Dovecot Tapestry Studio now honour the legacy of their forebears in what was once the main swim-ming pool. Although visitors cannot stray onto the Weav-ing Floor they can observe the looms from a viewing balcony on Thursdays, Fridays and Saturdays. Elsewhere in the building, the former Ladies' Bath, which recalls when pub-lic bathing was segregated, is now used as the Dovecot Gal-lery. Here contemporary art, craft and design is promoted through a vibrant exhibition programme sponsored by the charitable Dovecot Foundation.

Stairwell Weave-In is a site-specific installation by Shane Waltener at Dovecot Studios

When William Adam's Royal Edinburgh Infirmary was demolished several key architec-tural elements from the building were recycled. The ornamental gates, for example, were moved to the new Infirmary building on Drummond Street, which is now used by the University of Edinburgh's School of GeoSciences. Four Ionic pilasters from the façade were combined to form a monument to the Covenanters outside Dreghorn Barracks on Redford Road (EH13). The most important element, the surgical theatre in the attic of the building, was reworked as a gate lodge for Redford House almost opposite the barracks and can easily be identified by its oversized stone volutes.

Other locations nearby: 30, 32, 33, 34, 42, 43

32 Scotland's Oldest Concert Hall

EH1 1NQ (Old Town), St. Cecilia's Hall on Niddry Street
Bus 3, 5, 7, 8, 14, 29, 30, 31, 33, 35, 37, 45, 49 to South Bridge

Many visitors to Edinburgh will be unaware that an exceptional Georgian treasure lies hidden on Niddry Street (EH1). St. Cecilia's Hall is Scotland's oldest purpose-built concert hall yet time and urban development have gradually overshadowed it and the world-class collection of musical instruments it contains. Now the University of Edinburgh has reinvigorated this important building making it the focal point for early music in Scotland.

The hall finds its origin in a series of private concerts by a group of amateur gentlemen musicians and professional music teachers in honour of St. Cecilia, the patron saint of music. The first took place in 1695 and by 1728 their success had resulted in the birth of the Edinburgh Music Society. The need for a custom-made venue resulted in the building of St. Cecilia's Hall, which opened with an inaugural concert in December 1763. The building was designed by Edinburgh architect Robert Mylne (1733–1811), who is perhaps best remembered for designing London's Blackfriars Bridge.

At the heart of the building, which is said to have been inspired by the opera house in the Italian city of Parma, is a concert room surrounded by three galleries. Essentially unchanged since its construction, a contemporary account of 1779 describes it as being "oval in form, the ceiling a concave elliptical dome, lighted solely from the top by a lantern. Its construction is excellently adapted for music; and the seats ranged in the room in the form of an amphitheatre are capable of containing a company of about five hundred persons".

Perhaps the most colourful figure to have performed at St. Cecilia's was the Sienese *castrato* Giusto Ferdinando Tenducci (1736–1790), who in later years sang for Mozart. Tenducci was married briefly to a 15-year-old Irish girl, Dorothea Maunsell, by whom it was claimed he had fathered two children. In view of his condition, however, it seems more likely that the children were the offspring of Dorothea's second husband.

The recent renovations at St. Cecilia's include refurbishment of the historic façade, which had become overshadowed by the construction of the South Bridge, relocation of the public entrance so that it is visible from the Royal Mile, and restoration of the 18th century character of the concert room itself. Tiered seating and stages have been installed and display spaces redesigned, with an additional fourth gallery added to display instruments held formerly at the Reid Concert Hall. A glass-fronted Conservation Workshop and Teaching Pod allows visitors to witness various hands-on musical activities.

Most importantly around 40 of the world's best-preserved early keyboard instruments are now on show, including harpsichords, virginals, spinets, organs and fortepianos,

A French harpsichord displayed in St. Cecilia's Hall on Niddry Street

many of which can still be played. St. Cecilia's Hall can thus pride itself in being the only place in the world where it is possible to hear 18th century music played on contemporary instruments and in a concert hall of the same period.

Musical Instrument Museum Edinburgh – from which the St. Cecilia's Hall exhibits are drawn – ranks among the finest of its type in the world. Containing around 46,000 items, it encompasses more than 350 categories of instruments from accordions to zithers, and spans a period of 500 years. From a 1560s virginal to a 21st century flugelhorn, the various intruments have been created by 1300 different manufacturers from around the world. There are many less well-known instruments here, too, including one-stringed fiddles and finger-holed trumpets. It seems entirely fitting that some 90 categories of instruments have an Edinburgh provenance, including many bagpipes, chanters and drones.

Other locations nearby: 18, 19, 30, 31, 33, 34

33 A City beneath the Streets

EH1 1QR (Old Town), the South Bridge Vaults at 28 Blair Street
Bus 3, 5, 7, 8, 14, 29, 30, 31, 33, 35, 37, 45, 49 to South
Bridge (note: self-guided tours of the Vaults are available by
appointment through Mercat Tours on Blair Street)

Edinburgh in the first half of the 18th century was a city with a problem. Union with England and rising prosperity through banking was rapidly creating a new middle class elite that would soon facilitate the Scottish Enlightenment. Such developments, however, were at odds with the cramped medieval city. Edinburgh needed to expand beyond the limits of its Old Town as defined by the steep-sided ridge along which it was built. The two bridges built to facilitate this expansion remain the city's most ambitious engineering projects.

Work on the North Bridge was initiated in 1763 by the Lord Provost, George Drummond (1688–1766), a driving force behind the modernisation of Edinburgh. Completed in stone in 1772, it spanned the valley containing the recently-drained Nor' Loch between the High Street in the Old Town and Princes Street in the New Town. The bridge remained in use until 1896, when it was replaced by the girder bridge seen today.

Work on the South Bridge, which was designed to span the Cowgate gorge between the High Street and the growing University of Edinburgh on the Southside, was commenced in 1788. Consisting of 19 stone arches, it was completed three years later. Edinburgh was a superstitious place at the time and when the first person invited to cross the bridge died and was instead carried over in a coffin, it was considered cursed and many refused to use it!

Footfall increased though and as it did so did the commercial potential of the South Bridge. Tenements were built along either side of the bridge obscuring all of the arches except for the Cowgate arch. The upper storeys of these tenements contained shops facing onto the bridge itself. To create more useable space, floors were then inserted into the obscured arches creating around 120 vaulted chambers. Despite being dark, airless and without sanitation, these were used as workshops and storerooms by all manner of trades, including cobblers, cutlers, milliners and taverners. After a few years, however, it was discovered that the masonry of the bridge was not waterproofed and as water seeped in so these artisans moved out.

As early as 1795, the poor and disreputable were taking their place.

Inside the South Bridge Vaults beneath Blair Street

The presence of oyster shells, clay pipes, medicine bottles and broken crockery suggest petty thieves, prostitutes and illegal distillers lived here. It has even been suggested that the bodysnatchers Burke and Hare searched for victims in the vaults. As conditions deteriorated further, however, even these people left and by the mid-19th century the vaults lay abandoned.

Only in 1985 were the vaults re-discovered after a tunnel leading to them was found by former Scottish rugby player, Norrie Rowan, who owned the nearby Tron Bar. Now partially reopened, they have been re-purposed in a variety of ways. Those wishing to experience them in all their gloomy glory should head to Mercat Tours at 28 Blair Street (EH1), where by appointment visitors can take a self-guided tour. A separate guided ghost tour is available for those who believe the South Bridge may still be cursed!

Nearby at number 34a is Marlin's Wynd, the first of three unusual event venues created by the family of Norrie Rowan. What's interesting here are the remains of one of several closes swept away to make way for the South Bridge. Their second venture, the Rowantree at 255 Cowgate, was originally Lucky Middlesmass's Tavern, where key figures of the Scottish Enlightenment once met. The third is The Caves around the corner at 8–10 Niddry Street, where several of the original vaults have been restored and more remains pre-dating the Bridge have been revealed.

Other locations nearby: 15, 18, 19, 31, 32, 34

34 Darwin's Early Footsteps

EH8 9YL (Old Town), the University of Edinburgh's Old College on South Bridge
Bus 3, 5, 7, 8, 14, 29, 30, 31, 33, 37, 45, 49 to South Bridge

On 10th December 1831 the survey ship HMS *Beagle* departed England bound for South America. Onboard was a young Charles Darwin (1809–1882), whom the ship's captain had accepted as a fare-paying gentleman naturalist to keep him company. The scientific observations made by Darwin during the journey provided tantalising evidence for his nascent theories about evolution through natural selection. Such theorising would eventually result in his book *On the Origin of Species* (1859), which radically altered the way mankind viewed its origins.

Darwin's interest in natural history began as a child growing up in Shropshire. Encouraged by his father, who was a doctor, he collected insects and birds' eggs. In 1818 he joined his older brother, Erasmus, at a boarding school in Shrewsbury. When it came to studying the classics, however, Darwin proved inattentive. As a result his father removed him early and in 1825 sent both boys to study medicine at the University of Edinburgh.

At this time new university buildings known today as the Old College were being constructed on the South Bridge to designs by Robert Adam (1728–1792). The brothers lodged just around the corner at 11 Lothian Street (EH1) although the building was demolished when the National Museum of Scotland was constructed in the 1990s (a plaque marks the spot).

Although Darwin took little interest in his medical studies – he found the lectures dull and surgical procedures traumatic – it was in Edinburgh that his professional interest in the natural world was aroused. He paid regular visits to the Natural History Museum in the Old College, where the curator William Macgillivray (1796–1852) encouraged him to take observational notes during nature walks (see no. 102). The museum was housed in a neo-Classical hall designed by William Playfair (1759–1823), which today contains the university's public art collection known as the Talbot Rice Gallery (it gives a good impression of the stunning Playfair Library, which unfortunately is usually off limits).

Darwin also became friends with the Edinburgh-born zoologist Robert Grant (1793–1874), who taught him how to study marine invertebrates. The pair enjoyed examining local marine life together at Prestonpans on the Firth of Forth, where Grant had a residence. Darwin took lessons in taxidermy, too, from a neighbour on Lothian Street, John Edmonstone (1793–1822), a freed black slave who had explored the South American rainforest.

After two years, Darwin's neglect of his studies prompted his father to send him to Cambridge, where it was hoped an arts degree might be a first step towards becoming an Anglican parson. Again his days were filled with the pursuit of natural history although this time he did manage to pass his exams. It was shortly after graduating, whilst planning an expedition to Tenerife, that he secured his life-changing place on the *Beagle*.

Darwin's *On the Origin of Species* was first published in London by the company of Edinburgh-born John Murray (1745–1793). This explains the presence in the National Library of Scotland of the letter Darwin submitted with his original manuscript (see no. 9). Also in Edinburgh in the National Museum of Scotland on Chambers Street (EH1) is a scaly-throated earthcreeper stuffed by Darwin himself whilst aboard HMS *Beagle*.

Darwin studied at the University of Edinburgh's Old College

Overcrowding in the late 19th century saw the university expand southwards to George Square, where a series of wall plaques recall significant former students. Teviot Row House at 13 Bristo Square (EH8) opened in 1889 as the world's first purpose-built students' union building. The first purpose-built student accommodation was created in 1887 in a renovated former slum at 1 Mound Place (EH1) by the pioneering Scottish environmental town planner Sir Patrick Geddes (1854–1932) (see no. 5).

Other locations nearby: 31, 32, 33, 35, 42, 43

35 Mysteries at the National Museum

EH1 1JF (Old Town), the National Museum of Scotland
on Chambers Street
Bus 2 to Merchant Street, 23, 27, 41, 42, 67 to Chambers
Street; 35 to Forrest Road

Visitors to the National Museum of Scotland on Chambers Street (EH1) can travel the world without leaving Edinburgh. From the age of the dinosaurs to future technology, its galleries contain artefacts from most places and periods. It was formed in 2006 by the merger of two existing collections: the Museum of Scotland (founded as the National Museum of Antiquities of Scotland in 1858) and the Royal Museum (founded as the Edinburgh Museum of Science and Art in 1866). Despite the merger both retain their distinctive architectural character: the Royal Museum its Victorian neo-Renaissance building of 1888 and the Museum of Scotland its modern Corbusian building, erected when it relocated here from Queen Street in the 1990s.

A spectacular entrance to the museum is provided by the refurbished Victorian Grand Gallery. Based on the Crystal Palace, it consists of a light-filled atrium flanked by balconies supported on rows of cast iron columns. The disparate objects displayed – from a huge South Pacific feasting bowl to a 19th century lighthouse lens – provide a taster of the treasures to come. The same goes for the Window on the World, a vertical installation showcasing 800 diverse objects, including a girder from the infamous Tay Bridge. The Discoveries gallery beyond celebrates Scottish innovation and includes the world's oldest colour television invented by John Logie Baird (1888–1946).

It would take several trips to really appreciate the many themed galleries that follow: the Natural World, Art, Design & Fashion, World Cultures, and Science & Technology, which includes Dolly the sheep, the world's first cloned mammal. Space permits only a taster here, so what follows are three mysterious exhibits displayed in the Scotland Galleries.

The first (in the Early Peoples Gallery) is the Ballachulish Woman. This life-sized wooden sculpture with pebbles for eyes was found in 1880 on the shore of Loch Leven in Inverness-shire. It has been dated to around 600BC making it the oldest human figure found in Scotland. Undoubtedly female and probably young, the gravel embedded

These eight tiny coffins were found on Arthur's Seat

in the statue's base suggests it stood on a beach overlooking the dangerous straits linking Loch Leven with the sea. That the statue was surrounded by deliberately intertwined branches suggests it was a goddess to whom prehistoric travellers made offerings to safeguard their crossing.

Also found on a beach were the famous Lewis Chessmen (in the Kingdom of the Scots Gallery). These 11 gaming pieces made from walrus ivory were part of a much larger hoard of 93 items recovered in 1831 from a stone vault at Uig Bay on the Hebridean Isle of Lewis. The workmanship appears to be late 12th or early 13th century Scandinavian. That so many were found together representing four chess sets in total suggests they belonged to a merchant travelling from Norway to Ireland. The reason for their burial, however, remains unclear.

The third mysterious exhibit (in the Industry and Empire Gallery) is local to Edinburgh. In June 1836 a group of boys headed up to Arthur's Seat to hunt rabbits. There they discovered 17 miniature coffins in a small cave, each containing a tiny carved and dressed figure. The eight that survived have excited speculation as to their meaning ever since. Explanations have ranged from witchcraft and lucky charms to proxy burials honouring soldiers or even the victims of the body-snatchers Burke and Hare (see no. 43). The real reason will probably never be known.

Only a fraction of the National Museum of Scotland's holdings are displayed. The rest is stored at the National Museums Collection Centre at 242 West Granton Road (EH5). From butterflies to traction engines, the material here is as varied as it is vast. Research visits by appointment only (www.nms.ac.uk).

Other locations nearby: 34, 36, 37, 38, 42

36 The Chapel of the Hammermen

EH1 1JR (Old Town), the Magdalen Chapel at 41 Cowgate
Bus 2 to Merchant Street; 23, 27, 41, 42, 67 to Victoria Street;
35 to Forrest Road

Tucked away on the Cowgate (EH1) in the shadow of George IV Bridge is an easily-missed Edinburgh gem. The Magdalen Chapel at number 41 dates from the 16th century and incorporates some unique architectural features. It also occupies a key position in Edinburgh's religious history.

The chapel was commissioned in the early 1540s by one Janet Rynd, using a bequest left by her well-to-do husband, the wealthy moneylender Michael MacQuhane. The intended function of the chapel was twofold. Firstly it was to be the main place of worship of the Incorporation of Hammermen, an important craftsmen's guild comprising eight medieval professions (armourers, blacksmiths, cutlers, locksmiths, lorimers, pewterers, saddlers and shearsmiths). They had previously worshipped in an aisle of St. Giles' Cathedral. Secondly seven poor pensioners were to be accommodated in a hospital (almshouse) attached to the chapel. It would be their duty to pray for the repose of the soul of the MacQuhanes and also Mary, Queen of Scots.

Magdalen Chapel is an important place for several reasons. When completed in 1544 it was the last Roman Catholic chapel to be built in Edinburgh before the Reformation. Although today the Victorian street façade obscures the original building, the interior remains largely unchanged. Most significantly it contains the only examples of Scottish medieval stained glass still in situ, namely four roundel windows depicting the coats of arms of the two founders, as well as those of the Queen Regent, Mary of Guise (1554–1560), and the Lion Rampant of Scotland. The windows survived the iconoclasm of the Reformation because they originally looked out onto the Hammermen's private garden.

With the Reformation, the Magdalen Chapel became a centre for Presbyterianism, a form of Protestantism in which the Church is administered locally by a minister and a group of elected elders of equal rank. It might even have hosted the first assembly of the new Church of Scotland on 20th December 1560, with the reformer John Knox (c.1513–1572) in attendance.

Despite such tumultuous changes the chapel remained under the patronage of the Hammermen until 1857. During this time they added the distinctive steeple (1628) and a few years later the steeple bell cast in Flanders. The coats of arms of the different branches of the Incorporation of Hammermen adorn the walls and painted panels record bequests made by individual craftsmen.

This stained glass in the Magdalen Chapel predates the Reformation

During the Killing Time in the 1680s the chapel was used to prepare the bodies of martyred Covenanters for burial in Greyfriars Kirkyard (see no. 38). The table used can still be seen, as can the supposed sword of Covenanter Captain John Paton. Much later the chapel was also used by Edinburgh's Episcopalians and Baptists.

Restored in the early 1990s, the Magdalen Chapel is now the headquarters of the Scottish Reformation Society, which continues to defend and promote the ideals of the Protestant Reformation. Their website states that one reason for the Society's existence is to warn against pious Roman Catholic acts such as those of the MacQuhanes!

In 1615 the Magdalen Chapel was adapted to serve as the convening hall of the Edinburgh Trades, an organisation established in 1562 to represent the city's incorporated craftsmen's guilds, including the Hammermen. The raised dais where the guild 'deacons' met can still be seen at one end of the chapel. The organisation still exists, although many of its trades are now defunct, and is based at 61 Melville Street (EH3), where the current convening hall and a museum can be visited by appointment (www.edinburghtrades.org).

Other locations nearby: 9, 14, 35, 37, 38

37 Coffee with Harry Potter

EH1 1EN (Old Town), the Elephant House
at 21 George IV Bridge
Bus 2 to Merchant Street; 23, 27, 41, 42, 67 to Chambers
Street; 35 to Forrest Road

One of the great publishing sensations of recent years has been the *Harry Potter* series by J. K. Rowling (b. 1965). Turned down by a dozen publishers before being picked up by Bloomsbury, Rowling has sold half a billion copies. Although the idea of a young boy attending a school of wizardry came to Rowling fully-fledged in 1990 during a train journey between Manchester and London, it was in various cafés in Edinburgh that the first books were written.

Rowling arrived in Edinburgh in December 1993 from Portugal, where she had been teaching English. A jobless, single parent with a baby, she wanted to be closer to her sister. She brought three chapters of what would become *Harry Potter and the Philosopher's Stone* in her suitcase.

Determined to be an author, Rowling found the only way to be a mother and an author was to walk her child to sleep and then find a suitable café in which to write. One of these was Nicolson's at 6a Nicolson Street (EH8) owned by her brother-in-law. Now a restaurant called Spoon, it stands around the corner from the former Rutherford public house at 3 Drummond Street, once frequented by another Edinburgh author, Robert Louis Stevenson.

Rowling's favourite café was the Elephant House at 21 George IV Bridge (EH1), where she completed *The Philosopher's Stone*, *The Chamber of Secrets* and *The Prisoner of Azkaban*. From the back room she could see Edinburgh Castle, which surely inspired Hogwarts School of Witchcraft and Wizardry. Certainly in an interview with Rowling on the café's website she states that despite being English she always imagined Hogwarts to be located on a Scottish mountain alongside a loch (www.elephanthouse.biz). The school's Gothic flourishes were perhaps inspired by the turreted George Heriot's School on Lauriston Place (EH3), as were its four houses – Ravenclaw, Slytherin, Gryffindor and Hufflepuff – which correspond to George Heriot's Castle, Lauriston, Raeburn and Greyfriars.

Also visible from the Elephant House is the atmospheric Greyfriars Kirkyard, which inspired the graveyard of Little Hangleton in *The Goblet of Fire* (see no. 38). It is here that Harry Potter's nemesis,

Lord Voldemort, is restored to bodily form. Rowling has admitted that she sourced some of her characters' names from gravestones, so it seems likely that the grave of one Thomas Riddell inspired Voldemort's real name, Tom Riddle. Talking of names, might Potterrow near the University, named after an extramural medieval suburb lined with pottery stalls, have prompted Harry's own surname?

Just below the Elephant House is the narrow, curving Victoria Street, which is said to have inspired the magical shopping street, Diagon Alley. Weasleys' Wizard Wheezes, Gringotts, and Flourish & Blotts were based on a joke shop, bank and stationery store that once stood here. Before leaving

This view from the Elephant House helped inspire the world of Harry Potter

the Elephant House be sure to visit the toilets, which are smothered in Harry Potter graffiti.

One last location is room 552 of the luxurious Balmoral Hotel at 1 Princes Street (EH2). It was here in 2007 that Rowling completed work on the final Harry Potter book, *The Deathly Hallows*. To celebrate she opened a bottle of Champagne and scribbled her name on the back of a marble bust. The room has subsequently been renamed the J.K. Rowling Suite and represents a far cry from her first Edinburgh flat at 28 Gardner's Crescent (EH3) provided by the social services.

J.K. Rowling is today one of the wealthiest women in Britain and has used some of her money philanthropically. A fine example is the Anne Rowling Regenerative Neurology Clinic at 49 Little France Crescent (EH16) named in honour of her mother, who died from multiple sclerosis.

Other locations nearby: 9, 35, 36, 38

38 The Old Stones Speak

EH1 2QQ (Old Town), Greyfriars Kirk and Kirkyard
in Greyfriars Place
Bus 2 to Merchant Street; 23, 27, 41, 42, 67 to Chambers
Street; 35 to Forrest Road (note: Sunday services are given
in English and Scottish Gaelic)

People have been worshipping at Greyfriars Kirk for four centuries. As the first church built in Edinburgh after the Reformation, it occupies a prominent place in Scottish history. Its old stones have made it an important heritage site and these days it also doubles as a concert venue. Literary travellers come here, too, since the Kirkyard conjures up the image of Muriel Spark's Miss Jean Brodie, lecturing her pupils during an impromptu school outing.

Greyfriars stands on land that once belonged to the Franciscan Grey Friars, who came to Edinburgh in 1447 as medical missionaries. In 1559, with the Reformation in full swing, the order was dissolved and Mary, Queen of Scots (1542–1567) granted the land to the Town Council for use as a burial ground, to ease overcrowding in the churchyard of St. Giles, Edinburgh's parish church. Work on Greyfriars Kirk only began in 1602 and it was not completed until Christmas Day 1620. The American flag displayed in the Greyfriars Museum is a reminder that the Pilgrim Fathers landed in the New World on the same day.

Another momentous day for Greyfriars came on 28th February 1638, when the National Covenant was signed here. Over 4,000 members of the Presbyterian Church in Scotland signed in protest against the English style of worship imposed on Scotland by Charles I (1625–1649). An original copy is displayed in the nearby Museum of Edinburgh (see no. 24).

Unfortunately little remains of the original Greyfriars, which was a simple Late Gothic structure, with arcaded side aisles. Worshippers would have either stood or brought their own stools, the only furniture being the pulpit. The original north door, however, can still be seen inside the present porch. Its oak leaves and a cherub's head ornament in the doorframe survive, as does the oldest extant example of Edinburgh's coat of arms displayed above.

The original church ended where the great west arch now stands. Beyond once stood a squat tower, where the Council stored gunpowder. When this blew up in 1718 a second church was built on the ruins, so that Greyfriars now housed two separate congregations. The

Elaborately carved headstones in Greyfriars Kirkyard

scorching on some of the windows dates from 1845 when a fire gutted the building.

A move towards a less puritanical form of worship saw the installation in 1857 of the first stained glass in a Scottish Presbyterian church and in 1865 the first organ. Only in 1929 were the two congregations united and in 1938 to mark the tercentenary of the signing of the National Covenant, the dividing wall was torn down. Its former position can still be made out on the ceiling of the aisles.

The Kirkyard at Greyfriars is no less interesting, with nearly 100,000 people buried here. Notable graves include those of wigmaker-turned-poet Allan Ramsay the Elder (1684–1758), Father of Modern Geology James Hutton (1726–1797), chemist and discoverer of latent heat Joseph Black (1728–1799), founder of comparative linguistics James Burnett (1714–1799), businesswoman and girls' school founder Mary Erskine (1629–1707), and William McGonagall (1825–1902), the world's worst poet!

The most notorious grave is the drum-shaped mausoleum of 'Bloody' George Mackenzie (1636–1691), who as Lord Advocate to Charles II (1660–1685) was responsible for persecuting Scotland's Presbyterian Covenanters during the so-called 'Killing Time'. Following the defeat of the Covenanters in 1679 at the Battle of Bothwell Brig Mackenzie imprisoned 400 of them in a field alongside Greyfriars bounded by part of the old town wall (see no. 39). Those executed here are commemorated by the Martyrs' Monument erected in the Kirkyard

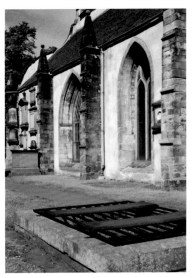

This mortsafe was used to protect fresh graves from bodysnatchers

in 1706 (others were hanged on the Grassmarket gallows, where another memorial can be found). Little wonder Mackenzie's domed mausoleum is said to be haunted.

When part of the field was later amalgamated into the Kirkyard for the construction of vaulted tombs, the area became known as the Covenanters' Prison. The heavy masonry and railings surrounding these vaults were intended as a deterrent to grave robbing before the Anatomy Act of 1832 regulated the supply of corpses for medical purposes (see no. 43). The pair of lockable iron cages alongside the church (known as *mortsafes*) provided a temporary solution to the same problem.

The Kirkyard's most endearing interment is undoubtedly that of Greyfriars Bobby, the loyal Skye terrier said to have watched over the grave of his dead master, John Gray, for 14 long years. The Lord Provost of Edinburgh, Sir William Chambers (1800–1883), who was also a director of the Scottish Society for the Prevention of Cruelty to Animals, was so touched by the story that he gave Bobby the collar displayed today in the Museum of Edinburgh (see no. 24). The grave where Bobby staged his vigil lies on the eastern path just north of the Kirkyard gates. When Bobby himself died in 1872 he was buried on unconsecrated ground near the gates, where a headstone was erected in 1981 by the Dog Aid Society of Scotland. A drinking fountain topped with a statue of Bobby unveiled outside the gates in 1873 is Edinburgh's smallest listed structure.

Only in 2011, however, did new research reveal that the Greyfriars Bobby story was a hoax created to attract visitors to the cemetery and a nearby restaurant. The real Bobby was a stray mongrel that was encouraged to stay put by being fed scraps. When it died in 1867 a second dog (this time really a Skye Terrier) was brought in to ensure that the story kept business healthy. It was this second Bobby that died in 1872 perpetuating a myth that would last more than a hundred years and spawn a Walt Disney movie along the way.

Other locations nearby: 9, 35, 36, 37

39 Exploring the Town Wall Ruins

EH3 9EX (Old Town), a tour of Edinburgh's ruined town walls including the Flodden Tower in the Vennel
Bus 2 to Grassmarket then walk up the Vennel; 23, 27, 35, 45, 47 to Lauriston Terrace then walk along Heriot Place

Several times during Edinburgh's history it was deemed necessary to erect town walls. Their purpose was not only defensive but also commercial in a bid to control trade, tax goods and deter smuggling. Demolished in piecemeal fashion from the mid-18th century onwards, their ruins still punctuate the landscape. It makes for an interesting excursion to locate them.

Edinburgh was formally established as a royal *burgh* around 1125 by David I (1124–1153). This granted the privilege of holding a market and the right to tax goods arriving for sale. Although no record survives of a wall at this time, it seems likely that a ditch or timber palisade was created to control the flow of goods. Since the castle on its rocky outcrop already defended the western approach, and there was a steep natural slope to the north of Old Town, this early boundary was most likely on the south and east sides of the *burgh*. This notion is supported by the earliest mention of defences, which include a south gate in 1214 and the Netherbow Port in 1369, which gave access to the Canongate, a separate *burgh* established by David in 1143.

The first documented wall, the King's Wall, dates from a charter granted in 1450 by James II (1437–1460) enabling the burgesses of Edinburgh to defend their town. This made Edinburgh one of only three Scottish towns to have medieval stone walls, the others being Stirling and Perth. A further charter granted by James III (1460–1488) ordered the demolition of houses to render the wall more effective. James also ordered the damming of a river valley in what is now Princes Street Gardens to create the marshy Nor' Loch, which further protected the northern approach.

The King's Wall ran along the south side of the Royal Mile from the middle of what is now Johnston Terrace to what is now St. Mary's Street, where it turned northwards. It had two ports, namely the Upper (or Over) Bow, in the vicinity of what is now Victoria Street, and the Nether Bow, on the Royal Mile, near Fountain Close. Unfortunately nothing definite remains of this wall although sturdy masonry in Tweedale Court and Castle Wynd has been attributed to it (see no. 18).

In 1513, James IV (1488–1513) led an invasion of northern England in support of the pro-French Auld Alliance. The Scots met the English on 9th September at the Battle of Flodden Field and were roundly defeated, with James killed in action. With an English invasion now anticipated (though never forthcoming), the construction of a new town wall in Edinburgh began. Seeing commercial potential in this, the town council built it farther south so as to encompass the Grassmarket and Cowgate areas of the *burgh*. Measuring 24 feet high and almost four feet thick, the so-called Flodden Wall was completed in 1560, by which time it encompassed an area of 140 acres and a population of 10,000.

Like the King's Wall it commenced on Johnston Terrace but then ran south alongside Granny's Green Steps (where it has been incorporated into a later church) and across the west end of the Grassmarket (marked by inscribed, lighter-colour paving stones). The West Port was located here – the street still bears this name – from where the wall continued up the Vennel. Here the Flodden Tower, the only preserved bastion of the town walls, replete with cross-shaped gun-loops, marks where the wall turned east and then south again, to incorporate Greyfriars Kirkyard, where pieces of walling embedded with later gravestones are still standing. From here the wall turned east again (marked by a line of cobbles in the pavement and a narrow gap in the buildings where Forrest Road joins George IV Bridge) to the Bristo and Potterrow Ports (again recalled in modern street names), both of which were located where the National Museum of Scotland stands now (see no. 38).

Still continuing east, the wall then passed the Kirk o' Field, where the university's Old College on South Bridge now stands. It was here that Lord Darnley (1545–1567), second husband of Mary, Queen of Scots (1542–1567), was murdered in 1567. It then ran to the end of Drummond Street and then turned north at the Pleasance thereby enclosing Blackfriars Monastery, which stood in what is today High School Yards (see no. 30). This stretch of the wall is well-preserved and includes a blocked archway that probably gave access to a now-demolished bastion.

The Cowgate Port stood at the foot of the Pleasance from where the wall then ran up St. Mary's Street to the Netherbow Port on the High Street, which was rebuilt 150 feet farther east of its original location in the King's Wall. Marked today by brass pavement plates, it was over the Netherbow Port that the heads of criminals executed at the Old Tolbooth jail were displayed; the area inside the gate was known as World's End, since the cost of re-entering the *burgh* meant poorer residents never left. From here, the wall then continued northwards to the Nor' Loch (since replaced by Waverley Station), terminating at the Flodden Wall's sixth and last gate, the New Port.

Edinburgh's third and final wall was built between 1628 and 1636. Known as the Telfer Wall after its master mason, John Taillefer, it was an extension of the Flodden Wall and was built to enclose 10 acres of land west of Greyfriars Kirk, which the town council had acquired in 1618. The land was subsequently sold to the charitable George Heriot's Trust and is now occupied by the school of the same name.

The Telfer Wall ran south from the Flodden Tower in the Vennel along Heriot Place. Today providing the western boundary for the school, this stretch remains largely intact. At Lauriston Place the wall turned east although the only part remaining here is that enclosing the southern extremity of Greyfriars Kirkyard. At the end of Teviot Place it then turned north along Bristo Place to re-join the Flodden Wall at the Bristo Port.

Part of the Flodden Wall in the Vennel, with Edinburgh Castle in the background

By the 17th century the King's Wall had been almost entirely absorbed into later buildings. The Flodden and Telfer Walls, however, were still periodically strengthened when circumstances dictated. The last occasion was when Bonnie Prince Charlie's troops approached Edinburgh in their bid to restore the exiled House of Stewart to the British throne. They gained access through the Netherbow Port sparking the 1745 Jacobite Rising, which was brutally suppressed at the Battle of Culloden a year later.

With Edinburgh's town walls now of little military or commercial use, and increasingly a hindrance to both traffic and development, the decision to demolish them albeit gradually was taken a year later.

Other locations nearby: 40, 41

40 A Tour for Bookworms

EH8 9DP (Old Town), a tour of independent bookshops
beginning with Edinburgh Books at 145–147 West Port
Bus 2, 35 to West Port; 23, 27, 45, 47 to Chalmers Street

Edinburgh is a place long steeped in the written word. It has not only inspired great literature through its local authors and landscapes but also promoted it through its many literary institutions and publishing houses. This prompted UNESCO to make Edinburgh the world's first City of Literature in 2004, an accolade reflected in part by the city's myriad independent bookshops.

This tour begins on West Port (EH1) in the Old Town, a colourful street containing several bookshops. Edinburgh Books at 145–147 is the city's largest secondhand outlet, with an eclectic stock covering most genres. The head of a stuffed water buffalo called Clarence lords over the proceedings and one of the basement rooms is given over to sheet music. Armchair Books farther along at number 72–74 is a more intimate experience, with handwritten labels, rickety library ladders and threadbare rugs adding to the charm. More old books are available at Peter Bell Books next door and beyond that is Scottish Pictures, which specialises in antique maps and prints.

Farther east on Candlemaker Row (EH1) are two very different bookshops. Transreal Fiction at number 46 focusses on science fiction, fantasy and related genres both in book and magazine form. Avizandum on the other hand at 56a is a specialist legal bookshop with an emphasis on Scots Law.

Moving up nearby West Bow – beyond the Dutch-gabled Crockett's Land at number 91 – is the Old Town Bookshop at 8 Victoria Street (EH1). This is an Aladdin's cave for devotees of art, architecture, Scottish history and topography. Supplying antiquarian books since 1978, it is a joy for those who appreciate the smell of old books and the sight of gilded leather bindings.

Another Old Town bookshop is the Old Children's Bookshelf at 175 Canongate (EH1). Comprising just two small rooms, the stock here embraces a hundred year's worth of children's books, comics and annuals. There are also biographies of children's authors, as well as adult titles by children's authors published under the shop's own Greyladies imprint.

Moving north now, McNaughtan's at 3a Haddington Place (EH7) is Scotland's oldest secondhand bookshop and one of its most elegant.

Opened in 1957 it not only offers a varied stock but also includes a gallery space added in 2010, which hosts exhibitions by local artists and photographers.

Completely different is Elvis Shakespeare at 347 Leith Walk (EH6), which as its name suggests specialises not only in secondhand books but also CDs, cassettes and vinyl records, especially punk, indie and alternative. Local writers and musicians often debut their new material here. Golden Hare Books over at 68 St. Stephen's Street (EH3) in Stockbridge also hosts book launches and prides itself in a carefully curated selection of contemporary fiction, poetry and art titles.

This tour concludes in the south with the Edinburgh Bookshop at 219 Bruntsfield Place (EH10), officially one of Scotland's best bookshops having won the Scottish Independent Bookshop of the Year award in 2014. Also here are

A stuffed water buffalo's head is a feature of Edinburgh Books on West Port

two student-friendly alternative bookshops on West Nicolson Street. Word Power Books at 43–45 (EH8) is a focus for Edinburgh's left-wing activists since 1994 and stocks an impressive selection of titles on political science, cultural and environmental studies, and social justice. The shop is also renowned for its support of small local presses and new writers, and organises the annual Edinburgh Independent & Radical Book Fair. The other is Deadhead Comics next door at 47, Edinburgh's biggest independent comic shop, which specialises in work by Scottish outsider artists such as John G. Miller.

Other locations nearby: 39, 41

41 Edinburgh on Fire

EH3 9DE (Old Town), the Museum of Fire
at 76–78 Lauriston Place
Bus 23, 27, 35, 45, 47 to Chalmers Street

The world's first municipal fire brigade was established in Edinburgh. This superlative fact is celebrated today at the city's Museum of Fire, which is housed inside a late Victorian former fire station at 76–78 Lauriston Place (EH3). At the time of writing there is talk of the Scottish Fire and Rescue Service selling off the building, so don't delay visiting this unique collection.

In the wake of the Great Fire of London in 1666, the first fire insurance companies were established, employing small teams of Thames watermen as firefighters. Their uniforms showed which company they worked for and they would only extinguish visibly insured buildings. In an overcrowded place like Edinburgh's Old Town, however, such a system was not workable. Several destructive fires in 1824 demonstrated clearly that extinguishing individual buildings would not stop widespread destruction.

So it was that later the same year 24 year-old James Braidwood (1800–1861) formed the Edinburgh Fire Engine Establishment (later the Lothian and Borders Fire and Rescue Service). The son of an Edinburgh cabinetmaker, his training as a surveyor had taught him much about construction techniques in the Old Town. As Master of Fire Engines he recruited local tradesmen, including masons, carpenters and plumbers, who helped set down the scientific fire-fighting prin-

One of several fire engines preserved at the Museum of Fire

ciples still used today. He also recruited mariners to haul the heavy engines and wheeled ladders up and down Edinburgh's steep streets.

In 1833 Braidwood left Edinburgh for London to spearhead what became the London Fire Brigade. It was there that he lost his life fighting an enormous blaze on Tooley Street. One of several memorial plaques outside the fire station in Lauriston Place recalls his heroic contribution and a statue in Parliament Square stands near the site of his original High Street fire station. The funds for the statue were raised by Dr. Frank Rushbrook, a retired fireman with the Lothian and Borders Service, and a benefactor of University of Edinburgh's Fire Laboratory.

The main display area of the Museum of Fire lies behind four large doors through which fire engines once sped. Fittingly a row of magnificently-preserved historic fire engines are parked there today. The oldest motor vehicle is a unique Halley Fire Engine built in Glasgow and purchased by Leith Fire Brigade in 1910. Other engines come from farther afield, including a Dennis engine of 1930 from Fraserburgh. A small side room contains a reconstructed fire control centre, replete with an old fashioned switchboard.

Another display area to the rear includes a hand-drawn pump used by the Edinburgh Fire Establishment when it was formed in 1824. A somewhat later horse-drawn pump from 1901 was used to protect the Tullis Russell paperworks in Fife. The stables here are a reminder that fire stations needed a supply of strong and healthy horses.

All around the museum are smaller artefacts illustrating the history of firefighting, including fire extinguishers, water hydrants, uniforms and the jump sheet invented by Braidwood. The oldest exhibits are the medieval 'cleikes of iron' used to pull thatch off burning roofs. The stairwell of the fire station has been cleverly used to show off the height of an extendable ladder and there is also a reconstructed Edinburgh close of the early 1800s, giving visitors an impression of the problems faced by the city's early firefighters.

Visitors requiring more information should ask the museum volunteer guides, most of whom are serving or retired fire brigade personnel with a passion for their profession.

In the nearby Edinburgh College of Art at 74 Lauriston Place (EH3) is the little-known Edinburgh Cast Collection, which includes one of only two casts ever taken from the Parthenon marbles.

Other locations nearby: 39, 40

42 Evidence of Stage Fright!

EH8 9FT (Southside), a tour of haunted theatres including
the Edinburgh Festival Theatre on Nicolson Street
Bus 2, 3, 5, 7, 8, 14, 29, 30, 31, 33, 37, 45, 47, 49
to Surgeons' Hall

Not only thespians but also ghosts tread the boards of Edinburgh's theatres. The earliest report relates to the Theatre Royal, which opened in 1769 at the corner of North Bridge and Waterloo Place (EH1). It is said that after each evening's performance, strange noises could be heard as phantom actors performed to an empty house. After being demolished in 1859 to make way for the General Post Office (now Waverley Gate), the name was transferred to the Queen's Theatre at the foot of Leith Street. The disgruntled ghosts must have transferred, too, since the re-named theatre and the three that came after it were all consumed by fire. The site today is occupied by an extension to St. Mary's Metropolitan Cathedral (see no. 65).

A haunted theatre still in business is the Edinburgh Festival Theatre on Nicolson Street (EH8). It occupies a site where theatres have stood since 1830 making it Edinburgh's longest serving theatrical venue. No less than six different establishments were here before the Empire Palace Theatre opened in 1892. Designed by the great British theatre architect Frank Matcham (1854–1920), its décor was lavish, with plasterwork elephants, nymphs and cherubs adorning the walls, and seating for 3000 people across four levels.

All the top artists performed here until 9th May 1911, when a disastrous fire occurred. The Munich-born illusionist Sigmund Neuberger (1871–1911), known as the Great Lafayette, was reaching the climax of his signature 'Lion's Bride' routine in which a woman about to be torn apart by a real lion is saved at the last moment by Lafayette disguised as one. At the critical moment a faulty lamp above the stage ignited the elaborate scenery. Although the audience escaped unharmed, those on stage were trapped when the lowered safety curtain jammed (the side doors had been locked at Neuberger's request to protect his stage secrets). Amongst the badly burned bodies retrieved was one assumed to be Neuberger although it turned out to be his identically-dressed stage double. The real body was retrieved two days later and laid to rest in Piershill Cemetery on Portobello Road (EH8). The imposing headstone there also carries the name of Neuberger's pet terrier, Beauty, a gift from Houdini that died just prior to Neuberger's final performance.

The Edinburgh Festival Theatre is said to be haunted by the Great Lafayette

After reopening in 1928 with the musical *Showboat*, the Empire remained popular, hosting the likes of Laurel and Hardy and Judy Garland until being turned over to bingo in 1963. Only after being given a new glass frontage in 1994 did it become the Edinburgh Festival Theatre, Scotland's premier dance and opera venue boasting the country's largest stage. All the while a tall, dark stranger said to be the ghost of the Great Lafayette has haunted the place. And perhaps the ghosts of the Theatre Royal are here, too, since several theatrical medallions salvaged from that building are displayed at the top of the stairs. Backstage tours of the Festival Theatre and its splendid sister venue, the King's Theatre at 2 Leven Street (EH3), are available by appointment (www.edtheatres.com).

Edinburgh has two other haunted theatres. The Royal Lyceum Theatre on Grindlay Street (EH3) opened in 1883, with a production of Shakespeare's *Much Ado About Nothing* starring actor-manager Henry Irving (1838–1905) and his leading lady Ellen Terry (1847–1928), who is said to return occasionally as a ghostly lady in blue. The Edinburgh Playhouse on Greenside Place (EH1), which opened originally as a cinema, is haunted by a ghost called Albert, who is thought to have been either a stagehand killed in an accident or a night-watchman who committed suicide.

Other locations nearby: 31, 34, 35, 43, 44

43 Beware the Bodysnatchers!

EH8 9DW (Southside), the Surgeons' Hall Museums
on Nicolson Street
Bus 2, 3, 5, 7, 8, 14, 29, 30, 31, 33, 37, 45, 47, 49
to Surgeons' Hall

The Royal College of Surgeons of Edinburgh is one of the oldest surgical organisations in the world. Its origins date back to 1505, when the Barber Surgeons of Edinburgh were formally incorporated as one of the city's trade guilds. From their premises in Surgeon's Square (now part of High School Yards) (EH1), the College elevated surgery from a manual craft to an academic discipline. Later in 1832 it relocated to the neo-Classical Surgeons' Hall on Nicolson Street (EH8) designed by William Henry Playfair (1790–1857). The College is still there today as are Surgeons' Hall Museums, which contain a fascinating if at times grisly collection of specimens and related artefacts.

In amongst the pickled organs and surgical implements are several items relating to the bodysnatchers Burke and Hare. They are a sobering reminder that Edinburgh as a pre-eminent centre of medical learning had a dark side. In the early 1800s the bodies of executed criminals were used for anatomical dissection but as sentences were increasingly commuted to deportation so the supply of cadavers dwindled. Unscrupulous criminals perceived a gap in the market and began digging up bodies from churchyards and selling them to anatomists.

The Scottish public was horrified, especially since they believed that a dissected body could not be raised at the Last Judgement. Until the 1832 Anatomy Act regulated the legal supply of corpses for medical purposes, those who could afford it protected their dead from the so-called Resurrection Men by installing low iron cages known as *mortsafes* over the grave until decomposition had set in. Examples can still be seen in Greyfriars Kirkyard (see no. 38).

The Irish immigrants William Burke (1792–1829) and William Hare (c.1792–c.1858) went one step further. In 1828 they murdered at least 16 people and delivered the bodies to the respected Edinburgh anatomist Dr. Robert Knox, who gave private dissection classes in Surgeon's Square (although the building is long-demolished it resembled the yellow-painted Chisholm House still standing). The grisly business was summed up in a contemporary skipping rhyme: "Up the close and doun the stair, But and ben wi' Burke and Hare, Burke's the butcher, Hare's the thief, Knox the boy that buys the beef."

The two were apprehended in November 1828 after one of their victims was recognised on Knox's dissection slab. Hare turned King's evidence in return for immunity and disappeared. Knox was cleared of any crime but his career was ruined. Burke was tried, found guilty of murder and hanged in the Lawnmarket in January 1829 before a crowd of thousands. In an ironic twist his body was publicly dissected the next day. Parts of his skin were used to cover a pocket book, which together with a death mask showing the mark of the hangman's noose, is displayed in the History of Surgery Museum, one of three collections that today make up the Surgeons' Hall Museums (the other two are the Wohl Pathology Museum and the Dental Collection).

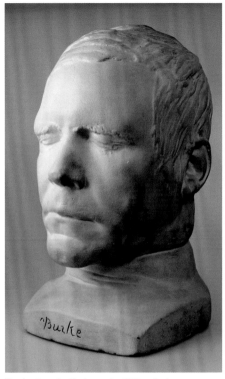

The death mask of bodysnatcher William Burke

Burke's skeleton (and a life mask of Hare) can be found in the University of Edinburgh's old-fashioned Anatomical Museum on Teviot Place (EH8). It is a reminder that Burke's sentence stipulated that he not only be hanged and dissected but also be put on public display. The museum is part of the Old Medical School, which includes a steeply-raked anatomy theatre installed in 1877 to a design by Robert Rowand Anderson (1834–1921). This can be visited during Edinburgh Doors Open Day (www.doorsopendays. org.uk).

A calling card case made from Burke's skin is displayed at The Cadies & Witchery Tours shop at 84 West Bow (EH1).

Other locations nearby: 30, 31, 34, 42, 44

44 Ways to Worship in Southside

EH8 9LD (Southside), three places of worship including the
Chapel of St. Albert the Great on George Square Lane
Bus 2, 41, 42, 67 to Bristo Place; 23, 27, 35, 45, 47 to Middle
Meadow Walk

Within easy walking distance of each other in Edinburgh's Southside
are three very different places of worship. The first is the Chapel of
St. Albert the Great in the back garden of the University's Catholic
Chaplaincy at 23 George Square (EH8). The two buildings could not
be more different though. The chaplaincy occupies one of Edinburgh's
first Georgian townhouses erected when the square was laid out in
1766 as part of the city's first suburb. By complete contrast, the chapel
is a modernist design completed in 2012 by Edinburgh architects Simpson & Brown. Indeed the choice of natural building materials used for
the chapel means it shares a more intimate connection to the garden
than the chaplaincy to which it belongs.

Four tree-like steel columns support a curved, oak-slatted canopy
that reaches ground level on one side; on the other is a wall built of
clay blocks clad with pale sandstone. The steel columns have been
left to rust so as to provide a naturalistic, paint-free finish. The angled
glazing cleverly helps illuminate the chapel without diverting the congregation's focus away from the altar, which is highlighted against the
garden by means of a plate glass gable. The result is a space that offers
students, staff and visitors a peaceful retreat throughout the week and
the Catholic community a focal point on Sundays.

Across the square at 50 Potterrow (EH8) is a rather different place
of worship. The Edinburgh Central Mosque opened in 1998 to accomo-
date the city's Muslim community. Designed by the Iraqi-born architect
Basil Al Bayati (b. 1946), its layout and decoration rely on traditional
Islamic principles, with the addition of a Scottish Baronial corner turret. Much of the cost was borne by King Fahd of Saudi Arabia.

The prayer hall with its vast carpet and chandelier is where Friday
prayers (*Jumu'ah*) and the five daily prayers (*salat*) take place. A thousand worshippers can be accommodated here, with the women occupying the balcony. Elsewhere in the building are segregated ablution
(*wudu*) rooms, a well-stocked library, and a funeral area for bathing
and enshrouding the dead. There is also a *halal* café called the Original
Mosque Kitchen (although the original chefs have now opened their
own enterprise simply called the Mosque Kitchen around the corner

The Chapel of St. Albert the Great in a garden on George Square Lane

in Nicolson Square). Guided tours of the mosque are available by appointment (www.edmosque.org).

The third place of worship is the City of Edinburgh Methodist Church at 25 Nicolson Square (EH8). Different again, this strait-laced chapel of 1816 was cleverly modernised in 2014 by the Glasgow-based architects Page\Park. Notably they joined the chapel and the neighbouring Epworth Halls (a Sunday School built in 1916) by means of a glazed two-door lift, which negotiates the buildings' various levels. A bright and friendly café is now located on the ground floor, with a conservatory opening out onto a garden, whilst on the upper level a new mezzanine creates a common level between the buildings. In the main worship space, the old pews have been removed and the floor levelled to allow for multi-purpose useage. In the gallery above, vertical planes have been inserted into the original raked seating to provide exhibition space and there is even a tiny artist-in-residence's studio.

In Leith other faiths practise their beliefs. They include the Hindu Mandir in a converted Presbyterian church on St. Andrew Place (EH6) and the Kagyu Samye Dzong Tibetan Buddhist Meditation Centre in the former Leith Bank at 25 Bernard Street (EH6). Scotland's first non-denominational place of worship, the Sanctuary, can be found in the Royal Infirmary of Edinburgh in Liberton (EH16).

Other locations nearby: 45, 46, 47

45 Signposts to the Past

EH3 9HW (Southside), a tour of the Meadows and Bruntsfield
Links beginning with Archers' Hall at 66 Buccleuch Street
Bus 41, 42, 67 to Meadow Lane

The Meadows and Bruntsfield Links look like many parks, with tree-lined walks, sports facilities and acres of mown grass. What makes them extraordinary, however, is their history as revealed through some intriguing signposts to the past.

The first is just outside the Meadows at 66 Buccleuch Street (EH3), where two bowmen are carved over a doorway. They identify the building as Archers' Hall built in 1777 as a club house for the Royal Company of Archers. Originally a private archery club for gentlemen and nobles, the Company used the Meadows for target practice. Since George IV's visit to Edinburgh in 1822 it has acted as the Sovereign's Bodyguard in Scotland.

Down one side of Archers' Hall runs Boroughloch. The name is a reminder that the Meadows was once water. Until the arrival of piped water in the 17th century, Edinburgh's Old Town sourced its drinking water here. The loch was drained in 1740 by the agriculturalist Sir Thomas Hope of Rankeillour (d. 1771) and made into a park.

On Melville Drive at the far side of the playground stand two pillars topped by a lion and a unicorn clutching the arms of Edinburgh. They were donated in 1881 by the printing firm of Thomas Nelson and Sons in gratitude for being given temporary premises here after their printing works burned down. This is also where the first football derby between Heart of Midlothian and Hibernian took place on Christmas Day 1875, and where 500 allotments were created during the Second World War in an effort to make Edinburgh self-sufficient.

Walk westwards now along Melville Drive to reach Jawbone Walk, which is entered through a whalebone arch. Back in 1886 this formed the Shetland and Fair Isle Knitters' pavilion at the International Exhibition of Industry, Science and Art. The centrepiece of the exhibition, which was opened by Queen Victoria's grandson, Prince Albert Victor, was a Grand Hall illuminated by electricity. The Prince Albert Sundial and the Memorial Masons' Pillars straddling Melville Drive are further remnants of the exhibition. Made from various types of stone, the pillars were designed by quarry owner Sir James Gowans (1821–90) to demonstrate the stonecutter's art (the Brassfounders' Pillar removed to Nicolson Square (EH8) served a similar purpose).

A detail of Archers' Hall on Buccleugh Street

Cross now to Bruntsfield Links on the other side of Melville Drive. Unlike the Meadows, this was always dry land and is all that remains of the Burgh Muir, a forest that once covered south Edinburgh. The undulating landscape here is the result of 16th century sandstone quarrying. The spurious suggestion that the undulations are burial mounds for plague victims is based on the fact that such people were indeed quarantined here in the 17th century. After disinfection, however, they were taken to huts elsewhere although some died en route, which explains the solitary headstone at 1 Chamberlain Road (EH10).

The rights of golfers to play on Bruntsfield Links date back to 1695. The Royal Burgess Golfing Society began playing here in 1735 making it the world's oldest short-hole course. Before they relocated to Musselburgh in the 1870s (and eventually to Barnton in the 1890s), they used the Golf Tavern at 30–31 Wright's Houses as their clubhouse. Built in 1771, it still hires out clubs and balls for free, making it the longest serving golf clubhouse in the world.

Nothing remains from the Scottish National Exhibition of 1908 held in Saughton Park on Balgreen Road (EH11). Over three million people came here to see a Senegalese tribe and take gondola rides on the Union Canal. These days they enjoy the Winter Gardens and Scotland's biggest skateboarding park.

Other locations nearby: 44, 46, 47

46 The Innocent Railway Tunnel

EH16 5XN (Southside), the Innocent Railway Tunnel
on East Parkside
Bus 14 to Bernard Terrace; 2, 30, 33 to Montague Street

The St. Leonard's area of Edinburgh, sandwiched between the Southside and Holyrood Park, appears unremarkable at first glance. Modern residential housing has seemingly obliterated whatever may have stood here previously – but look closer. In amongst the houses are several much older structures that bear witness to something extraordinary: the remains of Edinburgh's first public railway.

The first sign of the railway actually predates it. The lovely old house at 64 St. Leonard's Street (EH16) was built in 1734 and later leased to the engraver Robert Scott (1777–1841), whose son William Bell Scott (1811–1890) knew Pre-Raphaelite artist Dante Gabriel Rosetti (1828–1882). When it was restored in the 1980s it took the name Hermits & Termits (recalling two ancient crofts that once stood here) but before that it was known as the Coalyard House. This reflects the fact that in 1827 it was acquired by the Edinburgh & Dalkeith Railway for use as a coal depot office.

The Edinburgh & Dalkeith Railway opened in 1831 as a horse-drawn tramway to bring coal into the city from pits around Dalkeith. The engineer was James Jardine (1776–1858), who was also responsible for the final stages of draining Edinburgh's Nor' and Burgh Lochs, and who is credited with determining Mean Sea Level. The most difficult part of the line for him to construct was the long steep incline between Holyrood Park and the depot at St. Leonard's. It necessitated the construction of a third of a mile-long tunnel through which coal wagons were winched by stationary steam engine. The building that housed the engine can still be found at 19 St. Leonard's Lane.

The tunnel opening on the St. Leonard's side lies at the bottom of a ramp half way along East Parkside (EH16). It was one of three engineering features on the original 9 mile-long line, the others being an historically-important cast iron railway bridge over the Braid Burn at the junction of Duddingston Road West and Forkenford (EH16), and a conventional single-span stone-arched bridge over the North Esk in Dalkeith (EH22).

Within a year of its opening, much to the surprise of its promoters, the Edinburgh & Dalkeith began attracting fare-paying passengers. St. Leonard's thus became Edinburgh's first public railway station, the

The Innocent Railway tunnel is now used by walkers and cyclists

line's slow pace and horse-drawn technology earning it the nickname 'The Innocent Railway'.

In 1845 the Edinburgh & Dalkeith was acquired by the North British Railway as part of their plan to build a passenger line between Edinburgh and Carlisle. The gauge was increased for steam locomotives and passenger services into St. Leonard's curtailed. Instead a new station was opened at North Bridge (known later as Waverley) into which passenger services from Dalkeith were re-routed via Portobello (see no. 17). St. Leonard's then continued in its original role as a coal depot until 1968, when the line finally closed and the coal depot cleared for housing.

In 1981 the track bed of the old railway reopened as an off-road pedestrian and cycle path. Those entering the tunnel at St. Leonard's today will find it illuminated by electric lights rather than the original gas lamps. At the other end it opens onto Holyrood Park, where the path continues eastwards through the Bawsinch & Duddingston Nature Reserve and onwards through Niddrie Mains to Brunstane.

Between Dalkeith Road and Minto Street is the Blacket, a once-gated estate of grand Victorian villas. Abden House at 1 Marchhall Crescent today contains the Confucius Institute for Scotland. In the garden is a statue of former Edinburgh University student Huang Kuan, the first Chinese student to graduate in the West (1857).

Other locations nearby: 45, 47

47 Gin at the Dick Vet

EH9 1PL (Southside), the Summerhall Distillery and
Pickering's Gin at 1 Summerhall
Bus 42, 67 to Summerhall (note: guided tours
by appointment only)

Summerhall in Edinburgh's Southside is one of Europe's largest public arts venues. Formerly the University of Edinburgh's veterinary school, the site is today home to over 50 resident artists, musicians, artisans and other creatives. Some idiosyncratic local companies have found their home here, too, and none moreso than the Summerhall Distillery, Edinburgh's first exclusive gin distillery in over 150 years.

The school was founded in 1823 by Edinburgh veterinarian, William Dick (1793–1866), which explains its official name: the Royal (Dick) School of Veterinary Studies (Dick Vet for short). Summerhall's main buildings were purpose-built for the school, when it moved to the site in 1916. The former Anatomy Lecture Theatre, with its curved, tiered seating and vaulted skylight, survives intact. Notable alumni from the Dick Vet include Donald Sinclair, who inspired the character of Siegfried Farnon in *All Creatures Great and Small,* and John Boyd Dunlop, inventor of the pneumatic tyre. When in 2011 the school relocated to Esater Bush, the old buildings were converted for use as an arts hub.

Since 2013 the Summerhall Distillery has occupied the former dog kennels of the school's Small Animal Hospital. Here in a modest distillery, Marcus Pickering and Matthew Gammell hand-craft small batches of their Pickering's Gin. The recipe they use is based on an old handwritten Bombay recipe dating back to 1947, which they have fine-tuned for a contemporary palette. Nine botanicals are used – juniper, coriander, cardamom, angelica, fennel, anise, lemon, lime and cloves – each carefully measured and added to the grain spirit in a pair of copper stills. A custom-designed *Bain Marie* heating system provides gentle, all-over heat to the stills, which simmers the botanicals and accounts for Pickering Gin's remarkable smoothness. So smooth in fact that it can be enjoyed neat. In technical terms, the gin exhibits a clean fresh pine nose, with citrus notes, strongly aromatic in the mouth, with hints of licquorice, cinnamon and a sweet lavender-like softness, and a refreshingly crisp, dry finish.

As official gin sponsors of the Royal Edinburgh Military Tattoo and with orders now coming in from around the world, the Summerhall

Pickering's Gin is created in the Summerhall Distillery

Distillery must be doing something right. Visitors can find out if they agree by booking a guided tour during which they will witness the full distillation, bottling, and labelling process (www.pickeringsgin.com). Incidentally according to Marcus Pickering the peacock motif on his labels "evokes the premium nature of the gin and the social animals that drink it!"

Adjacent to the distillery is the Royal Dick, a unique bar and café. Drinkers are reminded that it was also once part of the Small Animal Hospital by the zoological specimens and scientific instruments in the glass-fronted wall cabinets. A pipe connecting the bar with the distillery makes this the only bar in Scotland offering gin on tap.

Another drinks manufacturer at Summerhall is the microbrewer Andrew Barnett, who trades as Barney's Beer. His presence is a reminder that even before the arrival of the veterinary school there was a brewery here established around 1710 (the old brewery well can still be seen at the northern end of the Small Animal Hospital). Barney's Beer is also available at the Royal Dick.

Guided tours are also available at the Edinburgh Gin Distillery at 1a Rutland Place (EH1), where visitors will see and taste gin distilled in a pair of stills called Caledonia and Flora. Tutored tastings and even gin making classes using baby stills are available (www.Edinburghgindistillery.co.uk).

Other locations nearby: 45, 46, 92, 93

48 Big Screen Edinburgh

EH3 9LZ (West End), the Cameo Cinema at 38 Home Street
Bus 10, 11, 16, 23, 27, 45 to Tollcross

Edinburgh has a dozen working cinemas, with more than 30 repurposed and many more demolished. It's a story repeated in most major cities and illustrates the public's on-off relationship with the big screen. Fortunately those claimed by the wrecker's ball have found immortality in the database of the Scottish Cinemas Project (www.scottishcinemas.org.uk).

Those that have been repurposed now serve a variety of uses. The Palace at 183 Constitution Street (EH6), for example, is now a pub and the George at 14 Bath Street (EH15) is a bingo hall. The Caley at 31 Lothian Road (EH1) contains a shop, as does the Monseigneur News Theatre at 131 Princes Street (EH2), the wavy-framed window above marking its former smoking lounge. The Central at 11 Casselbank Street (EH6) started life as a Turkish Bath before being converted into a cinema in 1920. It now serves as a church but retains Scotland's only plaster screen. The Playhouse at 18–22 Greenside Place (EH1), which opened in 1929, was once Edinburgh's largest cinema, with seats for more than 3,000 people. Now used as a theatre it retains its magnificent foyer and banked auditorium.

Of Edinburgh's historic working cinemas, the most interesting is the Cameo at 38 Home Street (EH3), which opened as the King's in 1914. Beyond the retro covered entrance, much of the original architecture remains intact, including a terrazzo-floored foyer and old fashioned ticket kiosk. The auditorium beyond, which features red plush seating and ornamental plasterwork, occupies the courtyard of the surrounding tenements. The roof once doubled as a drying green to hang out laundry making it the last example of a so-called 'back court' cinema.

In the days when silent films were screened here, accompanied by Madam Egger's Ladies' Costume Orchestra, there were 673 seats in the auditorium. The cinema was fitted for sound in 1930 and in 1949 it was renamed the Cameo by new owner, Jim Poole (1911–1998). He introduced foreign and arthouse films, and commenced an association with the Edinburgh Film Festival that continues today. A reduction in the number of seats means audiences can now enjoy greater comfort, as well as a drink in Edinburgh's first licensed cinema bar opened in 1963 by Sean Connery.

Considered one of Britain's best independent cinemas, the Cameo

The Cameo Cinema on Home Street is one of Edinburgh's oldest

has long attracted celebrities, including Orson Welles and Cary Grant. More recently Quentin Tarantino attended a screening of *Pulp Fiction* here and author Irvine Welsh was on hand at the world premiere of *Trainspotting*. The Cameo itself appeared in the film *The Illusionist* (2006).

Not far from the Cameo are two other interesting cinemas. Like the Cameo, the Filmhouse at 88 Lothian Road is an arthouse cinema. Opened in 1979 inside a converted church, it is the official home of the Edinburgh Film Festival, the world's oldest continually running film festival inaugurated in 1947. The Odeon at 118 Lothian Road opened as the Regal in 1938 and was rebranded the ABC in 1969. Although the auditorium was demolished in 2000, the original monumental façade still stands and now fronts an office block, with a miniplex in its basement. Nearby at 1 Spittal Street is the flat where scenic artist George Gibson was born. The view from here of Edinburgh Castle is thought to have inspired his painting of the Emerald City backdrop for the MGM film *The Wizard of Oz*.

This tour concludes in Morningside with the Dominion at 18 Newbattle Terrace (EH10). Opened in 1938 it is rendered in the glamorous late *Art Deco* style known as *Streamline Moderne*, including a central ceiling spine in the main auditorium that draws the eyes inexorably towards the big screen.

Other locations nearby: 49

49 Boots and Beer on the Union Canal

EH3 9PD (West End), the Leamington Lift Bridge at the
junction of Leamington Road and Lower Gilmore Place
Bus 1, 34, 35 to Gilmore Park; 10, 27 to Leamington Terrace

Anyone interested in industrial archaeology should visit Fountain-bridge. The area is located at the eastern terminus of the Union Canal, which together with the Forth and Clyde Canal connects Edinburgh to Glasgow. Opened in 1822 to bring coal into Edinburgh, the canal's importance declined from the 1840s onwards with the arrival of the railways. Despite this the area continued to attract various industries, which dominated Fountainbridge until the late 20th century. Although the land around the canal basin has now been largely cleared, there are still some industrial-era remains to be seen.

The Union Canal originally stretched almost 32 miles from its junction with the Forth and Clyde Canal at Falkirk to the Port Hope-toun basin in Edinburgh, which was located between Semple Street and Lothian Road (EH3). In the early 1920s this was drained and the *Art Deco* Lothian House built on the site. Thereafter the terminus lay a mile westwards at the Lochrin Basin. At the same time the Leamington Lift Bridge, which stood just outside the original basin, was shifted to the junction of Leamington Road and Lower Gilmore Place. Restored to

The Leamington Lift
Bridge on the Union
Canal

full working order in 2002, it features a wooden deck used by pedestrians and cyclists, which can be raised to allow boats to pass.

Nowadays Lochrin Basin is the centrepiece of Edinburgh Quay, an award-winning mixed-use development of offices, housing and leisure facilities. Back in the mid-19th century, however, the area would have looked very different. In 1856 an American entrepreneur established the North British Rubber Works on the north side of the canal. Eventually the premises covered 20 acres and employed over 8,000 workers producing everything from tyres to hot-water bottles. During the First World War a million pairs of trench boots were manufactured here and in 1958 the company manufactured Britain's first traffic cones.

After the factory closed in 1973 much of the site was taken over by the Fountain Brewery, which had been established in 1856 by William McEwan on the north side of Dundee Street. The brewery was named after local springs, which together with the nearby Caledonian Railway determined its siting. It too was hugely successful until its relocation in 2005 after which the Dundee Street site was cleared for the Fountainpark leisure centre. The sole surviving part of the rubber factory at the corner of Fountainbridge and Gilmore Park is set to be transformed into an arts centre.

Since the canal's revival in 2001 it has been possible to walk or cycle the towpath from the Lochrin Basin all the way to Glasgow. Within the borders of Edinburgh it takes in several photogenic spots, including Polwarth Parish Church, with its canalside garden, Ashley Terrace Boathouse at Lockhart Bridge (home to the Edinburgh Canal Society), and the Slateford Aqueduct, which carries the Union Canal over the Water of Leith. The canal crosses the Edinburgh Bypass at Hermiston by means of the modern Scott Russell Aqueduct, named after the Scottish naval engineer John Scott Russell (1808–1882), who helped streamline ships' hulls after observing wave patterns on the Union Canal.

Cruises are available courtesy of Re-Union Canal Boats (www.re-union.org.uk).

Two other remnants of old Fountainbridge stand on the street outside Lochrin Basin. They are the soon-to-be demolished Palais de Danse, a once-glamorous 1920s ballroom, where all the great dance bands played and Sean Connery worked as a bouncer, and across the road the former entrance to the Edinburgh Meat Market, adorned with a pair of bulls' heads. The market and abattoir moved here from the Old Town in the mid-19th century and in 1921 moved again out to Chesser.

Other locations nearby: 48

50 From Orphanage to Art Gallery

EH4 3DR (West End), the Scottish National Gallery of Modern Art at 75 Belford Road
Edinburgh Coach Lines Bus 13 to Gallery of Modern Art; Lothian Bus 19, 36, 37, 41, 47, 113 to Drumsheugh Place then walk

Two grand buildings on Belford Road (EH4) tell a remarkable tale of changing function and fashion. Both were built in the style of imposing country houses and yet served somewhat incongruously as orphanages. Today as the Scottish National Gallery of Modern Art that incongruity continues since they are now used to display the nation's collection of modern and contemporary art. Covering the period from 1900 to the present day, the holdings consist of paintings, drawings and prints, as well as sculptures, installations and video works.

The first Scottish National Gallery of Modern Art opened in 1960 in Inverleith House, a converted Georgian private home in Edinburgh's Royal Botanic Garden (see no. 82). With space running out, it relocated in 1984 to the former premises of the John Watson's Institution on Belford Road. This neo-Classical building designed by William Burn (1789–1870) had opened in 1828 as a refuge for orphans using a bequest left by a well-to-do Edinburgh solicitor. The building is known today as Modern Art One.

The first works encountered are outside including *6 Times* by Antony Gormley (b. 1950), a series of six iron men positioned between here and Leith Docks (although currently only this one and the last are visible) (see no. 78). Beyond is American landscape architect Charles Jencks' *Landform*, a spiralling grass mound reflected in three crescent-shaped pools, and Martin Creed's neon *Work No. 975 EVERYTHING IS GOING TO BE ALRIGHT* above the entrance.

Inside are works from the early 20th century, including pieces by Matisse, Picasso and Bonnard. A highlight here are works by the Scottish Colourists – Samuel John Peploe, John Duncan Fergusson, Francis Cadell and Leslie Hunter – who in the 1920s and 30s combined the vibrant colours of the French Impressionists with the painting traditions of Scotland to create an idiom all their own. Their subjects include island landscapes, Edinburgh interiors and fashionable models.

Modern Art One also includes a renowned collection of international post-war art, with works by Francis Bacon, David Hockney and Tracey Emin, as well as modern Scottish art by the likes of Joan Eardley, noted for her portraits of Glasgow street children, the Zen-influenced Alan Davie, and video artist Douglas Gordon, whose work *List of Names* is projected onto a stairwell. To the rear of the building the Water of Leith can be accessed by a long flight of steps.

Charles Jencks' *Landform* outside Modern Art One

Across the road from Modern Art One is Modern Art Two, which since 1999 has occupied the former Dean Orphan Hospital. Another imposing neo-Classical building, it was established in 1833 by the philanthropist and French teacher Louis Cauvin (1754–1825) to a design by Thomas Hamilton (1784–1858). The allotments at the entrance to the building date from 1940, when many school grounds were used to grow vegetables (see no. 39).

On permanent display here is a collection of works gifted by Leith-born sculptor Sir Eduardo Paolozzi (1924–2005), including his towering robot-like sculpture *Vulcan* and a reconstruction of his studio (see no. 65). It also contains a world class collection of Dada and Surrealist material, including works by Dalí, Magritte and Alberto Giacometti.

Several palatial schools built using philanthropic bequests stand nearby. Donaldson's on West Coates (1851) was designed in the style of an Elizabethan-cum-Jacobean palace by William Henry Playfair (1790–1857) and is currently being converted into apartments. Stewart's Melville College on Queensferry Road (1855) by David Rhind (1808–1883) and Fettes College on Carrington Road (1869) by David Bryce (1803–1876) are both now respected independent schools.

Other locations nearby: 51, 52

51 Ups and Downs in Dean Village

EH4 3BJ (West End), Dean Village at the bottom of Bell's Brae
Bus 19, 36, 37, 41, 47, 113 to Drumsheugh Place

The landscape of Edinburgh was shaped millions of years by volcanoes and glaciers. Consequently those exploring the city today encounter hills everywhere and between them concealed valleys. Most dramatic is the gorge carved out by the Water of Leith as it skirts the north-west reaches of the New Town. Nestling on the riverbank is Dean Village, a unique community of converted watermills, Victorian social housing and modern apartments.

The village lies at the bottom of Bell's Brae (EH4) on the Edinburgh side of Dean Bridge. History relates how in 1128 David I (1124–1153) granted the income from several watermills here to Holyrood Abbey. In those days the western limit of Edinburgh was the castle, and the Water of Leith, which rises in the Pentland Hills and empties into the Firth of Forth, was the most powerful river within easy reach.

A clue as to what type of mills operated here is provided by a 17th century carving over a blocked doorway facing the river. Depicting two crossed bakers' paddles used to remove loaves from a hot oven, it is the symbol of the Incorporation of Baxters (the trade guild for millers and bakers) and this was once their granary. Eleven flour mills providing flour to Edinburgh's burgeoning population were in operation here until the 19th century, when larger mills in Leith rendered them obsolete. One of them, the former West Mill, stands on the opposite side of the river and now contains apartments. Look out for the stone relief high up the building depicting a sheaf of wheat.

By the early 1800s the river was also being used by tanners, textile workers and blacksmiths, all benefitting from the fact that the main route west out of Edinburgh crossed the river here. This ended abruptly, however, in 1832, when Scottish engineer Thomas Telford (1757–1834) built Dean Bridge, which bypassed the village by carrying a new road directly over the gorge. Only the tanners survived and in 1886 their lot was improved by the proprietor of *The Scotsman*, John Ritchie Findlay (1824–1898), who overlooked the village from his home on Rothesay Terrace (EH3) (see no. 98). He financed the construction of Well Court on Damside to provide the tanners with improved housing. This remarkable red sandstone complex designed by architect Sydney Mitchell (1856–1930) features a communal courtyard for drying clothes and a clocktower to remind the workers to be home by 10pm on work days. Dean Village continued to decline though and the last tannery eventually shut in the 1960s. A decade later work began on transforming the village into the desirable place it is today, with Well Court as its focal point.

Returning to Bell's Brae, walk along Miller Row (part of the Water of Leith Walkway) past some old grinding stones from another mill. Pass beneath the towering arches of Dean Bridge to reach Dean Gardens, established in the 1860s by local residents. On the riverbank here can be found two mineral springs, first the sturdy

Well Court in Dean Village on the Water of Leith

St. George's Well and farther along, St. Bernard's Well, a neo-Classical temple erected in 1789 to a design by the artist Alexander Nasmyth (1758–1840). Their waters were once believed to cure everthing from bruises to blindness.

The counterpart to Bell's Brae on the opposite side of the river is Dean Path. At the top it passes Dean Cemetery, a fashionableVictorian burial ground. Graves include the dictionary publisher Robert Chambers (1832–1888), the inventor of the pneumatic tyre Robert William Thomson (1822–1873), and the suffragist and founder of the Scottish Women's Hospitals, Elsie Inglis (1864–1917). The English traveller Isabella Bird (1831–1904) is also here on account of her having married an Edinburgh surgeon.

Other locations nearby: 50, 52

52 A Splash of History

EH4 3BL (West End), the Drumsheugh Baths Club
at 5 Belford Road
Bus 19, 36, 37, 41, 47, 113 to Drumsheugh Place
(note: visits by non-members by appointment only)

Edinburgh is a sports-friendly city with facilities for everything from football, golf and roller skating to croquet, ice skating and even petanque, which is played in the summer months in Inverleith Park. When it comes to swimming, it is certainly not at the shallow end either. Remarkably Edinburgh has more Victorian pools still in use than any other city. Four from a total of 14 date from this period and still retain many of their original features.

The finest example is undoubtedly Drumsheugh Baths Club, which opened in 1882 at 5 Belford Road (EH4). This makes it the oldest swimming pool in Edinburgh. The Drumsheugh Baths Company employed architect Sir John James Burnet (1857–1938) to design the building as part of a broader development of this steep-sided area overlooking Dean Village. Having trained at the École des Beaux Arts in Paris, he came up with a Moorish design fashionable in bath-building at the time.

Unfortunately Burnet's building was consumed by fire just ten years later. Although it was rebuilt to the same design it bankrupted the original company and a new one was formed in 1902. The shareholders were all members who actually used the baths and so were

The Drumsheugh Baths Club is Edinburgh's oldest swimming pool

not driven solely by profit. Mostly local residents, including business people and doctors, it is a similar demographic that still uses the baths today.

At street level the baths comprise a discreet arcaded vestibule of red brick and stone, with inscribed wrought iron screens. The pool itself, which is 70 feet long, is situated farther down the slope, its original exercise rings and trapezes still suspended over the water. The impressive wooden hammerbeam roof pierced by two glass cupolas is supported on a series of brick arches atop ornate iron columns. Overlooking the pool at one end is the members' lounge, with a balcony leading to what was once a Turkish bath. This area now houses a gym and sauna but retains its Moorish tiles, vaulted ceiling and apse. Refurbishment in 2005 saw the pool retiled and the installation of new poolside changing cubicles all in keeping with the original design. The emphasis here is very much on charm, peace and privacy so visits by non-members are by appointment only (www.drumsheughbaths. com).

The only Victorian pool in Edinburgh to retain its Turkish bath *(Hammam)* is the Portobello Swim Centre at 57 The Promenade (EH15). Opened in 1901 to a design by City Architect Robert Morham (1839–1912), it comprises four rooms of varying temperature – *Tepidarium* (warm), *Caldarium* (hot), *Laconium* (very hot) and *Frigidarium* (cool) – and a bracing cold plunge pool to finish. Also here is a prototype therapeutic Jacuzzi called an *Aerotone*, invented in the 1930s by Granton-based engineer, William Oliver.

Of Edinburgh's two other Victorian-era baths, those on Glenogle Road (EH3) in Stockbridge, known affectionately as Glennies, were opened in 1897 and also designed by Morham. The Warrender Baths at 55 Thirlestane Road (EH9) in Marchmont opened a decade earlier and originally included a billiard hall and reading room. Numerous Olympic and Paralympic swimmers have trained here, including gold medallist David Wilkie (b. 1954).

The Royal Commonwealth Pool on Dalkeith Road (EH16), known locally as the Commie, is Edinburgh's only 50 metre pool. Built as part of a successful bid to bring the Commonwealth Games to Edinburgh in 1970, this modernist gem has been cited as a significant modern contribution to Scottish architectural heritage. Recently refurbished at great expense, it offers the unique experience of being able to see the distinctive outline of Arthur's Seat whilst swimming!

Other locations nearby: 50, 51

53 A Most Elegant Square

EH2 4DR (New Town), a stroll around Charlotte Square
beginning with the Georgian House museum at number 7
Bus 24, 29, 42 to Frederick Street; 10, 11, 12, 16, 41
to George Street

In 1791 the renowned architect Robert Adam (1728–1792) designed Charlotte Square, which was named in honour of George III's queen. The last element of the First New Town, it is located at the west end of George Street, where it mirrors St. Andrew Square to the east (see no. 61). Most commentators agree that it is the jewel in the New Town's crown and one of the most elegant neo-Classical squares in Europe.

Adam conceived Charlotte Square as a paradigm of the Georgian ideals of urban planning. Like the broad parallel streets laid out by the New Town's planner, James Craig (1739–1795), it offered the well-to-do citizens of late 18th century Edinburgh a means of escape from the overcrowded tenements of the Old Town, and provided a suitable backdrop for the Scottish Enlightenment (see no. 6).

This stroll begins on the north side of the square, which comprises nine separate town houses. The *feus* (building plots) here were put up for sale in 1792 just days after Adam's death. Fortunately he left behind finished plans and the house at number 7 was completed in 1796 for John Lamont, 18th Chief of the Clan Lamont. In the 1960s this property was acquired by the National Trust for Scotland and restored to its original condition. As the Georgian House museum it provides visitors with a rare glimpse of New Town life around 1800. The ground floor dining room is elegantly furnished with paintings, porcelain and silverware. Note the pewter chamber pot used by gentlemen after the ladies had retired to the upstairs drawing room! The life 'below stairs' of the servants is recreated in the large kitchen. Note too the cone-shaped torch extinguishers on the iron gateposts outside.

The adjacent properties are also of interest. Number 5 was the birthplace of Sir Leander Starr Jameson (1853–1917), who studied medicine in Edinburgh then relocated to South Africa to become Prime Minister of the Cape Colony. Number 6, Bute House, is today the official residence of the First Minister of Scotland, and number 9 was once home to the antiseptic pioneer Joseph Lister (1827–1912).

Number 12 on the west side of the square is where Sir John Marjoribanks (1763–1833), twice Lord Provost of Edinburgh, lived and at number 13 lived Sir William Fettes (1750–1836), benefactor of the col-

The north side of New Town's Charlotte Square, with the Georgian House on the left

lege that bears his name. Henry, Lord Cockburn (1779–1854), a Scottish lawyer, judge and literary figure lived at number 14. His interest in architectural conservation led to the formation of Edinburgh's civic trust, the Cockburn Association. This side of the square is interrupted by St. George's Church, which was completed in 1814 to an original Adam design adapted by Robert Reid (1774–1856). Since 1964 it has been used for archival storage by National Records of Scotland.

Number 24 on the south side of the square is where Field Marshall Douglas Haig (1861–1928), Commander of the British Forces during the First World War, was born (see nos. 24 & 81). Finally number 45 on the east side was once home to Sir Robert Philip (1857–1939), a pioneer in the treatment of tuberculosis. Perhaps such achievements were inspired in part by the glorious green space at the heart of Charlotte Square in which stands the Albert Memorial by sculptor Sir John Steell (1804–1891).

Telephone pioneer Alexander Graham Bell (1847–1922) was born at nearby 14 South Charlotte Street, where he first studied acoustics due to his mother's deafness. A monument on North Charlotte Street recalls the children's author Catherine Sinclair (1800–1864), who set up Edinburgh's first public fountain on Princes Street, the remains of which rest today in Gosford Place (EH6).

Other locations nearby: 54, 55

54 Around Edinburgh with Inspector Rebus

EH2 4JB (New Town), a tour in the footsteps of the fictional
detective John Rebus including the Oxford Bar
at 8 Young Street
Bus 24, 29, 42 to Frederick Street; 10, 11, 12, 16, 41
to George Street

The Scottish crime writer Ian Rankin was born in 1960 in Cardenden, a
former mining town in Fife, where in 1826 the last duel on Scottish soil
took place. Much to the disappointment of his parents, who expected
him to take up a trade, Rankin studied English Literature at the University
of Edinburgh. After graduating in 1982 he worked as a pig farmer,
a grape picker and played in a punk band before eventually settling
down as a best-selling novelist.

Rankin didn't set out to be a crime writer though. Indeed he considered
his first two books, *Knights & Crosses* (1987) and *Hide and
Seek* (1991), to be mainstream works more in tune with Robert Louis
Stevenson's *Strange Case of Dr Jekyll and Mr Hyde* (1886) and Muriel
Spark's *The Prime of Miss Jean Brodie* (1961). Both those authors recognised
the societal divisions within the Edinburgh of their time and
Rankin does the same. His books are set in a real albeit monochrome
Edinburgh of crime, sleaze and overworked police, far removed from
the bright lights and the tourist hotspots. And at their heart is the
believable but world-weary detective, Inspector John Rebus, a dishevelled
music-loving divorcee, who likes a drink and ignores his bosses.

Readers around the world have taken to the books and their anti-hero
protagonist prompting Rankin to pen another eighteen Rebus
titles in the intervening years, the latest being *Even Dogs in the Wild*
(2015). With translations into many languages and global sales of 30
million, Rankin has unwittingly but not unhappily become a leading
light of *Tartan Noir*, a crime fiction genre with distinct Scottish roots
and a hard-boiled edge drawn from modern American crime writing.

With so many readers having experienced Edinburgh through the
pages of Rankin's novels, it's not surprising that a good number want
to visit the real locales that inspired him. Part of the success of the
series is the way Rankin uses such places in his plots, for example in
Set in Darkness he references the new Scottish Parliament building,
and *The Falls* includes the sinister miniature coffins displayed in the

National Museum of Scotland (see nos. 29 & 35).

Those readers that do visit won't be disappointed and there are several ways of going about it. Independent travellers can download the free *Ian Rankin's Edinburgh* iPhone app. Devised by Rankin's publisher it includes tours of the Old Town, the Royal Mile, the New Town and the Water of Leith, together with exclusive photos and audio of Rankin describing Edinburgh's dark side. Others will enjoy the two-hour walking tour given with Rankin's blessing by Rebus Tours (www.rebustours.com). This departs every Saturday at midday from the Royal Oak at 1 Infirmary Street (EH1), a pub frequented by Rebus, and takes in St. Leonard's

The Oxford Bar on Young Street is a favourite with Inspector Rebus

Police Station, where Rebus works and the mortuary, where autopsies are carried out. Additionally the tour takes in several mainstream sights such as the Flodden Wall and Salisbury Crags, and along the way the guide gives selected readings from the books.

One location that every Rebus fan will want to visit is the Oxford Bar at 8 Young Street (EH2) in the New Town. This is Rebus' favourite Edinburgh watering hole and it's no coincidence that it is Rankin's favourite, too (he regularly enjoys a pint of Deuchar's IPA here). The Ox, as it is fondly known, is unusual in that it retains its original compartmentalised form, with a no-frills stand-up bar at the front. Above the bar hang photos of Rankin and the actor Ken Stott (b. 1954), who played Rebus on television.

Other locations nearby: 53, 55

55 Mysterious World of the Freemasons

EH2 3JP (New Town), the Lodge of Edinburgh (Mary's Chapel) No. 1 at 19 Hill Street
Bus 24, 29, 42 to Frederick Street; 10, 11, 12, 16, 41 to George Street (note: the Lodge is only open to masons)

Other than all being Scotsmen, what is it that connects Arthur Conan Doyle, Alexander Fleming, Harry Lauder and Thomas Telford? The answer is that they were once all freemasons. With its ritualised meetings and penchant for symbolism, freemasonry has always seemed mysterious to the unitiated. Edinburgh is doubly so, since it is home not only to Scotland's oldest masonic lodges but also to Scotland's Grand Lodge, the country's governing body of freemasonry.

The origins of freemasonry still baffle historians. Some have fancifully suggested a re-emergence of the Knights Templar after their suppression in the 14th century. It seems more likely, however, that it stemmed from groups of specialist medieval masons working in freestone, who established secretive guilds to protect their skills (bakers, brewers and other professions formed incorporations for the same reason). With the gradual admission of non-operative members to raise extra funds, they became builders in a philosophical sense and are known today for their charity work and espousal of good working practices.

Freemasonry in Edinburgh is recorded as far back as the early 1500s. Indeed the very first minutes of a masonic lodge anywhere in the world were taken down here in July 1599. This historic meeting took place in the Chapel of St. Mary on Niddry's Wynd, which was accordingly placed at number 1 on the Scottish Lodge Roll when the Grand Lodge of Scotland was established in 1736. The destruction of Niddry's Wynd in 1787 to make way for the South Bridge, however, means that Lodge Canongate Kilwinning at 23 St. John Street (EH8) (number 2 on the Roll) is now the world's oldest purpose-built lodge still in use.

Meanwhile the Lodge of Edinburgh (Mary's Chapel) No. 1 relocated and since 1893 it has occupied 19 Hill Street (EH2). This normal-looking Georgian house is distinguished by a lantern decorated with the familiar masonic dividers and set square. Over the door is carved a hexagram symbolising the balance between spirit and matter that masons strive for, within a circle representing universal harmony. Within the star is a flaming 'G' (for God, the Great Architect) and around it the date '1893' and the lodge's acronym 'LEMCNo1'. Less easy to decipher are the 16 runic signature marks of the lodge officials at the time.

Cryptic carvings identify a masonic lodge on Hill Street

Although the interior of the lodge is only accessible to masons, the Grand Lodge of Scotland completed in 1912 around the corner at 96 George Street (EH2) can be visited by the general public. The imposing Freemason's Hall is the highlight of any guided tour because it is here that representatives from the 32 provincial lodges meet and where the annual installation of the Grand Master Mason takes place. Since many lodges existed before the creation of the Grand Lodge these must be colourful affairs, as each lodge is permitted to retain its distinct rituals and regalia.

Another highlight is the Grand Lodge's museum, which houses the world's oldest masonic records, a painting showing the inauguration of 'Brother' Robert Burns in 1787, and numerous masonic 'jewels' (medals), ceramics and timepieces. The more eclectic items include a masonic Bowie knife from Texas (James 'Jim' Bowie was a freemason) and a masonic Zippo lighter!

Amongst the archives held at General Register House at 2 Princes Street (EH1) is the world's oldest document describing masonic ritual. Dating from 1696 it includes questions to be asked of someone seeking entry. They include describing the form of the world's first lodge, namely the porch of King Solomon's Temple, and explaining the details of a masonic embrace, known as the Five Points of Friendship.

Other locations nearby: 53, 54, 56

56 Cock Fights and Jamie Oliver

EH2 2LR (New Town), the Assembly Rooms
at 54 George Street
Bus 24, 29, 42 to Frederick Street; 10, 11, 12, 16, 41 to George
Street (note: the Assembly Rooms can only be visited during
advertised events and on Edinburgh Doors Open Day)

The construction of Edinburgh's New Town provided a very 18th century solution to the problem of an increasingly overcrowded city. Unlike the medieval Old Town, with its narrow closes and towering tenements, the New Town was laid out as an ordered grid befitting the rationality of the prevailing Scottish Enlightenment (see nos. 53 & 61). The principal street was named George Street (EH2) after the ruling monarch, George III (1760–1820), and was lined with imposing buildings. Of these the most storied is undoubtedly the Assembly Rooms at number 54.

Assembly rooms were built during the 18th and early 19th centuries as public gathering places for the well-to-do of both sexes. Those in Edinburgh were designed by local architect John Henderson and built by public subscription on a plot given by the town council. An outstanding example of Georgian neo-Classical architecture, the building comprises a hundred foot-long stuccoed ball and banqueting room on the first floor, with subsidiary rooms for suppers, teas and playing cards (the portico at the front of the building and the music hall to the rear were added later).

The inaugural event on 11th January 1787 was the Caledonian Hunt Ball, which attracted several hundred noblemen and their ladies. According to the local press the men did not leave until 8am the following morning. The very first event hosted at the Assembly Rooms, however, was rather different. It was a cockfight staged two years earlier between the gentlemen of Lanark and Haddington in one of the half-built rooms. The Scottish caricaturist John Kay (1742–1826) illustrated the event and in the audience can be seen the infamous Deacon Brodie (see no. 91).

Other significant events in the Assembly Rooms included a ball in 1822 attended by George IV (1820–1830), a benefit dinner for retired actors in 1827 at which novelist Sir Walter Scott revealed himself as the hitherto anonymous author of the popular *Waverley* novels, a concert in 1841 given by Hungarian pianist Franz Liszt (1811–1886), and in the same year a ceremony during which author Charles Dickens was made a Freeman of the City.

Despite the taste for formal events fading during the late 19th century, and with them many assembly rooms, those in Edinburgh continued to figure in the city's social life. Indeed they were extended as late as 1906. In 2012, after an extensive refurbishment, the Assembly Rooms reopened for a new generation. Parts of the building have now been given over to retail units, including a branch of Jamie Oliver's successful Italian restaurant chain, which occupies the very room where the cock fight

Thus we poor **Cocks**, *exert our skill & Brav'ry*
For idle **Gulls**, *and* **Kites**, *that trade in Knav'ry*

A cock fight in the half-built Assembly Rooms depicted by caricaturist John Kay

took place 200 years ago. The only cocks here these days are of the chargrilled variety!

Since the Assembly Rooms are only open to the public during special events and on Edinburgh Doors Open Day, a visit to the restaurant provides a great opportunity to get a glimpse of the building's splendid interior (www.doorsopendays.org.uk).

The New Town's other palace of pleasure was the Hopetoun Rooms opened in 1827 at 68-73 Queen Street (EH2). In October 1848 Frédéric Chopin (1810–1849) gave a two-hour concert here as part of a tour instigated by his devoted Scottish pupil, Jane Stirling (1804–1859). He lodged with the Polish émigré physician Adam Łyszczyński at 10 Warriston Crescent (EH3), where in view of his failing health he wrote his last will and testament. In 1871 the Hopetoun Rooms were taken over by a girls' school founded in 1694 by the Edinburgh businesswoman Mary Erskine (1629–1707). When the school moved away in 1966, the building was replaced by Erskine House.

Other locations nearby: 55, 59

57 The Skating Minister and Other Masterpieces

EH2 2EL (New Town), the Scottish National Gallery
on The Mound
Bus 23, 27, 41, 42, 67 to Mound Place; 1, 3, 4, 10, 11, 16, 19, 22,
25, 29, 30, 31, 33, 34, 37 to Princes Street Scott Monument;
Tram T50 to Princes Street

Between 1781 and 1830 an estimated two million cartloads of earth and rubble were removed during the construction of Edinburgh's New Town (see no. 61). This material was used to fill the Nor' Loch and to build The Mound (EH2), a ramp-like thoroughfare between the Old Town and Princes Street. Four of Edinburgh's great institutions have buildings here: at the top is the neo-Gothic twin-towered New College (containing the University of Edinburgh's School of Divinity and the Church of Scotland's General Assembly Hall) and the green-domed neo-Baroque Bank of Scotland (see no. 8); lower down is the neo-Classical Scottish National Gallery and overlooking Princes Street the matching Royal Scottish Academy, both designed by the great Scottish architect William Henry Playfair (1790–1857).

The Scottish National Gallery first opened to the public in 1859. Initially the exhibition space was shared with the Royal Scottish Academy, whence came several of the masterpieces seen today. The current permanent collection consists of two parts. Firstly, on the ground floor is a representative collection of European art from the Renaissance to the Impressionists. Here can be found Van Dyck's *The Lomellini Family*, *An Old Woman Cooking Eggs* by Diego Velázquez, Claude Monet's *Haystacks* and Paul Gauguin's *Vision after the Sermon*. A collection of Turner watercolours is displayed each January as stipulated a century ago by its benefactor.

The second part is the Gallery's Scottish collection in the basement. Notable here are works by Sir Henry Raeburn (1756–1823), Scotland's first significant portrait painter to remain based in his homeland (and not gravitate to London) following the Union with England in 1707. Born the son of a manufacturer in Stockbridge and later orphaned, Raeburn rose to become Portrait Painter to King George IV in Scotland, with a fine town house-cum-studio at 32 York Place (EH1). The portraits *Robert Adam* and *Mrs. Robert Scott Moncrieff* painted in the early 19th century are unmistakeable examples of his work in being so truthful and well-lit.

There is one work by Raeburn, however, which is remarkable for being so different to his usual formal portraits. *The Skating Minister* depicts the Reverend Robert Walker (1755–1808), minister at Cramond and later the Canongate Kirk, gliding serenely across the ice on Duddingston Loch. Walker's effortless pose would have been recognised as a difficult and sophisticated manoeuvre by his fellow members of the Edinburgh Skating Society, the world's first figure skating club.

That this small picture, which mysteriously only came to light around 1950, shows a figure in action has prompted

The Skating Minister is thought to be by Sir Henry Raeburn

some critics to query its attribution. Notably in 2005 a curator from the Scottish National Portrait Gallery suggested it was actually by French artist Henri-Pierre Danloux (1753–1809), who visited Edinburgh during the 1790s, when *The Skating Minister* was painted. Certainly there are stylistic similarities and the scale of the work has been compared to that of a French painter. But Raeburn fans are unconvinced and one need only look at his *Portrait of James and John Lee Allen*, also painted in the 1790s, to see similarities in dynamics and lighting.

Whoever the artist, and Raeburn does seem most likely, *The Skating Minister* is today one of Scotland's best-loved paintings, created during one of the most remarkable periods in the country's history, the Scottish Enlightenment.

The Royal Scottish Academy founded in 1826 has occupied the building overlooking Princes Street since 1911. It is unique in being Scotland's only independently-funded institution for the promotion of the arts. The building, completed in 1836, with the rooftop statue of Queen Victoria added in 1844, originally housed the Royal Institution for the Encouragement of Fine Arts in Scotland. It is today connected with the Scottish National Gallery by means of the Weston Link.

Other locations nearby: 8, 58

58 Scott-land!

EH2 2EJ (New Town), the Scott Monument in East Princes
Street Gardens
Bus 1, 3, 4, 10, 11, 16, 19, 22, 25, 29, 30, 31, 33, 34, 37 to Princes
Street Scott Monument; Tram T50 to Princes Street
(note: it may not be possible to climb the Scott Monument
in bad weather)

The death of Edinburgh-born novelist, playwright and poet Sir Walter
Scott (1771–1832) rightly caused a stir. Praised during his lifetime as
the inventor of modern historical fiction, his *Waverley* novels helped

reinvent Scottish culture at
a time when the Highlands
were still viewed in some
quarters as barbaric (see
no. 7). Edinburgh's main
railway station was named
Waverley in his honour and
a tower was erected on Corstorphine Hill, with further
memorials in Glasgow and
even New York's Central
Park. To this day Scottish
banknotes carry Scott's
likeness as a reminder that
he campaigned for Scot-
land's right to print its own
paper money.

The greatest memorial,
however, is the Scott Monument in East Princes Street
Gardens (EH2). Follow-
ing Scott's death in 1832,
a competition held to de-
sign it was won by George
Meikle Kemp (1795–1844),
a self-taught architect who
used a pseudonym to con-
ceal his lack of qualifi-

Bill Bryson compared the Scott Monument to a Gothic rocket ship   cations. Despite this the judges liked his design and in 1838 he was awarded the contract. The result is the world's largest writer's memorial.

Meikle's design consists of a massive Gothic spire of West Lothian sandstone soaring over 200 feet into the air. Best viewed from South St. David Street, it positively bristles with 64 figures from Scott's novels and a further 16 Scottish literary figures. At its base is a Carrara marble statue of Scott holding a quill pen by Sir John Steell (1804–1891), with his beloved dog Maida at his side. Not everyone was enamoured though including Charles Dickens, who compared it to "the spire of a Gothic church taken off and stuck in the ground". More recently the American travel writer Bill Bryson (b. 1951) has described it as a "Gothic rocket ship". Visitors enjoy climbing the dizzying 287 spiral stairs to enjoy the breezy views from the viewing platform at the top.

The Scott Monument is by no means the only memorial in Princes Street Gardens. Immediately to the east, for example, is a statue of the missionary David Livingstone by Amelia Robertson Hill (1821–1904), who was responsible for several statues on the Scott Monument and was one of Edinburgh's few 19th century female sculptors. Beyond The Mound, in West Princes Street Gardens, are more memorials, including the Royal Scots Regimental Memorial (1952), the Royal Scots Greys Memorial (1906), the Scots American War Memorial (1927) given by Scottish-Americans to honour Scottish troops who served in the Great War, and the magnificent Ross Fountain, which was purchased at the Great London Exposition of 1862 and shipped in pieces up to Leith.

More recent is the bronze statue of Wojtek, a bear that served in the Polish military during the Second World War and ended his days in Edinburgh Zoo. The smallest statue is that of Bum the Dog (2008), Edinburgh's twin city of San Diego's answer to Greyfriars Bobby, tucked inside the King's Stable Road entrance (see no. 38).

Beyond the Ross Fountain are the twin towers of St. Cuthbert's Parish Church at 5 Lothian Road. A church has stood here since 850 AD making it Edinburgh's oldest. It contains a rare Tiffany window depicting David and Goliath and an alabaster rendition of Da Vinci's *Last Supper* in the apse. The architect of the Scott Monument, George Meikle Kemp, is buried in the graveyard having drowned in the Union Canal before his work was unveiled. Agatha Christie married her second husband, archaeologist Max Mallowan, here, too. The neighbouring Church of St. John the Evangelist is also worth visiting for its Victorian stained glass, fan-vaulted nave, and filigree silver box shaped like an Ethiopian church.

Other locations nearby: 17, 57

59 Non Sinit Esse Feros

EH2 1JQ (New Town), the Royal College of Physicians
of Edinburgh at 9 Queen Street
Bus 23, 27, 61 to Hanover Street; 10, 11, 12, 16, 26, 44
to North St. David Street (note: the building can only
be visited by appointment)

Edinburgh's New Town is considered a masterpiece of town planning. Laid out in stages between 1767 and 1850, the area retains many of its original neo-Classical buildings (see nos. 53 & 61). One of the most striking is the Royal College of Physicians at 9 Queen Street (EH2). This ornate building is not only extremely well preserved but its interior is only rarely open to visitors.

The Royal College of Physicians of Edinburgh (RCPE) was founded by the Scottish physician Sir Robert Sibbald (1641–1722) and established by Royal Charter in 1681. The aims of the 21 founding Fellows were to advance medicine as a reputable science and to alleviate the suffering of Edinburgh's poor. Today the RCPE boasts some 12,000 members around the world and still works to maintain medical training standards. In this respect its motto *Non Sinit Esse Feros* – a misquote of the Roman poet Ovid's "Emollit Mores Nec Sinit Esse Feros" (Learning humanises character and does not permit it to be cruel) – seems particularly apt.

Initially the RCPE met in the private homes of its Fellows. Thereafter it convened in Fountain Close, off the High Street, where in 1729 it was instrumental in founding what became the Royal Infirmary of Edinburgh at the top of Infirmary Street (EH1) (see no. 31). The RCPE then built its own hall on George Street in 1781 only to relocate to its current premises on Queen Street in 1846. Two 18th century buildings were demolished to make way for it.

Designed by Edinburgh architect Thomas Hamilton (1784–1858), the building's façade is adorned with three figures: Asclepius, the Greek god of healing (left); Hygeia, the Greek god of cleanliness (centre); and Hippocrates, the ancient Greek physician considered the Father of Western Medicine. Either side of door are serpent-entwined rods associated with Asclepius and thought to represent the non-venomous snakes used in ancient healing rituals. Such snakes are also thought to represent the contradiction that medicine can either heal or harm.

The relatively narrow façade conceals a far larger-than-expected interior. On the Grand Staircase is a bust of James Young Simpson

(1811–1870), who in 1847 discovered the anaesthetic properties of chloroform in his home at 52 Queen Street. Also displayed is a portrait of Alexander Wood (1817–1884), the inventor of the hypodermic syringe. The Great Hall, which was doubled in size in 1865 by architect David Bryce (1803–1876), is a magnificent space with Corinthian columns, numerous busts and paintings, and a coffered ceiling. Bryce was also responsible for the equally impressive library, with its marble fireplaces and floor-to-ceiling bookcases containing many of the RCPE's 60,000 medical books. The magnificent building can be visited by appointment or as an invited guest during advertised special events.

The extravagant façade of the Royal College of Physicians on Queen Street

Such Victorian splendour contrasts greatly with the restrained Georgian elegance of the adjacent building at 8 Queen Street. Completed to a design by Robert Adam (1728–92) in 1771 and probably the first house on Queen Street, it was purchased by the RCPE in 1868. The intact Drawing Room is where the Council of the RCPE now meets.

To the rear of the buildings is a modern Physic Garden based on one created in 1671 near the Palace of Holyroodhouse by Robert Sibbald and another founding Fellow, Sir Andrew Balfour (1630–1694). The purpose of the original garden was to cultivate medicinal plants for prescriptions and to teach medical botany to students. It eventually developed into the Royal Botanic Garden Edinburgh in Inverleith (see no. 82).

Other locations nearby: 56, 60

60 The First Purpose-Built Portrait Gallery

EH2 1JD (New Town), the Scottish National Portrait Gallery
at 1 Queen Street
Bus 23, 27, 61 to Hanover Street; 10, 11, 12, 16, 26, 44 to North
St. David Street

The Scottish National Portrait Gallery founded in 1882 and opened to
the public in 1889 stands at 1 Queen Street (EH2). London's National
Portrait Gallery – the world's first – was founded in 1856 but didn't
move to Trafalgar Square until 1896. This means that the Scottish National Portrait Gallery was the world's first to occupy purpose-built
premises. Visiting the building today shows it to be every bit as interesting as the portraits it contains.

The Scottish historian and philosopher Thomas Carlyle (1795–
1881) was first to call for a Scottish National Portrait Gallery in which
to exhibit portraits of, but not necessarily by, Scots. When the funds to
build it were not forthcoming from London, the proprietor of *The Scotsman*, John Ritchie Findlay (1824–1898), stepped in and financed the
entire project. The result is one of the most remarkable of Edinburgh's
Victorian public buildings.

Built from red sandstone quarried in Dumfriesshire to a Gothic Revival design by Sir Robert Rowan Anderson (1834–1921), it is modelled
on the Doge's Palace in Venice. Such revivals had become fashionable
in the 1850s after the publication of John Ruskin's *Stones of Venice*.
Where the two buildings differ is in the decoration. In Edinburgh because of the gallery's lack of contemporary portraits of medieval Scots,
statues of them were used to embellish the façade. Later figures featured, too, including the political economist Adam Smith. All are by
David Watson Stevenson (1842–1904), who also contributed statues to
the Scott Monument (see no. 58).

In the main entrance hall an elaborate Arts and Crafts scheme of
decoration was employed. A dozen columns with gilded capitals form
an arcade supporting a first floor balcony. Across the surface of the
arcade is painted an extraordinary processional frieze of 150 notable
Scots from Saint Ninian to Robert Burns. One contemporary critic described the work by Englishman William Brassey Hole (1846–1917)
as "one of the most notable essays in mural decoration ever accom-
plished in this country". Also in the entrance hall is a gilded memorial

to John Ritchie Findlay, whose financial support made all this magnificence possible.

Fast forward now to the late 20th century, when the building was being shared with the National Museum of Antiquities and the display areas had become compromised. It was decided in 2009 that the museum would relocate to the Museum of Scotland on Chambers Street. The Portrait Gallery was then restored to its original layout but with improved access and visitor facilities. Reopened in 2011, the emphasis has now shifted from glorifying Victorian worthies to telling the story of the Scottish people from the Renaissance to the present day. The 17 refurbished galleries follow a chronological timeline and inevitably include works by the great masters of 18th century Scottish portrait

The richly decorated entrance hall of the Scottish National Portrait Gallery

painting (Allan Ramsay the Younger and Sir Henry Raeburn) and portraits of illustrious Scots (the oldest dated 1507 depicts James IV). But there's now much more besides, including depictions of golfers at play, death masks, and a parade of men in kilts. Portraits of more recent Scottish pioneers are especially popular and include comedian Billy Connolly, football manager Alex Ferguson and film actress Tilda Swinton. Thomas Annan's photos of Glasgow slums are a reminder that the Scottish National Photography Collection is also housed here.

Those responsible for the Gallery's transformation, namely Page\ Park Architects, have been sure to cater for the broadest possible audience. So while digitally-savvy visitors are engaging with the interactive Touchscreen Gallery, traditionalists will enjoy the studious atmosphere of the Victorian Library on the first floor, with its galleried shelves and collection of busts.

Other locations nearby: 59, 61

61 The New Town's Unsung Architect

EH2 2AD (New Town), the foyer of the Royal Bank of Scotland
at 36 St. Andrew Square
Bus 1, 3, 4, 19, 22, 25, 29, 30, 31, 33, 34, 37 to Princes Street
Waverley; Tram T50 to St. Andrew Square

Many people pass daily through the foyer of the Royal Bank of Scotland at 36 St. Andrew Square (EH2). What few realise, however, is that embedded in the floor is a circular bronze plate marking the point from where Edinburgh's New Town was measured out. With its rectilinear plan, elegant squares and fine terraces, the New Town is considered one of the finest pieces of European town planning.

Proposals for enlarging Edinburgh northwards were first mooted in the late 17th century. Considering the overcrowded and insanitary conditions of the Old Town, where ancient tenements were in the habit of collapsing, the issue of expansion was a pressing one. It was not until 1766, however, that George Drummond (1688–1766), Lord Provost of Edinburgh, managed to persuade the Town Council to support the project and to stage a competition for its design. In so doing he hoped to attract back to Edinburgh those aristocrats who had relocated to London in 1603, when James VI became James I of England. In preparation Drummond had already instigated the draining of the Nor' Loch and the construction of the North Bridge, which would connect the Old Town with the New (see no. 33).

The competition was won by the young Edinburgh architect and draughtsman, James Craig (1739–1795). His proposal for a symmetrical grid-iron arrangement of three main streets (Princes Street, George Street and Queen Street) and two lesser streets (Rose Street and Thistle Street), with narrower streets running at right angles and a square at each end (St. Andrew Square to the east and Charlotte Square to the west), was considered a rational one in tune with the ongoing Scottish Enlightenment. A copy of the plan is displayed in the Museum of Edinburgh (see no. 24).

Construction on what became known as the First New Town began in 1768, with St. Andrew Square. The original idea to build a church here, however, was thwarted by Edinburgh MP Sir Lawrence Dundas (1710–1781), who built a Palladian mansion on the site instead. This was acquired in the 1820s by the Royal Bank of Scotland for use as its head office and extended to include the glorious domed banking hall seen today (see no. 8). St. Andrew's Church meanwhile was shunted farther along George Street, where during the Disruption of 1843 the Free Church of Scotland was formed.

That Craig was only responsible for the layout of the First New Town and not its buildings, however, has meant he is often overshadowed by the architect Robert Adam (1728–1792). It was Adam who designed the magnificent Georgian terraces adorning Charlotte Square, the final element

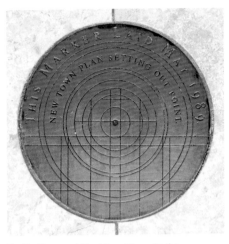

The New Town was laid out from this spot in the Royal Bank of Scotland

of the First New Town completed in 1820 (see no. 53). This has led some to assume incorrectly that Adam was responsible for everything.

Craig's contribution was further obscured when the increasing demand for property prompted the construction of the Northern New Town in the space between Queen Street Gardens and the Water of Leith. Although Craig's grid-iron plan was used as a template, the architects here produced fewer buildings of note, indeed as one progresses northwards from Heriot Row so the elegance diminishes. There are still some superb building though, including the former Broughton Place Church, which is now a beautiful saleroom for the auctioneers Lyon & Turnbull. Also noteworthy is Jamaica Street (EH3), its curious circular plan echoing Craig's "windy parallelograms" that are such a distinctive feature of the First New Town. Kay's Bar at number 39 is a cosy hideaway pub housed inside a former Georgian coach house, which was used by a wine and spirit merchant in the Victorian period.

By this time, however, Craig was long dead having succumbed to consumption in 1795. Although he had submitted other designs for Edinburgh and Glasgow after working on the First New Town, his lack of business acumen and headstrong criticism of the Town Council meant he never worked at the same level again. Burdened with debts he was buried in an unmarked grave in Greyfriars Kirkyard and his drawings and equipment sold to pay his creditors. Only in the 1930s did the Saltire Society erect a gravestone for the man who helped transform Edinburgh from 'Auld Reekie' to the 'Athens of the North'.

James Craig's grid-iron plan still dominates the New Town

Fortunately Craig's clear vision for the First New Town endures to this day and he would still recognise his grid-iron plan. The ultimate accolade came in 1995, when UNESCO recognised the First New Town as one of Britain's finest urban ensembles and made it part of the broader Edinburgh World Heritage Site.

The world-famous Princes Street (EH1) was originally going to be named St. Giles Street after Edinburgh's ancient patron but George III (1760–1820) objected because the name was already that of a notorious London slum. Instead it was named Princes Street after the future Duke of York. Not so well known is Ann Street (EH4) in the north-western corner of the Northern New Town. Named after the wife of artist Henry Raeburn (1756–1823), who purchased and developed the Deanhough Estate here in 1813, it was considered by Sir John Betjeman "the most attractive street in Britain". J.M. Barrie (1860–1937), the author of *Peter Pan*, was so charmed that he based his novel *Quality Street* on it. Another interesting street is India Street (EH3). The physicist James Clerk Maxwell (1831–1879) lived here at number 14, where a small museum celebrates his contribution to electromagnetic theory and the modern measurement of colour. At the north end of the street are the lovely India Street Gardens planted in 1822 and still enjoyed exclusively by local residents.

Other locations nearby: 60, 62, 63

62 An Historic Pub Crawl

EH2 2AA (New Town), a tour of historic pubs beginning with
the Café Royal at 19 West Register Street
Bus 1, 3, 4, 19, 22, 25, 29, 30, 31, 33, 34, 37 to Princes Street
Waverley; Tram T50 to St. Andrew Square

Amongst the holdings of the National Galleries of Scotland is a painting called *Poets' Pub*. The work of portrait painter Alexander 'Sandy' Moffatt (b. 1943), it depicts a group of Scottish 20th century writers in an amalgam of three of their favourite New Town pubs: the Café Royal, the Abbotsford and Milne's Bar. All three are still in business and together make a great historic pub crawl.

The Café Royal at 19 West Register Street (EH2) is surely Edinburgh's grandest pub. Built in the 1820s as a gas and plumbing showroom, it was converted into a pub in the 1860s. The typically Victorian fittings include a polished mahogany bar, brass foot-rails, marble floors and ornate ceilings. A special feature is the magnificently-carved walnut screen bisecting the interior. On one side is the Oyster Bar and Buffet adorned with stained glass windows depicting outdoor pursuits: on the other is the Circle Bar, with Royal Doulton panels of famous inventors. These were acquired in 1886 at the International Exhibition of Industry, Science and Art held on the Meadows (see no. 45).

The Oyster Bar and
Buffet of the Café
Royal on West Register
Street

Next Stop is Rose Street to the west. At a recent count, Edinburgh had over 700 pubs, so it's not surprising that some streets have more than one. Rose Street is a case in point and has even spawned its own drinking game – the Rose Street Challenge – in which punters have a drink at each of the street's dozen watering holes. Close proximity to the Scott Memorial explains why a couple of them honour the famous author, including the Abbotsford at 3–5 Rose Street (EH2) named after Scott's residence near Melrose. Opened in 1902, the highlight of this ornate Edwardian pub is the island bar hewn from Spanish mahogany. Note, too, the tall Aitken Founts used to raise cask beers from the cellar by air pressure rather than the English suction method.

During the 1950s and 60s the Abbotsford was popular with the Rose Street Poets, whose number included Hugh MacDiarmid, Norman MacCaig, Sorley MacLean and Sydney Goodsir Smith (all of whom feature in the *Poets' Pub* painting). They spearheaded the Scottish Renaissance during the first half of the 20th century, when likeminded writers and artists merged their interest in modern philosophy and technology with folk traditions and declining languages. The Rose Street Poets also frequented the nearby Milne's Bar at 35 Hanover Street (EH2). Here they would congregate for lively poetic and political debate in a room dubbed the Little Kremlin.

Another pub crawl can be made along the Royal Mile. The White Horse Inn at 266 Canongate (EH8) established in 1742 is the oldest pub on the Royal Mile and doubles as the Laughing Horse comedy venue during the Edinburgh Fringe. Farther along in Fleshmarket Close (EH1) is the tiny Halfway House offering third-of-a-pint glasses of beer and Cullen Skink soup in its cosy single room. Also in this steep close is Jinglin' Geordie named after the wealthy court goldsmith George Heriot (1563-1624), who bequeathed money to found the school that bears his name.

Off the Royal Mile at 80 West Bow (EH1) is the Bow Bar, which looks old but isn't. Opened only in the 1980s it is decorated with vintage trade advertisements. It does, however, serve Deuchar's IPA from the Caledonian Brewery at 42 Slateford Road (EH11), Edinburgh's oldest working brewery founded in 1869.

This tour ends with the White Hart Inn at 34 Grassmarket (EH1). Established in 1516, its customers have included Robert Burns, William Wordsworth and the bodysnatchers Burke and Hare. An inscription on the pavement outside recalls where a bomb dropped by a German Zeppelin exploded in 1916.

Other locations nearby: 61, 63

63 The Archivists' Garden

EH1 3YY (New Town), the Archivists' Garden between General Register House at 2 Princes Street and New Register House at 3 West Register Street
Bus 1, 3, 4, 19, 22, 25, 29, 30, 31, 33, 34, 37 to Princes Street Waverley; Tram T50 to St. Andrew Square

Two unique buildings stand at the east end of Princes Street (EH1). General Register House and New Register House are purpose-built repositories for Scotland's national records and a paradise for those in search of Scottish ancestry and history. In the courtyard between them is the Archivists' Garden, which celebrates the link between plants and Scotland's history.

General Register House at 2 Princes Street is probably the world's oldest archive building still serving its original function. Designed by the Scottish neo-Classical architect Robert Adam (1728–1792) and opened to the public in 1789, it is the headquarters of National Records of Scotland, which looks after Scotland's national archives and gathers population data. Alongside it at 3 West Register Street is New Register House, opened in 1861.

A path leading upwards through the peaceful Archivists' Garden

With registration in Scotland having become compulsory in 1855, this building provided much-needed extra storage for Scotland's birth, death and marriage records. Designed by Robert Matheson (1808–1877), its Italianate style complements that of Adam.

Historians and genealogists have long been drawn to both buildings. The records of Scotland as an independent kingdom are here, including the Declaration of Arbroath (1320) asserting Scottish independence, the Act of Union with England (1707) that led to the creation of Great Britain, and records of the Scottish Parliament that preceded it. Also here are modern records of government and the devolved Parliament, including court and kirk session records, wills, property registers, and documents relating to railways, shipbuilding and landed estates. In addition to Statutory Registers from 1855 onwards, the Old Parish Registers date back to the 16th century and include the proclamation of banns of marriage of Mary, Queen of Scots and Lord Darnley.

Family research is carried out in the Scotlands People Centre on the ground floor of both buildingss. At the heart of General Register House visitors can see the magnificent Adam Dome, beyond which a staircase leads up to the Historical Search Room. The Matheson Dome was added in 1871 to house additional records. The main architectural feature of New Register House is also a dome, lined with four miles of tiered bookshelves – red volumes for births, black for death and green for marriages.

In 2010 the courtyard separating the two Register Houses was transformed into the Archivists' Garden. Designed by Edinburgh landscape architects Gross Max using a plant palette conceived by the Royal Botanic Garden Edinburgh, it features 57 species connected in some way with Scotland's collective memory, whether through events such as birth, death and marriage or famous Scots, heraldry, tartan, and the notion of homecoming.

The garden highlights the longstanding role of plants in Scottish culture and tradition. Visitors are reminded of the forgotten habit of planting an apple tree to celebrate the birth of a boy and a pear for a girl, how plants inspired clan badges and Scotland's national flower (the thistle), and the connection between Robert Burns and the Cowslip *(Primula veris)* mentioned in his *Lass of Cessnock Banks*. The Bell Heather *(Erica cinerea)* has a link to tartan though its purple dye and acts as a reminder that the Scottish Register of Tartans is administered by National Records of Scotland.

It should be mentioned that whilst Scotland's archives are of necessity arranged in an orderly manner, the human mind is not always like that. Living memories are often random and incomplete, and that's reflected in the garden, which is laid out in abstract flowing patterns, much like the surface of the human brain.

Those chasing elusive relatives can continue their search at the Scottish Geneaology Centre at 15 Victoria Terrace (EH1), where grave inscriptions, military records and maps are held on microfilm.

Other locations nearby: 21, 61, 62

64 A Scottish Acropolis

EH7 5AA (New Town), the monuments on Calton Hill
Bus 34, 113 to Regent Bridge; 1, 4, 19 22, 25 to Leith Street

Amongst the graves of the Canongate Kirkyard is that of the painter Hugh William Williams (1773–1829), who was known as 'Grecian Williams'. It is thought that the sobriquet 'Modern Athens' (hence 'Athens of the North') was first applied to Edinburgh in 1822, when Williams exhibited his watercolours of Athens alongside views of Edinburgh, and asked onlookers to see similarities between the two (at the time Edinburgh's New Town was being hailed as a triumph of enlightened town planning). Fittingly the backdrop to his grave is provided by the monument-topped Calton Hill, Scotland's very own Acropolis.

There are several ways to climb Calton Hill, the most dramatic being via the staircase on the south side at the junction of Waterloo Place and Regent Road (EH7). Look out for the plaque on the right commemorating three Scottish singers (one of whom is an ancestor of violinist Nigel Kennedy) and the whitewashed Rock House on the left, where Robert Adamson (1821–1848) and David Octavius Hill (1802–1870) pioneered photography in Scotland.

Upon reaching the summit, the monuments of Calton Hill reveal themselves. First is the soot-blackened Observatory House built

William Playfair's classical tribute to philosopher Dugald Stewart on Calton Hill

in 1777 to a design by New Town planner James Craig (1739–1795) (see no. 61). Leith optician Thomas Short (1711–1788) commissioned it as part of a proposed observatory but he died before its completion in 1792 (the telescope it contained would eventually be claimed by Short's daughter Maria, who eventually relocated it to the Camera Obscura on Castlehill (EH1) (see no. 3)).

Of the observatory nothing remains since in 1818 the New Observatory designed by William Henry Playfair (1790–1857) was built on the same spot. With a cruciform plan, four temple-like porches and a dome on the roof, it was the first of several neo-Classical structures on Calton Hill reflecting the fashionable Greek Revival. The main purpose of the observatory was to observe the transit of stars through the meridian and thereby keep the observatory clock accurate. Accurate timekeeping was important for navigation, and mariners would bring their ships' chronometers here for adjustment.

In 1896 underfunding forced the New Observatory (by now called the Royal Observatory) to relocate to a new site on Blackford Hill (see no. 103). The old buildings on Calton Hill were then refurbished and reopened two years later as the City Observatory. A new stand-alone building called the City Dome, inspired by the Tower of the Winds in Athens, was also built at this time. Until 2009 the observatory was administered by the Astronomical Society of Edinburgh since when Edinburgh Town Council in partnership with the Collective Gallery have been redeveloping the site as an arts and restaurant venue. The City Dome is already being used for exhibitions, with the rest set to reopen in 2017.

Whereas the observatories on Calton Hill were sited here for practical reasons, the other monuments seen today were erected purely to exploit the dramatic aspect. The first of them, the Nelson Monument, was completed in 1816. Designed by Robert Burn (1752–1815) in the Gothic style to match that of Observatory House, it takes the form of a giant upside-down telescope. Over the entrance is the date 1805, marking the Battle of Trafalgar, and an inscription urging the people of Edinburgh to follow Nelson's noble example. Weather permitting, the Trafalgar flag signal "England expects that every man will do his duty" is still flown here on Trafalgar Day (21st October).

In 1854 a time ball was installed at the top of the Nelson Monument. Triggered by the observatory clock to drop precisely at 12 noon GMT on weekdays, it could be seen by shipping in the Firth of Forth. This equates to 1pm during British Summer Time, which means that for half the year the dropping coincides with the firing of the One O'Clock Gun at Edinburgh Castle. Both were once connected by a telegraph wire but today are triggered manually. Magnificent views await those able to negotiate the monument's 143 spiral steps.

In a similarly patriotic vein, work commenced in 1826 on the nearby National Monument. Intended to commemorate Scottish soldiers and sailors killed during the Napoleonic Wars, its architects William Playfair and Charles Robert Cockerell (1788–1863) envisaged a replica of the Parthenon in Athens. Unfortunately by this time the enormous cost of the building the New Town had bankrupted the Town Council and only only half the funds required were forthcoming. The project was abandoned in 1829 leaving the dozen massive Doric columns seen today. Playfair described it as "the pride and the poverty of Scotland", whilst others dubbed it "Edinburgh's Disgrace".

The unfinished National Monument on Calton Hill

Around the same time as the National Monument was being built, the so-called Playfair Monument was also underway. Forming one corner of the enclosure surrounding the New Observatory, this scholarly mix of the Tomb of Theron at Agrigento and the Lion Tomb at Cnidos was designed by William Henry Playfair in memory of his uncle, the scientist and mathematician Professor John Playfair (1748–1819).

Calton Hill's neo-Classical ensemble was completed in 1831 with Playfair's graceful rotunda to the philosopher Dugald Stewart (1753–1828), who is buried in the Canongate Kirkyard below. It follows the form of the Choragic Monument of Lysicrates in Athens.

> The Royal High School on Regent Road (EH7) below Calton Hill dates from 1829 and it too was rendered in the neo-Classical style. In the 1970s it was refitted as New Parliament House but when devolution was delayed until 1997 it was superceded by the custom-built Scottish Parliament at Holyrood (see no. 29). The building is currently awaiting a new use.

Other locations nearby: 21, 63

65 The Manuscript of Monte Cassino

EH1 3JD (New Town), The Manuscript of Monte Cassino outside St. Mary's Metropolitan Cathedral at the foot of Leith Street
Bus 7, 8, 14, 22, 25, 49 to Leith Street; 10, 11, 12, 16 to York Place; Tram T50 to York Place

St. Mary's Metropolitan Cathedral at the foot of Leith Street (EH1) is the mother church of Scottish Catholicism and the National Shrine of St. Andrew. So when it came to installing public sculpture in the cathedral forecourt something really special was needed. What better therefore than *The Manuscript of Monte Cassino* by Leith-born sculptor Sir Eduardo Paolozzi (1924–2005). Eyecatching, allegorical and a popular climbing frame for youngsters, it ticks a lot of boxes for passers-by.

The name in part reflects the fact that Leith-born Paolozzi was the son of immigrants from the Cassino area of southern Italy. When Italy declared war on Britain in June 1940, he was interned for three months at Saughton Prison in Stenhouse. During this time his father, grandfather and uncle were all drowned, when the ship transporting them to Canada was sunk by a German U-boat.

In 1943 Paolozzi commenced his studies at the Edinburgh College of Art, transferring a year later to London's Slade School of Fine Art. It was at this stage of the war that the historic abbey at Monte Cassino was destroyed by Allied bombing in an effort to dislodge German forces. After the war Paolozzi relocated to Paris, where he was greatly influenced by Surrealist sculptors such as Braque, Giacometti and Brâncuşi.

On his return to Britain in 1949 Paolozzi forged his own career in a variety of media, including screenprinting and textiles, and became a leading proponent of the Pop Art movement. He became especially renowned for his sculpture, notably of man-machines and deconstructed human forms. For his efforts he was made Her Majesty's Sculptor in Ordinary for Scotland in 1986 and later knighted.

It was Paolozzi's special connection with Edinburgh that prompted the town council and local entrepreneur Tom Farmer of Kwik Fit car servicing fame to commission *The Manuscript of Monte Cassino*. Cast in Germany and unveiled in 1991, it consists of a huge human foot, an

Part of Sir Eduardo Paolozzi's *The Manuscript of Monte Cassino*

open palm and a part of a limb. Paolozzi was tight-lipped about the meaning of the work beyond stating that Edinburgh warranted sculpture of the right scale because the city had long drawn inspiration from the Classical world. This certainly explains the giant foot, which recalls that of Emperor Constantine in Rome.

Passers-by must interpret the rest. The disjointed format, for example, might reflect the destruction of war, the foot representing the dispersal of victims and the hand representing the need for alms. Balanced on the hand is a ball, with geometric indentations and two mating locusts, references perhaps to genetic engineering and the Bible. Around the foot runs a Latin inscription penned 1,200 years ago by an exiled Italian monk. The piece therefore seems to speak of destruction and regeneration.

More of Palaozzi's work, including his robot-like *Vulcan* and the contents of his studio, is displayed in the Scottish National Gallery of Modern Art on Belford Road (EH4) (see no. 50). His man-machines are also used to great effect in the Early People's Gallery of the National Museum of Scotland on Chambers Street (EH1).

St. Mary's Metropolitan Cathedral was established as St. Mary's Chapel in 1814. It became the seat of a new Archdiocese of Saint Andrews and Edinburgh in 1878, three centuries after the execution of the previous Archbishop. Since Scotland's original relics of St. Andrew had been lost when St. Andrew's Cathedral in Fife was destroyed during the Reformation, further relics were acquired, which are stored today in reliquaries beneath an icon of the saint. The diagonal cross or saltire on the Scottish flag is a reminder that St. Andrew, the country's patron saint, was crucified.

Other locations nearby: 66, 67, 68

66 The Home of Holmes

EH1 3JT (New Town), the statue of Sherlock Holmes
in Picardy Place
Bus 7, 8, 14, 22, 25, 49 to Leith Street; 10, 11, 12, 16
to York Place; Tram T50 to York Place

One of the most enduring fictional supersleuths is Sherlock Holmes, accompanied as always by his dependable sidekick Dr. John Watson. But whereas many of the detective's cases were set squarely in Victorian England, it was in Edinburgh that his creator, Sir Arthur Ignatius Conan Doyle (1859–1930), was born. And it is there that both men are remembered in different ways.

Conan Doyle was born in Edinburgh's New Town on 22nd May 1859 at 11 Picardy Place (EH1) (the name recalls a colony of French silk-weavers that settled here in 1730). Unfortunately the section of street containing Doyle's home was demolished in 1970 and is now a traffic island. A modest brass plaque on the wall at 2b Picardy Place, however, states that the house stood nearby and a pub named in Doyle's honour stands opposite at 71–73 York Place.

Most importantly a life-sized bronze statue of Sherlock Holmes by the sculptor Gerald Ogilvie Laing (1936–2011) stands in the same area. Inscribed on Holmes' trademark pipe is the text "Ceci n'est pas une pipe" (This is not a pipe). The words echo those written by Belgian surrealist René Magritte beneath his famous painting of a pipe, *The Treachery of Images*. Alongside Holmes' foot is an ominously large footprint assumed to be that of the giant dog in Doyle's hugely successful tale, *The Hound of the Baskervilles*.

In 1864 Doyle and his siblings were housed temporarily at various addresses across Edinburgh due to their father's drinking (a surveyor and a skilful caricaturist, his work is held at the City Art Centre). When the family reconvened in 1867 it was in a squalid tenement at 3 Sciennes Place (EH9). A year later aged nine Doyle was sent away by his well-to-do uncle to Jesuit schools in Lancashire and then Austria, although he later rejected Catholicism and became an agnostic.

Back in Edinburgh between 1876 and 1881 Doyle studied medicine at the city's Royal College of Surgeons. He lived at 23 George Square (EH8), where a wall plaque marks the spot. He also studied botany at the Royal Botanic Garden and began writing short stories. Although his first effort, *The Haunted Grange of Goresthorpe*, was rejected (the original manuscript is held at the National Library of Scotland), *The*

Mystery of Sasassa Valley, a story set in South Africa, was printed in 1879 in *Chambers's Edinburgh Journal*.

After his graduation Doyle established a medical practice in Plymouth. Whilst waiting for patients he wrote more fiction, including his first published work featuring Holmes and Watson, *A Study in Scarlet* (1886), which received positive reviews.

Doyle admitted to modelling the analytical Holmes on Dr. Joseph Bell (1837–1911), one of his college lecturers, and may have based Watson on another, Sir Patrick Heron-Watson (1832–1907). Many more successful stories followed after Doyle moved to London in 1890. One of them, *The Lost World* (1912), was inspired by the volcanic Salisbury Crags in Edinburgh's Holyrood Park (see no. 96). The main protagonist Professor Challenger was based on another of Doyle's lecturers, Professor William Rutherford (1839–1899).

A statue of the fictional sleuth Sherlock Holmes watches over his creator's birthplace

Doyle had a longstanding interest in mysticism and after the death of his son in the Great War began looking for signs of spirit beings. This resulted in one of his lesser-known works *The Coming of the Fairies* (1922) and explains the presence in Edinburgh today of the Sir Arthur Conan Doyle Centre at 25 Palmerston Place (EH12). This imposing Victorian mansion built in 1881 for William McEwan (1827–1913), founder of Edinburgh's Fountain Brewery, is home to the Edinburgh Association of Spiritualists (see no. 49).

Other locations nearby: 65, 67, 68

67 These Shops are Different

EH7 4AA (New Town), a tour of idiosyncratic shops including
Valvona & Crolla at 19 Elm Row
Bus 7, 10, 11, 12, 14, 16, 22, 25, 49 to Elm Row; 1, 4, 5, 19, 26, 34,
44, 45 to Leopold Place

Powerful retail chains have colonised the high streets of too many cities. In doing so they are creating generic street scenes that defy a sense of place. Fortunately Edinburgh's historic architecture goes some way to discouraging the habit, so the city retains plenty of independent stores.

Typical is the Italian delicatessen Valvona & Crolla at 19 Elm Row (EH7), Scotland's longest established independent specialist food shop. It was founded in 1934 by Alfonso Crolla and Raffaele Valvona to provide Leith's Italian immigrant community with affordable continental produce. By the time Italy declared war in 1940, Raffaele had retired and Alfonso and his son, Victor, were interned as aliens. Alfonso died when his ship to Canada was torpedoed leaving Victor to pick up the business again in 1945. From then on he specialised in fine Italian meat, cheese, oil and wine, a practice continued today by Victor's nephew, Philip Contini.

A very different emporium is Cranachan & Crowdie at 263 Canongate (EH8). Despite being on the tourist-filled Royal Mile, this shop contains some high quality Scottish products, including oatcakes, tablet (a brittle fudge), black bun (a rich fruit cake in pastry) and shortbread. For whisky you can do no better than visit Cadenhead's at 172 Canongate (EH8), Scotland's oldest independent bottler established in 1842. Those with a sweet tooth will also enjoy Lickety Splits at nearby 6 Jeffrey Street (EH1), a modern shop selling old fashioned boiled sweets in jars.

Back on the Royal Mile at 63 High Street (EH1) is John Morrison Kiltmakers offering 1500 woven wool kilts off the peg, and a further 5,000 tartans for made-to-measure. Kinloch Anderson at 4 Dock Street (EH6) sells the sporrans, kilt pins, *sgian-dubhs* and ghillie brogues to go with them. Bagpipes Galore at 20 Haymarket Terrace (EH12) completes the ensemble. And should your kilt ever need cleaning visit Kleen Cleaners at 10 St. Mary's Street (EH1), the only dry cleaner in Scotland awarded a Royal Warrant.

Away from the Royal Mile at 30a Victoria Street (EH1) is the flagship branch of I. J. Mellis, a traditional cheesemonger selling Scot-

Inside Italian delicatessen Valvona & Crolla on Elm Row

tish and international cheeses. Around the corner at 5 Cowgatehead is Mr. Wood's Fossils, perfect for those interested in meteories and mammoth hair, and at number 13 is Fabhatrix, where Scottish tweed headwear is manufactured on the premises. Armstrongs along the way at 81–83 Grassmarket (EH1) is Britain's largest pre-owned clothing store established in 1840, and almost as old is Napiers the Herbalists at 18 Bristo Place (EH1) established in 1860.

Bruntsfield to the south is a paradise for foodies and includes the Dig-In community fruit and vegetable shop at 119 Bruntsfield Place (EH10). Also here is Wm. Christie's venerable family butchers at number 186 and George Hughes' fishmongers at number 197. S. Luca closeby at 16 Morningside Road (EH10) sells traditional Italian ice cream.

New Town revels in its sophistication and is home to the world famous coat manufacturer Crombie at 63 George Street (EH2). Also here is 21st century Kilts at 48 Thistle Street, the home of celebrity-endorsed kilts in pinstripe and leather. This tour finishes in Stock-bridge with Those Were the Days at 26 St. Stephen Street (EH3), a vintage clothing store specialising in bridal wear, and Sheila Fleet, an Orcadian jeweller, at number 18.

No survey of Edinburgh shops would be complete without mentioning Jenners at 48 Princes Street (EH2). It was founded in 1838 by two English drapers, Charles Jenner and Charles Kennington, using money won at Musselburgh Races. The current premises were custom-built after fire destroyed the original building in 1892.

Other locations nearby: 65, 66, 68

68 Edinburgh's Sistine Chapel

EH3 6BB (North & West Suburbs), church murals
in the Mansfield Traquair Centre at 15 Mansfield Place
Bus 8 to Mansfield Place, 7, 14, 22, 25, 49 to Leith Street;
10, 11, 12, 16 to York Place; Tram T50 to York Place

Overlooking the Broughton Street roundabout at 15 Mansfield Place (EH3) is a Victorian church with a difference. Not used for worship since the 1970s, the former Catholic Apostolic Church contains a remarkable series of Victorian murals. So impressive are they that the building has been dubbed "Edinburgh's Sistine Chapel".

The Catholic Apostolic Church was a religious movement established in England in 1831 in preparation for the imminent Second Coming of Christ. An elaborate liturgy was devised based on the Eastern Orthodox, Roman Catholic and Anglican Churches, with an emphasis on processions, ornate vestments, music and incense.

Suitably impressive church buildings were an important element, too, as witnessed by the Church of Christ the King in London's Bloomsbury. In Edinburgh the movement's governors (known as Apostles) commissioned the Scottish architect Sir Robert Rowand Anderson (1834–1921), who had trained in the office of renowned Gothic Revival architect, George Gilbert Scott (1811–1878). The building he designed in neo-Romanesque style was completed in 1885, its magnificent barrel-vaulted nave devoid of aisles, giving the congregation an uninterrupted view of the colourful rituals taking place.

Mural painting played a significant part in several of Anderson's other commissions, notably the University of Edinburgh's McEwan Hall and the Scottish National Portrait Gallery (see no. 60). It is therefore no surprise, that the church was also painted. The task was given to Dublin-born Phoebe Anna Traquair (1852–1936), a leading light in the Arts and Crafts Movement, who had moved to Edinburgh in 1874 after marrying a Scots palaeontologist. Inspired by Renaissance art, Celtic manuscripts, the Pre Raphaelites and the religious visionary William Blake, she commenced work in 1893 on the two largest wall spaces. Facing the visitor upon entry into the church are four cherubim beneath a rainbow filling the great chancel arch. On the west wall behind is a painted representation of the all-important Second Coming. Scenes from the Old and New Testaments adorn the south and north walls of the nave respectively, and in the chancel side aisles are illustrations from the Parable of the Ten Virgins.

A detail of the murals in the Mansfield Traquair Centre

The various techniques used by Traquair can still be detected. She broadly mapped out the larger spaces, which she usually filled with saturated colour, and then worked freehand with more delicate tones in the quieter areas. Every possible surface is decorated though and with all kinds of imagery: humans and angels, animals and birds, and patterns everywhere. A distinctive feature is her use of gilded plaster known as *gesso* for haloes, trumpets and the decorative borders

The murals were not completed until 1901, the same year that the last of the original governors of the Catholic Apostolic Church died. Since ministers could only be ordained by a governor, further ordinations in the church were not possible. When the last minister of the Edinburgh congregation died in 1958, the elaborate liturgy could no longer be celebrated, and so the congregation moved out.

For the next three decades the abandoned church gradually deteriorated. Traquair's superbly-executed murals would have stood the test of time were it not for penetrating damp causing damage to the painted plaster. Fortunately help arrived in the 1990s, when the Friends of Mansfield Place Church and the Mansfield Traquair Trust joined forces to secure the future of the building. As a result, a comprehensive restoration of the old church was carried out by Historic Scotland in 2000–2005. The building now serves as a unique events venue and as headquarters for the Scottish Council of Voluntary Organisations.

Phoebe Traquair's murals also adorn the choir hall behind St. Mary's Cathedral on Palmerston Place (EH12).

Other locations nearby: 65, 66, 67

69 Hibs and Hearts

EH7 5QG (North & West Suburbs), the Easter Road football
stadium in Albion Place
Bus 1, 35 to Brunswick Road

On 21st May 2016 a late header from team captain David Gray saw
Hibernian Football Club win the Scottish Cup. Their 3-2 triumph
against Rangers ended a 114-year wait to lift the trophy. Such victories
are always a source of local pride but none moreso than for Leith-
based Hibs. Since being amalgamated reluctantly with Edinburgh in
1920, Leithers have understandably taken every opportunity to reas-
sert their independence.

The club was founded in 1875 by Irish immigrants from the Cowgate area of Edinburgh and that origin is reflected in the club's name
(Hibernia was the Roman name for Ireland), colour (emerald green)
and badge (the Irish harp alongside Edinburgh Castle and a Leith
ship). For the first two years matches were played on the Meadows,
including the first match against rival Edinburgh club Heart of Midlothian on Christmas Day 1875. Good natured competition between the
two clubs has been ongoing ever since.

Despite some initial resistance to Irishmen participating in Scottish
football, Hibs quickly established themselves and in 1887 became the
first east coast team to win the Scottish Cup. The club moved to Leith
in the late 1870s and after joining the Scottish Football League in 1893
settled permanently at Easter Road (EH7). They play all their home
matches in the stadium there, which is also now home to the Hibernian Historical Trust.

As official historian to the club, the Trust presents the team's history to the public through its extensive archives and collection of foot-
balling artefacts. A permanent exhibition called *The Changing Face of
Easter Road* charts the history of the stadium and can be visited as part
of a stadium tour available by appointment (www.hibernianfc.co.uk).
It acts as a reminder that originally the stadium had vast banks of ter-
racing on three sides, which meant that it could hold crowds in excess
of 60,000.

The record attendance for any football match played in Edinburgh
was set at Easter Road on 2nd January 1950, when Hibs played Hearts
before a 65,860-strong crowd. Such huge audiences were drawn by the
success of the Famous Five, a notable forward line comprising Gordon Smith, Bobby Johnstone, Lawrie Reilly, Eddie Turnbull and Willie

The Famous Five stand at the Easter Road stadium

THE FAMOUS **5** STAND

Ormond. They helped Hibs win the Scottish League Championship on three occasions between 1948 and 1952. The team has also won the Scottish League Cup three times, most recently in 2007 after which the club's unofficial anthem, *Sunshine on Leith* by local band The Proclaimers, was played to an ecstatic crowd. These days the stadium is all-seated, with four stands and a capacity of just over 20,000. The North Stand is named in honour of the Famous Five and their likeness can be seen above the entrance.

Hibs is one of three Scottish Professional Football League clubs in Edinburgh, the others being Edinburgh City, a part-time senior club based at the Meadowbank Stadium, and Hearts, Hibs' Edinburgh derby rivals based at Tynecastle Stadium in Gorgie. The only Scottish Premiership in the city, Hearts is Edinburgh's oldest football club having been formed in 1874 by a group of friends from the Heart of Midlothian Dancing Club. Their badge is based on the Heart of Midlothian mosaic on the Royal Mile and their club colour is maroon (see no. 13). Tours of Tynecastle Stadium, where home games have been played since 1886, are available by appointment (www.heartsfc.co.uk). Participants will hear the inspiring tale of players who fought in the Great War and never returned, their sacrifice recalled in a monument on the Haymarket.

Not far from Tynecastle is Murrayfield Stadium, the largest in Scotland and the home of Scottish Rugby Union. Tours are available (www.scottishrugby.org).

70   The Legend of Saint Triduana

**EH7 6EA (North & West Suburbs), St. Triduana's Chapel
in the grounds of St. Margaret's Parish Church
at 176 Restalrig Road South
Bus 19, 21, 25, 34, 49 to Restalrig Road South (note: the
outside is visible but interior visits by appointment only)**

There was a time when the east Edinburgh suburb of Restalrig was a separate village. The name means 'swampy ridge' and it evokes those far off times, as do the remains of a castle on a crag overlooking Lochend Park. Another ancient remnant is St. Triduana's Chapel in the grounds of the Church of St. Margaret at 176 Restalrig Road South (EH7). Now surrounded by modern housing, its stones tell a fascinating tale.

Restalrig first appears in the history books in the 12th century but the legend of Saint Triduana is much older. High-born in Turkey sometime between the 4th and 8th centuries, the beautiful and virtuous Triduana is said to have accompanied Saint Regulus on his flight with Saint Andrew's relics from Greece to Scotland (in reality the relics probably arrived with Saint Augustine in 597). For several years Triduana then led a cloistered life as a nun in Forfar. Famously when the Pictish Prince Nectan offered his hand in marriage on account of her beautiful eyes, she plucked them out and sent them to him on a skewer! After this extraordinary act of self-mutilation, Triduana crossed the River Forth and settled at Restalrig, devoting her remaining years to prayer and fasting. Legend has it that during her lifetime Restalrig became a place of pilgrimage for those seeking a cure for eye diseases.

Legend aside, charters confirm that a parish church was standing in Restalrig by the late 12th century, although it is unclear if it was built because of Triduana's story. Whatever the reason, around 1480 James III (1460–1488) added a two-storey hexagonal chapel royal to the church, where priests could say masses for him. It was a unique building for its time, "a sumptuous new work" as Pope Innocent VIII (1432–1492) described it a decade later, when he raised the church to collegiate status.

What little remains of the chapel's upper storey today suggests a high vaulted structure illuminated by large traceried windows. By contrast, the lower storey or undercroft remains largely intact. Resembling a chapter house, it has a ribbed vault springing from a central pier. The

St. Triduana's Chapel in Restalrig

floor lies below ground and a pump is required to keep it from flooding. For this reason there may once have been a holy well here.

Although James III was killed at the Battle of Sauchieburn in 1488, James IV (1488–1513) continued with benefactions at Restalrig until his death at Flodden, as did James V (1513–1542), who in 1515 completed the building. By this time the church boasted 32 altars, eight canons under a dean, and two choirboys, and the chapel undercroft had been fitted with an altar dedicated to Triduana.

All this magnificence was short-lived though and in 1560 the first General Assembly of the Reformed Church of Scotland decreed that "as a monument of idolatrie, Restalrig should be utterly casten downe and destroyit". As a result the congregation relocated to South Leith Parish Church (EH6) (see no. 76).

Not until 1836 was the church at Restalrig rebuilt (although only a few windows and a blocked doorway from the original building remain) and only in 1912 did it become a parish church again (the congregations of Restalrig and neighbouring Lochend were united as St. Margaret's in 1992). St. Triduana's Chapel was excavated and restored in 1907, with a statue of the enigmatic Saint Triduana placed at the apex of its new roof.

Other locations nearby: 71

71 The Story of the Craigentinny Marbles

EH7 6PR (North & West Suburbs), the mausoleum of William
Henry Miller on Craigentinny Avenue
Bus 19 to Christiemiller Avenue

A suburban estate of 1930s bungalows is hardly the place one expects to find a magnificent neo-Classical mausoleum. But that's exactly what awaits the explorer in Craigentinny, and its owner's story is every bit as bizarre as the monument's location.

The mausoleum of William Henry Miller (1789–1848) rears up directly opposite the front door of 4 Craigentinny Crescent. Erected in 1856 to a design by prominent Scottish architect David Rhind (1808–1883), it takes the form of an ancient Roman tower tomb on the Appian Way. Back in the 1850s of course there were no houses here, just open fields flanking the road to Portobello.

Two sides of the mausoleum are adorned with large bas-reliefs depicting scenes from the Bible: Moses and the Israelites escaping Egypt on one side and the pharaoh's army being destroyed by the Red Sea on the other. Carved by the eminent Victorian sculptor, Alfred Gatley (1816–1863), they represent contrasting notions of fear and celebration. It was these sculptures that led to the mausoleum being dubbed the Craigentinny Marbles because of their passing resemblance to the Elgin Marbles in the British Museum.

William Henry Miller certainly had the resources to be remembered forever. A well-to-do landowner and MP for Newcastle-under-Lyme, he inherited Craigentinny House on nearby Loaning Road from his father. He was also a serious book collector and created one of the finest private libraries of his time. Such was his pedantry regarding books that he was nicknamed 'Measure Miller' after his habit of carrying a ruler to measure potential new additions to his collection.

Despite spending much of his life in England, Miller developed a liking for Edinburgh and chose Craigentinny as his final resting place. He died there relatively young and without heirs, and his opulent burial arrangements soon aroused public interest. His last will and testament stipulated that not only would his grave be marked by an imposing monument but also that his body should lie at the bottom of a 40 foot-deep stone-lined shaft, with a stone slab placed on the coffin. And all for a staggering £20,000.

But public interest didn't stop there. There was also talk of Miller, a confirmed bachelor, not having been quite what he seemed in life. One report at the time noted that "he was averred to be a changeling – even a woman, a suggestion which his thin figure, weak voice, absence of all beard and some peculiarity of habit, seemed to corroborate." His eccentric burial arrangements were construed by some to have been a means of ensuring the secret never got out.

But such conjecture seems unfair to Miller. Certainly he was a private man and few were ever allowed to inspect his library but on the other hand he hardly shied away from public

This extraordinary mausoleum towers over an estate of bungalows in Craigentinny

life and ran for election no less than seven times. The most probable explanation for his curious burial arrangements is that he wanted his tomb to be both impressive and to act as a deterrent to bodysnatchers. Edinburgh was still reeling from the grisly activities of the grave robbers Burke and Hare, so those with money did all they could to protect their mortal remains.

One of the reasons for Edinburgh bringing Leith within its boundaries in 1920 was to acquire the large swathes of land which Leith controlled, including Craigentinny. This enabled Edinburgh to expand northwards and in a period of just 20 years much of the area was covered with low density bungalows.

Other locations nearby: 70

72 Protestants, Plague Pits and Golf

EH6 7EN (North & West Suburbs), Leith Links at the junction
of Duncan's Place and John's Place
Bus 7, 10, 12, 14, 16, 22, 25, 49 to Foot of the Walk

Leith Links officially became a public park in 1888 as part of the Leith Improvement Plan. At that time the area was levelled and divided by paths lined with salt-tolerant trees. Despite this makeover the colourful history of the place is still discernible in the landscape.

An important event on the Links occurred on 25th July 1559, when the Protestant Lords of the Congregation met here with the Catholic Queen Regent, Mary of Guise (1554–1560). The Lords were a group of Scottish nobles, who favoured a Scottish-English alliance and church reform along the lines promoted by the cleric John Knox (c. 1513–1572) (see no. 22). Mary's goal, however, was to strengthen the Auld Alliance between Scotland and Catholic France, which had existed in one form or another since 1295 (Mary's coat of arms showing Scotland impaled with Lorraine is displayed in South Leith Parish Church on nearby Kirkgate).

At the time of the meeting, Mary had been driven from Edinburgh by the Lords (see no. 72). A truce was agreed in the name of religious tolerance but it didn't last. French troops arrived to bolster Mary's ambitions prompting the newly-crowned Elizabeth I (1558–1603) to send an English army to besiege them. The two mounds on the Links, known as Giant's Brae and Lady Fyfe's Brae, are alleged to be artillery mounds from this time. Mary's unexpected death in 1560 decided events by enabling the Protestants to take control of Scotland. Her grandson, James VI (1567–1625), then achieved the union of the Scottish and English crowns as James I (1603–1625).

Between the 14th and 17th centuries, Edinburgh and Leith experienced several outbreaks of plague. One in 1645 was probably typhus introduced by Scottish Covenanter troops returning from the Siege of Newcastle. Those infected were quarantined in huts on the Links and their clothing fumigated in kilns like the converted dovecote still standing in Lochend Park. Approximately half the population of South Leith perished and were buried in plague pits on the Links, one of which has been identified in the triangle of land alongside Wellington Place.

On a lighter note, the Links have played an important part in the

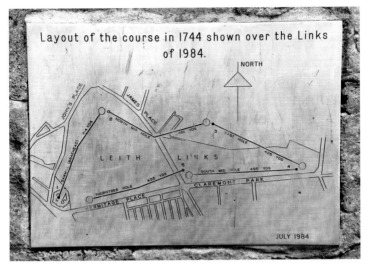

Layout of the course in 1744 shown over the Links of 1984.

NORTH

LEITH LINKS

JULY 1984

Leith Links is where the world's first golf club was formed

history of golf (the word 'links' being Scots for a golf course). Although it is unclear where and when golf was first played, it is first documented in a Scottish parliamentary edict of 1457, when James II (1430–1460) banned "ye golf" in an attempt to encourage archery (see no. 45). Golf is first mentioned in Leith in 1554 during a dispute between the cordiners of the Canongate and the "gouff ball" makers of North Leith.

In 1681 the Links played host to the world's first international golf match, between Scotland and England, with local boy Andrew Dickson the first ever caddy. It was organised by the Duke of Albany (later James VII/II) in a bid to dispel a claim that the game was invented in England. John Paterson of the victorious Scottish side used his prize money to purchase a house on the Canongate still known as Golfer's Land.

The most important match on the Links occurred in 1744 during which the Honourable Company of Edinburgh Golfers set down the official rules of the game. Based today in Muirfield, they are regarded as the world's first organised golf club. The position of the five 400 yard-long holes used in the match is shown on a commemorative stone cairn on Duncan Place. Although golf has been banned on Leith Links since 1905, a commemorative match marking the club's 250th anniversary was played in 1994 by golfers using 18th century equipment.

Other locations nearby: 73, 74, 75, 76, 77

73 A Trainspotting Tour of Leith

EH6 8HL (North & West Suburbs), a tour of locations
associated with the book Trainspotting beginning
at 2 Wellington Place
Bus 7, 10, 12, 14, 16, 22, 25, 49 to Foot of the Walk

There's no wall plaque marking 2 Wellington Place (EH6) in Leith but perhaps there should be. After all it was here in a top floor flat that Scottish author Irvine Welsh (b. 1958) penned his debut novel *Trainspotting*. Published in 1993, and spawning a hugely successful film three years later, it quickly attained a cult following by portraying a starkly different version of the cosy, culture-rich Edinburgh familiar to most visitors.

Trainspotting concerns a group of friends, boozers and heroin users in Leith in the 1980s. Set against a backdrop of economic depression and hard living, it taps into the youth subculture of the time. Tellingly the book was rejected from the Booker Prize shortlist because it offended the sensibilities of two judges.

Now almost 25 years later both book and film remain popular (a film sequel is slated for 2017) and there are even *Trainspotting* tours available courtesy of Leith Walks (www.leithwalks.co.uk). Whilst the locations visited won't match those seen in the film, many of which were filmed in an abandoned cigarette factory in Glasgow, they are those that inspired Welsh to write his book in the first place.

First stop is the former Leith Central Station on Duke Street, which closed in 1972 (although the decline in passengers actually began in the 1940s, when housing estates were built close to major local employers such as the Granton Gas Works). After spending time in London, the book's anti-hero Renton returns to Leith, where he visits the derelict station with the psychopath Begbie. A drunkard approaches them and asks jokingly whether they've come to do some trainspotting. Renton notices that Begbie is oddly subdued afterwards but then lashes out at a pedestrian on Leith Walk. It dawns on Renton that the drunkard is Begbie's father. The incident gave rise to the book's tongue-in-cheek title.

Only the station's Victorian frontage remains today, including the old fashioned Central Bar at 7–9 Leith Walk. In 1992 Edinburgh Council demolished the rest of the station and opened Leith Waterworld on the site but then sold it off in 2013 for redevelopment. Local residents were furious that a popular albeit unprofitable local amenity was being passed over in favour of re-furbishing Edinburgh's better-known Royal Commonwealth Pool. The huge covered train shed and platforms were also demolished to make way for a sprawling Tesco superstore.

Farther along Leith Walk at number 180 is a party pub called the Mousetrap. Until just a few years ago this was the spit-and-sawdust Volunteer Arms, or "The Volley" as Beg-bie calls it in *Trainspotting*. A regular drinking hangout for Renton and his cronies, it is here that Begbie indulges his taste for random acts of vio-lence. Struggling with an early morning hangover, for exam-ple, he hits a man with a pool cue for putting him off his game by eating crisps. The change of ownership at "The Volley" and the fact it no longer opens at 7am is evidence of Leith's slowly shifting demographics.

Third and final stop is the Muirhouse shopping centre on Pennywell Road (EH4). After failing to score any heroin,

The clock tower above the former Leith Central Station

Renton makes do with some opium suppositories that quickly play havoc with his bowels. Rushing to the toilet at the back of the centre's betting agency he relieves himself and in a memorably scatalogical scene fishes for the suppositories in the overflowing toilet bowl. Now boarded up, the shopping centre is an example of how one council regeneration scheme after another has failed here. The demolition of social housing has fragmented longstanding communities leaving local businesses without custom. Proof were it needed that enforced gentri-fication doesn't work everywhere.

Other locations nearby: 72, 74, 75, 76, 77

74 Deep-Fried Haggis and Irn-Bru

EH6 8LS (North & West Suburbs), a tour of old Leith
pubs and shops including the Mermaid Takeaway
at 43–45 Leith Walk
Bus 7, 10, 12, 14, 16, 22, 25, 49 to Foot of the Walk

Leith is in the throes of regeneration and much of what once defined
the former port community is slowly being swept away. For better or for worse Leith as depicted in Irvine Welsh's novel *Trainspotting* is becoming a thing of the past. Corners of the old Leith remain
though and they are worth celebrating in the face of advancing gen-
trification.

Take the pubs for instance. Although the Volunteer Arms of *Trainspotting* fame is no more, the Central Bar in the old railway station at
7–9 Leith Walk is still in business, and the Port O' Leith at 58 Constitution Street (EH6) remains as rowdy as ever (see no. 73). Both provide
a stark contrast to nearby Nobles, a recently made-over Victorian pub
offering curated beers and artisan pub food. The Boundary Bar at 379
Leith Walk (EH6) also revels in its history, its name recalling the days

Fried Food	SUPPER	SINGLE
CHICKEN BREAST STEAK (2)	3.80	2.50
CHICKEN NUGGETS (8)	3.90	2.60
CHIP RUMP STEAK	3.80	2.50
PEPPERED RUMP STEAK	3.90	2.60
BBQ KING RIB	3.90	2.60
CHEESE N BURGER	3.50	2.20
VEGGIE BURGER	3.30	2.00

Fried delights at the Mermaid in Leith

when Leith and Edinburgh were separate towns and the pub straddled the border. Until Leith's reluctant assimilation into Edinburgh in 1920, it offered longer licensing hours. Closing time in Edinburgh was 9.30pm so drinkers would simply walk out of a door on the Edinburgh side and re-enter the pub through a door on the Leith side! The two doors remain part of the frontage.

Several traditional Leith shops are worth tracking down. Borland's at 7 Croall Place (EH7) has been selling darts and televisions since 1925 and the Laundrette at 342 Leith Walk is as much a social club as a place to wash clothes. Storries at number 279 is an open-all-hours bakery, their steak pies the stuff of legend. Leith Athletics farther down at number 208–210 sells kits for the long-established football club and Canderson's at number 102 purveys old fashioned sweets in hand-weighed bags. Leith Barbers at 1 Great Junction Street is interesting for its boxing photos, which are a reminder that Leith Victoria at 28 Academy Street is Scotland's oldest boxing club and contains the UK's first Museum of Boxing.

This tour finishes with the Mermaid takeaway at 43–45 Leith Walk (EH6). Although fish and chips are advertised outside, it's the other deep-fried items on the menu that are noteworthy here. The Scottish crime writer Ian Rankin (b. 1960) has stated that the Mermaid is his favourite Edinburgh takeaway and famously accompanied American chef Anthony Bourdain (b. 1956) on a visit. Bourdain was moved to admit that he was "adrift in a sea of guilty pleasures in Scotland, the indisputable home and world champion of indiscriminate deep frying". Amongst the delicacies on offer are deep-fried Haggis and King Rib (a sweetened patty of minced pork), washed down with Salt'n'Sauce (a mixture of vinegar and brown sauce) and Irn-Bru. Described by Rankin as "the nectar of the gods", Irn-Bru is a bright orange carbonated soft drink first produced in Falkirk in 1901. It is considered Scotland's other national drink after whisky and is as popular here as Coca-Cola. Although Irn-Bru is not made from metal girders as its adverts once claimed, it really does contain 0.002 % ammonium ferric citrate.

The origins of Haggis, a savoury pudding of sheep's heart, liver and lungs mixed with onion, oatmeal and suet all boiled inside the animal's stomach, are ancient. The recipe is first recorded around 1430 in England as *hagws* or *hagese* but has been inextricably linked to Scotland since 1787, when Robert Burns (1759–1796) penned his *Address to a Haggis*. It is traditionally served at Hogmanay with 'neeps and tatties' and a wee dram of whisky.

Other locations nearby: 72, 73, 75, 76, 77

75 Shopping for Fleas

EH6 5HE (North & West Suburbs), the Ramsay Cornish
Vintage Lane Sale at 15–17 Jane Street
Bus 7, 10, 12, 14, 16, 22, 25, 49 to Foot of the Walk
(note: the sale takes place on Thursdays only)

Edinburgh is hardly unique in hosting markets for the sale of antiques and local produce. What is sometimes unusual though is the setting. There is an antiques market on the first Sunday of the month, for example, in the Meadowbank Stadium on London Road (EH8) and a Friday food and craft market inside Edinburgh Waverley railway station (EH1). The city's popular Saturday food markets include the Tram Stop Market on Picardy Place (EH1), Stockbridge Market on Kerr Street

(EH3), Leith Market in Dock Place (EH6) and the Grassmarket Weekly Market (EH1). The Grassmarket incidentally is named after the grazing pens used to hold livestock awaiting sale before the original market's closure in 1911. Most dramatic is the Edinburgh Farmers' Market each Saturday on Castle Terrace (EH1), with the castle as its backdrop.

Two Edinburgh antique flea markets that deserve special attention are both located in Leith. The first is the Vintage Lane Sale staged by the auctioneers Ramsay Cornish outside their premises, a former 18th century wine warehouse at 15–17 Jane Street (EH6). This unique Edinburgh institution dates back a hundred years and

The Ramsay Cornish Vintage Lane Sale takes place each Thursday

takes place at 11am sharp each Thursday. The items for sale are varied – from garden tools to stuffed animals – and are typically piled high on tressle tables. The key is to arrive when viewing begins at 9.30am, have a good rummage and then wait by anything you like. When the sale proper begins the auctioneer will move down the tables accepting bids for each item in turn. The highest bidder wins and all unsold items go for a pound.

Ramsay Cornish also stage over 60 regular indoor auctions each year, including a weekly General Furnishings & Collectibles auction, a bi-monthly specialist Antiques auction, and a quarterly Silver & Jewellery auction. All take place on a Saturday at 11am, with viewings the day before and on the morning of the sale itself from 9.30am.

The second is the Out of the Blue Flea Market held on the last Saturday of each month in the Drill Hall at 36 Dalmeny Street (EH6). Built in 1901 for the Royal Scots (Lothian Regiment) to a design by Sir Robert Rowand Anderson (1834–1921), the building was converted into a community arts and education centre in 2003. A mural down the side of the hall recalls the Gretna Rail Disaster, which occurred in 1915 at the Quintinshill Junction in Dumfriesshire. A troop train carrying young men from the 7th (Leith) Battalion of the Royal Scots to Liverpool, where they were to depart for Gallipoli, collided with a local train, the wreckage from which was then struck by a Glasgow-bound express. Over a hundred of the 226 people killed were soldiers and their bodies were laid out in the Drill Hall prior to burial in Rosebank Cemetery on Pilrig Street (EH6) (a memorial stands against the Broughton Road perimeter and the company's colours hang in South Leith Parish Church). It remains the worst rail disaster in British history. Considering Leith's maritime links it is not surprising that Rosebank Cemetery also contains many headstones inscribed 'drowned' or 'lost at sea', as well as the names of shipowners, masters and chandlers.

Georgian Antiques at 10 Pattison Street (EH6) in Leith is not a market but is also worth a visit. It is said to be the largest antiques shop in Scotland and is housed in a five-storey former whisky warehouse. It is frequented not only by the public but also by interior designers and television prop companies.

Other locations nearby: 72, 73, 74, 76, 77

76 Old Stones of Leith

EH6 6BZ (North & West Suburbs), a tour of historic Leith
buildings beginning with Trinity House Maritime Museum at
99 Kirkgate
Bus 7, 10, 12, 14, 16, 22, 25, 49 to Foot of the Walk then walk
along Kirkgate

Edinburgh and Leith blend seamlessly on street plans but it wasn't always that way. In the 18th century it took an hour to travel between the two and despite Leith being amalgamated reluctantly with Edinburgh in 1920, their characters remain distinct. Established as a medieval port for Edinburgh, Leith has seen its fortunes fluctuate. With the rough-edged seaport in the throes of reinvention, now is the time to visit the historic locations that tell its story.

It begins in 1128 with the establishment of Holyrood Abbey by David I (1124–1153), who granted land and harbour rights in North Leith to the abbey's Augustinian canons. They established a village for fishing and shipbuilding along Sandport Street/Quayside Street (EH6) on the north shore of the Water of Leith. South Leith on the opposite side was controlled by the lairds of Restalrig and centred on The Shore, where ships offloaded their cargoes for collection by Edinburgh's merchants (see no. 77).

This tour begins in South Leith with Trinity House at 99 Kirkgate, which was established in 1380 by Leith's seafarers to help destitute sailors and to improve safety at sea. A cargo tax facilitated construction of an almshouse here in the 1550s, which was replaced by the present Georgian building in 1816. It is still used by the Incorporation of Masters and Mariners and contains a fascinating maritime museum. The grandeur of the Convening Room illustrates how important seafaring once was in Leith (since 1956 dockers have congregated at Leith Dockers Club at 17 Academy Street).

Opposite Trinity House is South Leith Parish Church, a former chapel dedicated in 1487 by Leith's seamen. It was damaged in 1560 when English warships opposed to the Catholic Queen Regent, Mary of Guise (1554–1560) bombarded Leith. Her unexpected death prompted the return from France of Mary, Queen of Scots (1542–1567), who lodged briefly in the home of merchant Andrew Lamb on Burgess Street (see no. 72). When South Leith's original parish church in Restalrig was demolished during the Reformation, the chapel grew into the church seen today (see no. 70).

Behind Trinity House at the corner of Giles Street and Henderson Street are the Vaults. They were built in 1682 to store imported wine and in the 1880s converted for whisky storage. Both industries are still represented by the wine bar on the ground floor (formerly the auction room of the Vintners' Guild) and the Scottish Malt Whisky Society on the first floor. This makes the the Vaults Scotland's oldest continually-used commercial building. A relief depicting the 17th century 'stingmen' (wine porters) of Leith is embedded in the perimeter wall (see no. 24).

At the end of Henderson Street – passing Russell Dempster's magnificent mural of Leith-born artist Eduardo Paolozzi on the way – cross the Water of Leith to enter North

Leith's seafaring legacy is celebrated at Trinity House on the Kirkgate

Leith. Walk along Sandport Place to the end of Dock Street, where alongside a disused church stands a ruined arch. It is the remains of Leith Citadel, a huge pentagonal fort built in 1656 by Cromwell to regulate port traffic following his defeat of the Royalist Scots. Threatened with losing control of the port, Edinburgh was forced to finance the fort's construction and after the Restoration of the monarchy was forced to pay again to re-purchase the land. It should not be confused with Leith Fort, a Georgian barracks built in 1779 and demolished in 1955 (a gate survives on North Fort Street).

This tour finishes on Commercial Street, which is lined with old bonded warehouses and the former Leith Nautical College. It was in a factory here in 1868 that Rose's Lime Juice was manufactured to stave off scurvy in seamen through the adequate provision of vitamin C.

Other locations nearby: 72, 73, 74, 75, 77

77　Where George Came Ashore

EH6 6QN (North & West Suburbs), a tour of the old Port
of Leith beginning at 28 The Shore
Bus 16 to Bernard Street; 22, 35, 36 to Broad Wynd

On the quayside in Leith outside 28 The Shore (EH6) is a low metal panel emblazoned with a gold crown. It marks the spot where on 15th August 1822 George IV (1820–1830) stepped ashore from his ship *The Royal George*. It was the first visit of a reigning monarch to Scotland in almost two centuries and greatly improved George's popularity north of the border. Orchestrated by Sir Walter Scott (1771–1832) to include tartan pageantry, the visit also elevated the kilt to become part of Scotland's national identity. Thereafter the king got into an open carriage and made his way up to Edinburgh cheered along by huge crowds.

These days The Shore seems a long way from the open water of the Firth of Forth. That's because the harbour has grown so much since the king's visit. It is difficult to imagine that The Shore was the original port, where tall masted ships docked, while their crews loaded fish, coal, grain and hides for export to northern Europe and the Mediterranean. They would return later with wine, fruit, spices and cloth, the taxes for which were paid in the neo-Classical Customs House on the opposite shore (it is depicted in Alexander Carse's magnificent painting of the king's arrival hanging in Leith's former Town Hall at 81 Constitution Street).

More evidence for the old port can be seen farther upstream beyond the Commercial Street bridge. The name of the 15th century King's Wark pub at 36 The Shore recalls that James I (1406–1437) commissioned shipbuilders' workshops, merchants' accommodation, warehouses and taverns here in an attempt to stimulate the port's growth. Up to this time the harbour was little more than the mouth of the Water of Leith, where ships offloaded cargoes directly onto the river bank. He must have been successful because in 1720 Scotland's first dry dock was excavated on the opposite bank, where a row of trees is growing today. This allowed ships to be taken out of the water for repairs.

Downstream at the bottom end of The Shore is a stone tower. In 1685 the king's master mason Robert Mylne (1633–1710), who worked on Edinburgh Castle and the Palace of Holyroodhouse, was granted land along The Shore to build a sea wall, several tenements and a windmill. The tower seen today would originally have had a wooden top storey with sails. The crenellations were added during the Napoleonic War, when the windmill was converted into a signal tower relaying flag messages to incoming ships.

Alongside the tower is the former Seamen's Mission built in 1833 to provide mariners with decent accommodation, a recreation room and a chapel. Today it is a hotel and overlooks a new plaza containing the Merchant Navy Memorial unveiled in 2009. The work of Edinburgh sculptor Jill Watson (b. 1957), it commemorates the sacrifice made by Scottish sailors in two World Wars as well as in peacetime service along the trading routes of the world.

During the 19th century ships grew too large for the old port. Accordingly it was expanded northwards from here, firstly by means of the Queen's Dock begun in

Where King George IV stepped ashore in Leith in 1822

1833 (alongside the Plaza) and then by the Victoria and Albert Docks in 1851 and 1869 respectively. They can be seen beyond the impressive wrought iron swing bridge installed in the 1870s, which has now been superceded by the new bridge carrying Ocean Drive. A Christian Salveson harpoon gun nearby is a reminder that whaling was also once important in Leith. Several more docks were added later creating the sprawling seaport seen today although most are now abandoned and awaiting redevelopment.

Other locations nearby: 72, 73, 74, 75, 76

78 All Aboard a Floating Palace

EH6 6JJ (North & West Suburbs), the Royal Yacht *Britannia*
moored at Ocean Terminal on Ocean Drive
Bus 11, 22, 34, 35, 36 to Ocean Terminal

Despite being the largest enclosed deep-water port in Scotland, the Port of Leith is giving up its traditional role. The old quaysides once bustling with sailors and dock workers are now frequented by those in search of retail and leisure facilities. The change is encapsulated by the rotting West Pier at the end of which is an iron figure by sculptor Antony Gormley (b. 1950). The solitary figure overlooks Ocean Terminal, a modern shopping centre designed by Terence Conran (b. 1931) on the site of Henry Robb's shipyard, which closed in 1983. All that remains of the shipyard is a steel paint shed, where the pier makes landfall, built of welded steel plates like the hull of a ship.

A more upbeat piece of maritime history is the Royal Yacht *Britannia* berthed alongside Ocean Terminal. Launched at John Brown's Clydebank shipyard in 1953, *Britannia* served the British Royal Family for 44 years before being decommissioned in 1997 at Portsmouth in the presence of the Queen. During her career *Britannia* made 968 official voyages and travelled over a million nautical miles.

Britannia was the 83rd and last Royal Yacht in a tradition stretching back to 1660. Fortunately the tradition of scuttling decommissioned vessels was not observed and instead *Britannia* found a resting place in Edinburgh, where she is maintained as a museum ship by the Royal Yacht *Britannia* Trust. Detractors have questioned why a Clydebank ship would be brought to Leith, a place with which she has few links and at a time of Scottish devolution? It is a valid point but there's no denying the positive impact her presence has had in attracting 300,000 annual visitors to the old docks.

A visit to *Britannia* is a memorable experience. Her conversion from floating place to tourist attraction has been a sensitive one and none of her glamour has been lost in the process. Visitors reach her from Ocean Terminal by bridge, whereupon a tower containing stairs and a lift provide access to all areas of the ship. It's at this point that one realises how big *Britannia* is and why she required a 250-strong crew.

Like a stately home, *Britannia* has an upstairs for the passengers and a downstairs for the staff. The tour commences upstairs at the front, where the bridge and admiral's chair is located (*Britannia* was traditionally captained by an admiral). The admiral's day cabin and sleeping quarters are here, with the officers' accommodation and wardroom below. The upper three decks to the rear of the vessel contain the Royal Family's sun lounge and bedrooms, with a grand staircase connecting them to the State Dining Room and Drawing Room decked out in 1950s chintz. It is here that the likes of Mahatma Gandhi and Nelson Mandela were entertained.

Also of interest is the ship's sick bay, laundry and engine room, and don't miss the on-board Rolls Royce Phantom V rolled out for state visits.

Only in the bowels of the ship will the visitor find the relatively cramped triple-stacked bunks on which most of the crew slept.

The Royal Yacht *Britannia* is moored permanently at Ocean Terminal

Berthed alongside *Britannia* is the Royal Barge and the racing yacht *Bloodhound*. Built in 1936 and owned by the Royal Family during the 1960s, *Bloodhound* accompanied *Britannia* when the Royal Family took their annual family holiday around the Western Isles. She is also owned by the Royal Yacht *Britannia* Trust and can be chartered privately.

Moored in the nearby Prince of Wales Dock is the Vine Trust Barge. This decommissioned Ministry of Defence fuel barge has been adapted to serve as the Trust's floating Centre for Global Citizenship, which advises on overseas volunteering opportunities. Visits by appointment only (www.vinetrust.org).

Other locations nearby: 79, 80

79 Hidden History in Newhaven

EH6 4LW (North & West Suburbs), a tour of Newhaven
beginning in Fishmarket Square
Bus 11, 16 to Fishmarket Square; 7 to Newhaven Church;
10 to Annfield

For a taste of the sea in Edinburgh most people head to the beach at Portobello or the pretty village of Cramond (see nos. 84 & 99). Fewer probably make for the former fishing village of Newhaven between Leith and Granton. For city explorers this is a pity since hidden amongst its modern buildings are some intriguing historical remains.

Visitors to Newhaven should begin their tour at Fishmarket Square (EH6) overlooking the harbour. This open space is interesting because it was the original site of the harbour. When James IV (1488–1513) decided to expand the Royal Scots Navy he found the existing port of Leith too shallow for the purpose. Instead in 1504 he ordered the excavation of a custom-built Royal Dockyard at Newhaven (meaning 'new harbour') for the construction of his new warship *Michael*. Laid down here in 1507 and launched in 1511, the *Michael* was the largest ship afloat and measured an impressive 240 feet in length. Under the terms of the Auld Alliance the *Michael* supported the French against the English but after the Scottish defeat at the Battle of Flodden in 1513 she was sold off.

Although the Royal Dockyard did not survive James IV, Newhaven reinvented itself as a fishing village and ferry terminus providing pilots on the Firth of Forth. Herring and oysters were landed here and the harbour also played a role in the whaling industry, as recalled in the name Whale Brae at the top of Newhaven Road. The old whalemaster's house still stands midway along Park Road. The present harbour is Victorian and features a lighthouse and fishmarket, which today also contains a seafood restaurant.

Newhaven Main Street, which runs along the top of Fishmarket Square, is also of interest. Here one gets the feeling of the prehistoric raised beach on which the village was originally built. Unfortunately the street was partially obliterated when Newhaven was redeveloped in the 1950s and 60s, which accounts for the modern three-storey flats down one side. Some of those on the north side, however, were rebuilt in their original form and retain the 'forestair' characteristic of many Scottish fishing villages. This leads to the living area at first floor level, the ground floor being used for storing fishing nets.

Another reminder of the old harbour is the ruined walls of the Chapel of St. Mary and St. James in Lamb's Court, which is thought to have been erected for the king's shipwrights. The 16th century Newhaven Stone on a wall in Auchinleck Court probably came from the long-vanished Trinity Mains Farm, an estate owned by Trinity House in Leith, whose arms appear on the tablet (see no. 76). A copy of the stone is displayed in Victoria Primary School on Main Street, Edinburgh's oldest working primary school founded in 1844. Its foyer contains a tiny museum open during term time by appointment (tel. 0131 476 7306).

Forestairs like this one in Newhaven are a traditional feature of Scottish fishing villages

Newhaven began losing its identity with the construction of Leith's Western Harbour in the 1930s, when a huge new breakwater subsumed Newhaven's harbour at its landward end. With the subsequent retreat of port activities from the Western Harbour, the breakwater has been expanded through land-fill and is now fast becoming a small town in its own right, with plans for 17,000 new homes.

This maritime tour can be extended westwards to Granton. Although the once-common fishing trawlers have long departed, the harbour here is still used by yachts. At 22 West Harbour Road (EH5) is the former Northern Lighthouse Board Depot. For much of the 20th century lighthouse supplies were stored here and the lantern was used for training and testing lighthouse lights.

Other locations nearby: 78, 80

80 A Workshop for Sculptors

EH6 4JT (North & West Suburbs), the Edinburgh Sculpture Workshop at 21 Hawthornvale
Bus 7, 11 to Dudley Crescent; 10, 16 to Hawthornvale (note: the building is open to visitors during exhibitions with tours by appointment)

Google the words 'Edinburgh' and 'workshops' and it will become apparent how many opportunities there are to be crafty in the Scottish capital. Everything is available here from tapestrying and enamelling to mosaicking and cooking curries. Of the many venues where these workshops take place, one of the most impressive is the Edinburgh Sculpture Workshop (ESW) at 21 Hawthornvale (EH6). The UK's first purpose-built, open access sculpture production facility, it boasts a striking position in an old Newhaven railway cutting.

The architectural history of the ESW is well worth relating. Set up in 1986 by a group of Scottish sculptors, it was for several years housed in a drafty old railway shed on what had been a Caledonian Railway branch line servicing the docks at North Leith and Granton (the intact Newhaven station still survives nearby at 85 Craighall Road). In 2003 a fundraising campaign was launched to create a new building better suited to contemporary artists, one that would also facilitate interaction between artists and their audience. With contributions forthcoming from several public bodies and private initiatives, local arcitects Sutherland Hussey Harris were commissioned to design the structure in two phases.

The first phase, known as the Bill Scott Sculpture Centre, after the respected Scottish sculptor and educationalist, was completed in 2012. Consisting of 30 artists' studios, it straddles the former railway embankment concealing them from the street. Workshops for wood, metal, plaster and other media are arranged around a covered courtyard, with space for educational and administrative functions, and two self-contained apartments for artists-in-residence and visiting speakers.

The second phase resulted in the Creative Laboratories, which were completed in 2014. By contrast this building consists of a cloistered courtyard visible from the street, lined with bays where artworks can be displayed. There is also a café here, which opens onto the courtyard and a terrace, where events and exhibitions can be staged. A pathway traversing the space between the two areas connects the street with a cycleway that runs behind the facility.

Both phases of construction were rendered in brick-clad concrete not only to ensure durability but also to reflect Newhaven's industrial heritage. The same goes for the lighthouse-like tower rising above the Centre. This freestanding structure, which is over 90 feet high with a light shining out from a large aperture at the top, can also be used as an exhibition space.

It is important to stress that the aims of the ESW are two-fold. On the one hand artists are supported in their careers through the provision of space, facilities, funding and training. On the other there is a commitment to public engagement and finding new ways of bringing artists and the public closer

A lighthouse-like tower announces Newhaven's Edinburgh Sculpture Workshop

together. Accordingly young and old, teachers and laypersons alike are all welcome at the Centre's regular exhibitions, talks and other activities, including evening sculpture courses. Guided tours of the buildings themselves are available on request.

Edinburgh's other workshops include the Scottish Mineral and Lapidary Club in a converted Victorian bonded warehouse at 16–20 Maritime Lane (EH6) and the Stills: Centre for Photography at 23 Cockburn Street (EH1), Scotland's largest open-access darkroom. Those interested in tapestry will enjoy the Dovecot Studios housed in a converted Victorian swimming pool at 10 Infirmary Street (EH1) (see no. 31). Just outside the parameters of this book is the Ratho Byres Forge in a converted dairy farm on Freelands Road (EH28) and the Gogar Cabinetworks in a former Victorian church at 194 Glasgow Road (EH12).

Other locations nearby: 77, 78

81 Five Million Poppies a Year

EH7 4HJ (North & West Suburbs), Lady Haig's Poppy Factory at 9 Warriston Road
Bus 8 to Rodney Place; 23, 27 to Cannonmills-Brandon Terrace
(note: guided tours by appointment only)

On 28th June 1919 the First World War officially ended with the signing of the Treaty of Versailles. The hostilities, however, had ended the previous year at the 11th hour of the 11th day of the 11th month. In Commonwealth nations that day is observed as Remembrance Day, which in the UK and Canada is accompanied by the wearing of poppies. They recall those that grew in the churned-up battlefields of Flanders, their red colour symbolising the blood shed there.

The wearing of remembrance poppies began in 1921 and was inspired by the poem *In Flanders Fields* by Canadian army doctor Lieutenant-Colonel John McCrae. They were first worn in number by the American Legion to remember fallen American soldiers. From there the custom spread quickly to Britain, where it was promoted by Edinburgh-born Field Marshall and founder of the Royal British Legion, Douglas Haig (1861–1928) and his wife (see nos. 24 & 53).

Today the sale of poppies by Royal British Legion volunteers in the weeks leading up to Remembrance Day generates considerable finan-

Lady Haig's poppy factory in Warriston

cial support for British military personnel and their families. Not everyone realises, however, that the poppies come in two distinct varieties. Those in England, Wales and Northern Ireland have two red petals and a green leaf and are made at a factory in Richmond. Those in Scotland have four petals with no leaf and are made in the Edinburgh district of Warriston.

To see Scottish poppies being made book a guided tour of Lady Haig's Poppy Factory at 9 Warriston Road (EH7) (www.ladyhaigspoppyfactory.org.uk). The original factory opened in March 1926 in the grounds of Whitefoord House on the Canongate, with "two workers, a pair of scissors and a piece of paper"! The present factory opened in 1965 in a former printing works and employs a workforce of 40 ex-Servicemen. This explains the palpable feeling of military organisation and there probably needs to be since five million poppies are handmade here each year, as well as 10,000 wreaths and remembrance crosses. The factory also maintains the 25,000 collection tins used across Scotland during the annual Poppy Appeal.

Visitors will see how the red paper for the poppies arrives into the factory in large rolls and is then passed through a cutting and crimping machine. The shaped petals are then placed onto the green plastic stem and secured by the black button-shaped centre (termed a *pistil* by botanists).

Inevitably the wearing of poppies courts some controversy today, with several public figures questioning their political correctness. After all, poppies are only ever worn by the victors. Irish nationalists refuse to wear them and some even see them as a symbol of continuing Western imperialism. It is therefore worth noting that whilst Lady Haig's is run as a commercial venture under the auspices of the charity Poppyscotland, it quite separately strives to provide dignity through work. Many of those employed in the factory are registered disabled and gain considerable comfort and security from working here.

Opposite Lady Haig's is Warriston Cemetery at 42 Warriston Gardens (EH3). Opened in 1843 by the Edinburgh Cemetery Company and designed by city architect David Cousin (1809–1878), it was Edinburgh's first Victorian garden cemetery. Celebrated incumbents include James Young Simpson (1811–1870), who discovered the anaesthetic properties of chloroform, and newsagency magnate John Menzies (1808–1879). Warriston was the model for several other Edinburgh cemeteries designed by Cousin, namely Dalry, Dean, Newington and Rosebank. Contact the Friends of Warriston Cemetery for a guided tour (www. restinpixels.us).

Other locations nearby: 82

82 Planthunting at the Botanics

EH3 5LR (North & West Suburbs), the Royal Botanic Garden
Edinburgh on Inverleith Row
Bus 8, 23, 27 to Royal Botanic Gardens (East Gate)
(note: the garden is also accessible through the West Gate
on Arboretum Place)

When Edinburgh's busy streets get too hectic, there is no better place to retreat than the Royal Botanic Garden in Inverleith (EH3). Located one mile north of the city centre, these historic 26 hectares provide not only a tranquil place to unwind but also a fascinating world-class centre of botanical science. And unlike its English counterpart at Kew, entry except for the glasshouses is free.

The story of the Botanics, as locals like to call the garden, begins in 1671, when it was founded as a physic garden by two adventurous doctors, Robert Sibbald (1641–1722) and Andrew Balfour (1630–1694). They had met in France after travelling extensively in Europe and saw the need for a garden in Edinburgh to train physicians in the use of herbal remedies. Accordingly they leased a modest plot near the Palace of Holyroodhouse and there began cultivating medicinal plants. Ten years later the pair founded the Royal College of Physicians of Edinburgh (see no. 59).

In 1684 a second garden was created, where platform 11 of Waverley railway station now stands, and in 1763 the two gardens were merged at a site on Leith Walk. In the early 1820s the garden moved again, this time to its current site in Inverleith. Transplanting machines invented by the garden's curator, William McNab, were used to transport the larger specimens. Gradually over the next 50 years the garden was expanded, including the acquisition of Inverleith House, a Georgian home built in 1774 for landowner Sir James Rocheid (1715–1787). Used to house the garden's director – and much later the first Scottish National Gallery of Modern Art – it serves today as an exhibition space.

The collection of plants at the Botanics expanded with the British Empire, with Scottish planthunters criss-crossing the globe for new and unusual species. Commemorated in the garden's herbarium and library they include David Douglas (1799–1834), who introduced the Douglas Fir from North America, Robert Fortune (1812–1880), who transported Chinese tea plants to India on behalf of the British East India Company, and the aptly-named George Forrest (1873–1932), who brought back more than 30,000 plant specimens.

The Amazonian water lilies at the Botanics really can support a child

Nearly 15,000 different species from around the world are grown at the Botanics and its three regional branches today, representing around 7% of all known plant species. They are cultivated in a variety of attractive habitats, including a spectacular rock garden, an alpine house, a woodland garden containing a grove of Sierra Redwoods, and a temperate palm house built in 1858, the highest of its kind in Britain. The more recent Plants & People House constructed in 1967 contains rainforest vegetation around a central pond in which the giant Amazonian water lilly *Victoria* is grown. Visitors love hearing that its enormous floating pads can support a child!

Other special features at the Botanics include the Queen Mother's Memorial Garden, with its Bog Myrtle parterre, Britain's largest plant fossil unearthed at nearby Craigleith Quarry, and the Chinese Hillside, the largest collection of Chinese plants outside China. Of particular interest is the Demonstration Garden, a new educational space, which includes the original gatehouse-cum-botany school used when the garden was on Leith Walk. Known as the Botanic Cottage it was rebuilt here in 2014, where it continues its teaching function.

South of the Botanics is the former village of Stockbridge. There is some quirky architecture here including William Henry Playfair's Church of St. Stephen's Stockbridge at 105 St. Stephen Street (EH3), which boasts Europe's longest clock pendulum, and the Stockbridge Colonies, a cluster of parallel Victorian streets running off Glenogle Road built to provide affordable housing for artisans.

Other locations nearby: 81

83 An Edwardian Home Preserved

EH4 5QD (North & West Suburbs), Lauriston Castle
at 2a Cramond Road South
Bus 41 to Davidson's Mains or 29, 37 to Silverknowes
Terminus, then walk (note: guided tours of the interior only)

Northwest Edinburgh out beyond Queensferry Road is a hotch potch of former farming villages, golf courses and modern housing estates. In amongst them just off Cramond Road South stands lovely Lauriston Castle. Overlooking the Firth of Forth and Cramond Island, this idiosyncratic building remains unchanged since its last owner died in 1926. As such it is a time capsule of comfortable Edwardian life in a Scottish country house.

A Lauriston Castle stood on the site in medieval times but this was destroyed during the so-called Rough Wooing of 1544, a war declared by Henry VIII in a failed attempt to marry off his son, Edward, with the infant Mary, Queen of Scots. Although Henry's seaborne forces ransacked the area they were unable to take Edinburgh Castle and so retreated.

The core of the present Lauriston Castle is an L-shaped tower house with turrets, built around 1590 by Sir Archibald Napier (1534–1608), Laird of Merchiston and Master of the Scottish Mint. Of the castle's many subsequent owners the most colourful was undoubtedly John Law (1671–1729), the son of a Scottish goldsmith and banker. Bored with the family business, Law gambled in London, where in 1694 he killed a man in a duel. Upon receiving the death sentence he escaped to Holland and then Switzerland, where he began speculating in foreign exchange and securities. Eventually in 1703 he returned to Scotland and set up home at Lauriston Castle. There he devised a plan to establish the first Scottish national bank issuing banknotes as credit. When the idea was rejected by the Scottish Parliament he took his ideas to France instead, where he proposed a similar scheme to pay off the country's crippling national debt. Although it made Law the world's first millionaire, the massive speculation and ballooning stock prices that accompanied the scheme led to its demise, prompting Law to flee to Venice, where he died a pauper.

Another banker to own Lauriston was Thomas Allan (1777–1833), and it was he who in 1827 commissioned prominent architect William

Burn (1789–1870) to extend the original tower house in the Scottish Baronial style. The final owner of Lauriston was William Robert Reid (1854–1919), proprietor of a leading Edinburgh cabinet-making business, who acquired the property in 1902. He installed modern plumbing and electricity, and together with his wife, Margaret, created the series of Edwardian interiors seen today. Having no children the Reids bequeathed the property to the nation on condition it be preserved unchanged. As a result, today's visitor can still enjoy their collections of Italian furniture, Eastern rugs, Blue John ornaments and so-called Crossley Wool Mosaics. Made in Halifax during the mid-19th century these copies of popular Victorian paintings are neither stitched nor woven but rather created from wool pile glued onto a linen

Turrets and chimneys at Lauriston Castle

background. Look out for the doggy *Dignity and Impudence* and the oft-reproduced *Monarch of the Glen*. No less interesting are the castle's more workaday features, including the early stapling machine in Mr. Reid's study, and the old kitchen clock and housekeeper's quarters.

The castle's glorious gardens were originally laid out in the 1840s by William Henry Playfair (1790– 1857) and are renowned for their monkey puzzle trees, bluebell wood and croquet lawns. A more recent feature is the Japanese Friendship Garden designed by Takashi Sawano, which was unveiled in 2002 to celebrate the twinning of Edinburgh with Kyoto. The cherry blossoms and Japanese maples are beautiful.

84 A Walk to Cramond Island

EH4 6NS (North & West Suburbs), a walk through the village of Cramond
Bus 41 to Cramond Glebe Road (note: Cramond Island can only be reached by foot during the two hours either side of low tide)

Anyone looking for history, adventure and some sea air should take the bus to Cramond. Just five miles from the city centre, this delightful waterfront village is located where the River Almond joins the Firth of Forth. Attractions include a ruined Roman fort, a medieval tower house and an offshore island reached by a tidal causeway.

Visitors are advised to alight the bus at Cramond Glebe Road, where there is a sign for the village. Setting off in that direction it is worth reflecting that although Cramond has been part of Edinburgh since 1920, it has a very long history of its own. Indeed archaeologists have unearthed evidence for a Mesolithic campsite here of nomadic hunter-gatherers dating back to around 8500 BC. This makes Cramond the earliest known site of human settlement in Scotland.

Shortly after passing the 18th century Manse, where the skating minister Reverend Robert Walker (1755–1808) in Henry Raeburn's famous painting lived, Cramond Kirk appears on the right (see no. 57). Rebuilt in 1656 it retains a sturdy medieval tower from the 1400s and occupies the site of Cramond's first place of Christian worship built around 600. The Kirkyard is especially interesting since it contains the remains of a Roman fort uncovered in 1954. The Romans arrived here in 142 AD and by order of Emperor Antoninus Pius (138–161) built a fort and harbour to protect the Antonine Wall. The fort was later used as a base by African-born Emperor Septimius Severus (193–211) in his campaign against Scotland's rebellious tribes.

The fort was rectangular in plan, with walls 15 feet high and a gate on each side. Inside were barracks, workshops, granaries and a commander's house, whilst outside there was a bath building and civilian settlement. An extraordinary Roman survival is the Cramond Lioness dredged from the river in 1997 by a local boatman. Depicting a lion devouring a shackled man, the sandstone sculpture probably once adorned the tomb of a military commander and is now displayed in the National Museum of Scotland on Chambers Street (EH1) (almost as extraordinary is Eagle Rock, a boulder apparently carved with a Roman eagle, on the shoreline on the opposite side of the river).

After the Romans departed in 212, Cramond was occupied by the Votadini, a tribe of Iron Age Celts, who named their settlement *Caer Amon* ('fort on the river') from which the name 'Cramond' is derived. Thereafter little is known of Cramond's history until the medieval period, when the first Cramond Kirk was built. In the 1400s a summer residence was created here for the Bishops of Dunkeld, in whose diocese Cramond lay. What remains is a charming tower house at the end of Kirk Cramond. The Lairds of Cramond lived here until the 1680s, when they built the imposing Cramond House nearby, which was visited by Queen Victoria (1837–1901).

Returning to Cramond Glebe Road descend now to the village proper, which is made

One of several iron grave markers in Cramond Kirkyard

up of late 18th century lime-harled cottages typical of the Lothians. That no houses stand on the right-hand side except for the Cramond Inn is because these were cleared in 1826 to improve the appearance of the Laird's estate.

Beyond is the waterfront created in the 1930s over a shoreline of glacial boulders. The most interesting buildings here are the former maltings and brewhouse at 2 Riverside, once part of the original village inn. They are now used by the Cramond Heritage Trust as a local history museum.

At the far end of the waterfront is a tidal causeway giving access to Cramond Island. Lying almost a mile out to sea, the island can only be reached by foot during the two hours either side of low tide (see www.seabritain.co.uk). The causeway runs at the foot of a row of concrete pylons constructed as an anti-shipping boom during the Second World War, when the island was fortified to prevent enemy vessels entering the Firth of Forth. Where the causeway joins the island are emplacements for a 75mm gun and spotlight, and in the north-east

The submerged causeway leading to Cramond Island

corner of the island are more emplacements and two engine rooms that powered the defences. Also on the north side are the concrete footings of the barracks, where the island's garrison lived.

Archaeological evidence suggests that prehistoric people visited the island and the Romans probably did, too. More recently it was used for farming and was once renowned for its oyster beds. A jetty on the island's north-west shore may be medieval and there are remains of a 19th century farmstead in the centre, where sheep were kept until the 1960s.

Return now to the bus stop on Cramond Glebe Road and walk down School Brae. Here can be found evidence for Cramond's time as an industrial centre. Along the riverbank are the remains of several water-powered iron mills, which during the late 18th and 19th centuries produced shovels, nails and even shackles for slave boats. Downstream, for example, stands the manager's house and workers' cottages of the long-demolished Cockle Mill (now a café and B&B), with a silted up dock opposite from where finished goods were barged down to the Firth and eventually shipped as far away as India. Upstream at Cramond Falls are the ruins of the Fairafar Mill, with its impressive weir and race. The square socket holes in the rock face opposite once supported a horse-drawn tramway used to transport rock from nearby Craigie Quarry down to another set of docks, where it was then shipped to Leith and used in the building of the New Town. Between 1771 and 1860 these mills were owned by the Cadell family, whose idiosyncratic cast-iron grave markers can be found in Cramond Kirkyard.

85 Highs and Lows on Corstorphine Hill

EH12 6UP (North & West Suburbs), a walk up and down
Corstorphine Hill off Clermiston Road
Bus 26 to Clerwood then take the gated track and walk uphill

It is said that Edinburgh is like Rome and built on seven hills. One of them is Corstorphine Hill, a long, low ridge to the west beyond Murrayfield. Barely 530 feet high and mostly forested, it doesn't look much from afar. But hidden among the trees are some historic structures that make a visit worthwhile.

The best approach is from the Clerwood bus stop on Clermiston Road (EH12). On one side is the sort of housing that has encroached onto the lower slopes of the hill in recent times. On the other is a gated track that beckons the explorer into Corstorphine Woods. As the path runs uphill it passes a lovely Victorian walled garden, which once supplied the kitchen of nearby Hillwood House. Recently restored by

The lookout tower on top of Corstorphine Hill

the Friends of Corstorphine Hill, the garden is open to visitors.

Continue walking to the top of the hill, where there are manmade features ancient and modern. The oldest are rocks carved with Neolithic or Bronze Age 'cup marks': the most recent are the ugly but necessary radio masts used by Edinburgh Airport. The most obvious feature is Corstorphine Hill Tower erected in 1872 to commemorate Edinburgh-born writer, Sir Walter Scott (1771–1832). With buttressed corners and a battlemented parapet, it is built from 350 million-year old volcanic dolerite quarried on the hill itself. There is a wonderful view across the Firth of Forth from the top of the tower, which is open on Summer Sunday afternoons and during Edinburgh Doors Open Day (www.doorsopendays.org.uk).

The footpath north from the tower leads through the Corstorphine Hill Local Nature Reserve, which forms part of the coast-to-coast John Muir Way. Continue walking for just over half a mile to reach Barnton Quarry, where there is a graffiti-covered concrete structure. This is a former Second World War operations room for RAF Fighter Command. In 1952 a three-storey Cold War-era bunker was built beneath it in which information from radar surveillance stations across Scotland was correlated. In the early 1960s the bunker was reassigned as a self-contained regional seat of government in the event of Scotland's central government collapsing. Operational until the 1980s, it was damaged by fire in the 1990s. Enthusiastic volunteers are now gradually restoring the site.

It is a short walk to Clemiston Road North, where the bus can be taken back to the Clerwood Terminus. The Corstorphine story then continues half a mile south across St. John's Road on Kirk Loan. Here stands Corstorphine Old Parish Church, a sturdy medieval building endowed as a collegiate church in the 15th century and occupied by Cromwell's troops in 1560. A couple of streets away in St. Margaret's Park is the late 16th century Dower House, with crow-stepped gables and a lime-harled façade typical of the Lothians. Home to the Corstorphine Heritage Centre, it contains a small museum containing a slice from the 400 year-old Corstorphine Sycamore.

This tour finishes on nearby Dovecote Road, which is named after a well-preserved dovecote that once served long-vanished Corstorphine Castle. Measuring almost 90 feet at the base, it has space for over a thousand nests!

Those returning to Edinburgh along Corstorphine Road should watch out for the statue by Scottish sculptor Alexander Stoddart (b. 1959) depicting the parting on Corstorphine Hill of David Balfour and Alan Breck Stewart in Robert Louis Stevenson's *Kidnapped*. It stands on the left opposite Western Place and was unveiled in 2004 by Sean Connery.

The House of Shaws in *Kidnapped* was probably inspired by the now-ruined 17th century Cammo House on Cammo Walk (EH4). Its former estate is today a public wilderness containing the original stables and a crenellated 19th century water tower.

Other locations nearby: 86

86 Penguins on Parade

EH12 6TS (North & West Suburbs), RZSS Edinburgh Zoo
at 134 Corstorphine Road
Bus 12, 26, 31, 100 to Edinburgh Zoo

The animals of RZSS Edinburgh Zoo (Royal Zoologocal Society of Scotland) have roamed the slopes of Corstorphine Hill (EH12) for over a century. The diverse collection and breeding programme of endangered species have made it the city's most popular paid attraction after Edinburgh Castle. But it wasn't Edinburgh's first zoo. That opened in 1840 on East Claremont Street (EH7), where it featured Bruin the bear and a lion named Wallace. The conditions, however, were less than ideal and it closed in 1857.

Fast forward half a century and the current Zoo finds its origins with the Edinburgh solicitor, Thomas Hailing Gillespie (1876–1967). Imbued with a passion for zoology, he was determined to create an animal park in the city. Although the cold climate initially presented a problem, Gillespie was encouraged by Carl Hagenbeck, who had established a zoo in Hamburg in 1907. In 1909 Gillespie founded what was to become the Royal Zoological Society of Scotland and in 1913 he secured a south-facing site on Corstorphine Hill. The Scottish National

Penguins on parade at Edinburgh Zoo

Zoological Park opened later the same year, with Gillespie remaining its director until 1950.

The zoo's long association with penguins began in January 1914, when three king penguins arrived at Leith Docks on a Christian Salvesen whaler. They were the first penguins ever seen outside the South Atlantic and the subsequent hatching of a king penguin chick at the Zoo in 1919 was a world first. These days the Zoo is home to colonies of king, gentoo and rockhopper Penguins, which are kept in a landscaped area called Penguins' Rock. Most days the penguins take a stroll around the zoo with their keepers. The parade started by accident in 1950, when several of the birds escaped, much to the delight of the visitors. It should be noted, however, that it is the decision of the penguins alone to leave their enclosure – they are never coaxed out with food – so very occasionally the parade is cancelled if they are not in the mood!

The zoo's most famous penguin is Nils Olav, a king penguin adopted as a mascot in 1972 by the Norwegian King's Guard during their participation at the Edinburgh Military Tattoo. Nils received the rank of lance corporal and in 2008 his successor, Nils Olav II, was awarded a knighthood. In 2016 Sir Nils was further promoted to Brigadier in a ceremony attended by over 50 Norwegian soldiers.

Penguins aside, the Zoo offers its visitors plenty of other animal experiences. The Budongo Trail named after the Zoo's field work in the Ugandan forest is a state-of-the-art enclosure housing a troop of common chimpanzees. Living Links is a field station for the study of primate behaviour and contains squirrel monkeys and tufted capuchins. Brilliant Birds is a walk-through aviary alive with nicobar pigeons and Bali starlings. The Zoo is also home to Scottish wild cats, giant anteaters, Asiatic lions, meerkats, Sumatran tigers and pygmy hippos, and is the only zoo in Britain currently housing giant pandas.

Visitors should not overlook the gardens at the Zoo. This part of Corstorphine Hill was once a nursery owned by the botanist and gardener Thomas Blaikie (1750–1838), who planted several aristocratic gardens in France. His legacy is continued at the Zoo, which today boasts one of the most diverse tree collections in the Lothians.

Seafaring has long brought Norwegians to Edinburgh, with others escaping here during the Second World War. A former Norwegian Seaman's Church stands at 25 North Junction Street (EH6) in Leith and on 17th May each year Edinburgh hosts the largest Norwegian Independence Day parade outside Oslo.

Other locations nearby: 85

87 Digging for Happiness

EH14 2LZ (South & East Suburbs), the Redhall Walled Garden at 97 Lanark Road
Bus 44 to Redhall Bank Road

Edinburgh has an admirable record when it comes to community gardening. The number of people willing to garden collectively is growing and worthwhile initiatives are sprouting across the city. In many instances the aim is to grow not only wholesome seasonal produce but also community ties. This is certainly the case with the Barony Community Garden in Broughton (EH3), the Grove Community Garden in Fountainbridge (EH3), the Portobello Community Orchard (EH15), and North Edinburgh Grows in Muirhouse (EH4). There are two gardens, however, which go a step further by using horticulture as a route to real happiness.

The Redhall Walled Garden and its summerhouse

The first is Redhall Walled Garden at 97 Lanark Road (EH14). Since 1983 under the watchful eye of the Scottish Association for Mental Health (SAMH), groups of patients have been rehabilitated here through hands-on organic gardening. It goes without saying that the staff believe strongly in the therapeutic benefits of working outdoors, as well as the value of conservation and sustainable food production. So successful are they that many of the patients, or 'trainees' as they prefer to be known, pursue gardening as a career after leaving.

The garden's lovely setting on the banks of the Water of Leith has seen it become a visitor attraction in its own right. Visitors are made most welcome and are free to explore the various features, including a magnificent herb garden, a bee and butterfly garden, a bog garden and a reconstructed Iron Age roundhouse, all created by the trainees. Teas are available in the summer and there is a plant sales area for those wanting souvenirs.

The garden also includes a red-brick Palladian summerhouse. This dates from the mid-18th century when the garden was created to grow produce for Redhall House, which stands on the opposite side of the river. Built in 1758 using red sandstone from Redhall Castle, which stood nearby until it was destroyed by the troops of Oliver Cromwell, the house is abandoned at the time of writing. Its hexagonal dovecote on Redhall House Avenue, however, has been restored and embedded in its façade is an armorial tablet taken from the castle.

Edinburgh's other great therapeutic garden, the Royal Edinburgh Community Gardens (RECG), can be found in the grounds of the Royal Edinburgh Hospital on Morningside Terrace (EH10). The hospital was established in 1807 by the physician Andrew Duncan (1744–1828) after he witnessed the tragic plight of one of his patients, the poet Robert Fergusson (1750–1774). Fergusson died unnecessarily in the old Edinburgh lunatic asylum following mental health problems brought on by a head injury (the site at 11 Bristo Place (EH1) is now occupied by the aptly-named Bedlam Theatre). Duncan ensured that in his new hospital those with mental health issues would be treated in a far more humane way.

The gardens themselves were established in 2010 by the Cyrenians, an organisation dedicated to helping those excluded from society. Part of an NHS Lothian initiative, the purpose here is to encourage the recovery of patients by promoting social inclusion through gardening with others. Open to the public several days a week, the gardens contain vegetables plots, fruit trees and herb gardens. Walks, workshops, team building exercises and a range of other activities and events are organised here on a regular basis.

The concept of therapeutic gardening was pioneered in 1824 by Dr. William Lowe, who rented Saughton Hall on Balgreen Road (EH11) as an Institute for the Recovery of the Insane. Although the hall is long gone, the lovely Saughton Park still bears witness to his and his patients' endeavours.

88 Where the War Poets Wrote

EH14 1DJ (South & East Suburbs), the War Poets Collection on the Craiglockhart Campus of Edinburgh Napier University at 219 Colinton Road
Bus 36 to Napier Craiglockhart Campus; 4, 10, 27, 45 to Craiglockhart Campus (note: open during term time only; visitors must report to the reception desk on arrival to collect a visitor's badge and sign the visitors' book)

The Craiglockhart Campus at 219 Colinton Road (EH14) is one of three campuses used by Edinburgh Napier University. Law and business courses take place here in a striking collection of adapted historic buildings and modern purpose-built venues. The oldest part is the former Craiglockhart Hydropathic, which was used as a military hospital during the Great War.

The Craiglockhart Hydropathic opened in 1880, when the practice of using water in the treatment of human illness was experiencing a fashionable revival. Built in the Italianate style, with lawns that hosted the Scottish Croquet Championships between 1897 and 1914, the huge building was requisitioned in 1916 as a psychiatric hospital for the treatment of shell-shocked soldiers. Its most famous patients were Wilfred Owen (1893–1918) and Siegfried Sassoon (1886–1967), whose anti-war poems were first published in the hospital's magazine *The Hydra*. Their poignant story is recounted today in the War Poets Collection, a free public exhibition on the Craiglockhart Campus.

Wilfred Owen's anti-war poems were first published in *The Hydra*

The studious and romantic Wilfred Owen discovered his poetic vocation in 1904 during a holiday in Cheshire. Not surprisingly when war came he enlisted reluctantly in the Artists' Rifles and in 1916 was commissioned as a second lieutenant in the Manchester Regiment. Once in the trenches of northern France, however, he suffered a series of traumas, as a result of which he was diagnosed with neurasthenia (shell shock) and sent to Craiglockhart.

It was whilst recuperating there in 1917 that Owen met fellow poet Siegfried Sassoon. Motivated by patriotism, Sassoon had already joined the British Army by the time war broke out in 1914. He accompanied the Royal Welch Fusiliers to France, where a meeting with the writer Robert Graves (1895–1985) inspired his preference for literary realism. Increasingly depressed by the horrors of war, Sassoon became suicidally brave on the battlefield. Then in 1917 after a spell of leave he refused to return to duty and penned his famous anti-war letter *Finished with the War: A Soldier's Declaration*, which was read out in the House of Commons. Rather than being court-martialled he too was sent to Craiglockhart to be treated for shell shock.

Encouraged by his doctor to write down his experiences, Owen's poems on the horrors of trench and gas warfare exhibit a combination of his own romantic notions and Sassoon's gritty realism. The result was a poetic synthesis both potent and sympathetic that stood in stark contrast to the public's perception of war and the patriotic verse of earlier war poets such as Rupert Brooke (1887–1915). One of Owen's best-known works written at Craiglockhart is *Anthem for Doomed Youth*, with its lines "What passing-bells for these who die as cattle? Only the monstrous anger of the guns".

Owen was discharged from Craiglockhart in late 1917 after being judged fit for light regimental duties. He returned to active service in France the following year, prompted by Sassoon's return from the battlefield, this time a victim of friendly fire. Owen now saw it as his duty to continue the 'warts and all' reportage that Sassoon had pioneered. He was killed in action on 4th November 1918 exactly one week before the signing of the Armistice. Sassoon survived the war and thereafter tirelessly promoted Owen's work helping to make him the greatest war poet of all time.

The ruins of Craiglockhart Castle, a 15th century tower house, can be found at the Glenlockhart Road entrance to the campus. On Wester Craiglockhart Hill behind the campus are the remains of a prehistoric vitrified fort.

89 Walking around Colinton

EH13 0JR (South & East Suburbs), a walk around Colinton
beginning at Colinton Parish Church on Dell Road
Bus 18, 45 to Colinton Village then walk along Spylaw Street;
10 to Barnshot Road; 16 to St. Cuthberts

Colinton in Edinburgh's southern suburbs is a former village with plenty of history. This round walk begins at Colinton Parish Church on Dell Road (EH13), which is notable today for its Victorian Italianate bell tower. The first church on the site, however, was built back in 1095 by Ethelred, a son of Malcolm III (1058–1093). It is a reminder that Colinton was originally founded here because the site offered a convenient fording point on the Water of Leith.

Colinton Manse behind the church was once occupied by Robert Louis Stevenson's grandparents. As a child he played in the garden here and found inspiration for what would become his *Child's Garden of Verses*. In 2013 a bronze

This Italianate church lies at the heart of Colinton

statue of Stevenson was unveiled outside the church by Scottish crime writer Ian Rankin (b. 1960), who admitted that without Stevenson's *Strange Case of Dr. Jekyll and Mr. Hyde* he would not have dreamt up his fictional character, Detective Inspector Rebus (see no. 54).

Walk to the top of Dell Road now, where a signpost points to Colinton Dell. Through this steep-sided glen, which stretches as far as Slateford, flows the Water of Leith (see no. 51). The riverside walkway passes ancient woodland and the sites of old watermills that once produced textiles, paper and snuff. As recently as the 1960s, the Caledonian Railway's Balerno line also ran along here servicing the mills, and until 1943 it carried passengers, too (the impressive Dell Tunnel can be explored where the B701 crosses the river).

Take the footbridge over the river and walk along an old mill race to reach Katesmill Road. This leads up to Merchiston Castle School in the grounds of which can be found the 16th century Colinton Castle. Slighted in 1650 by Oliver Cromwell (1599–1658) during his invasion of Scotland, it was later repaired and then partially demolished in the 18th century by the artist Alexander Nasmyth (1758–1840) to create the picturesque ivy-clad ruin seen today.

The name of the school is confusing in that Merchiston Castle actually stands four miles north-east at 10 Colinton Road (EH10). It was there that the school was founded in 1833 before being relocated to Colinton in 1930. Built by the Napier family in the 1450s, Merchiston Castle is more correctly a tower house, where John Napier (1550–1617), the inventor of logarithms, was born. Today it stands at the heart of the university that bears his name.

Exit the school now to join Colinton Road and turn right at the Army School of Bagpipe Music. Between Redford Road and Thorburn Road are the Arts and Crafts-style Colinton Cottages designed by Sir Robert Lorimer (1864–1929) and now used as sheltered accommodation. The tour finishes on Westgarth Avenue at St. Cuthbert's Episcopal Church, which retains a splendid painted ceiling designed by the architect Robert Rowand Anderson (1834–1921), who was once a member of the congregation.

In the 1870s Robert Louis Stevenson's father leased a house at Swanston in the Pentland Hills. The country air helped Stevenson's weak chest and the scenery was frequently woven into his literature. The ancient right of way to Swanston can still be followed through Braidburn Valley Park (passing Comiston Springs Wellhead) and along Cockmylane to Caiystane Gardens, where a detour onto Caiystane View reveals the Caiy Stone, a 5,000-year old standing stone. Caiystane Drive then runs into Swanston Road, which crosses the Edinburgh City Bypass to reach Swanston Golf Course. Swanston Cottage, used by the Stevensons, stands on the right. Straight ahead, beyond the trees, the 18th century thatched hamlet of Swanston appears like a real-life *Brigadoon*.

90 The Morningside Wild West

EH10 4QG (South & East Suburbs), the Morningside Wild
West at 14 Springvalley Gardens
Bus 5, 11, 16, 23, 36 to Springvalley Gardens

Tucked away behind busy Morningside Road is something wholly unexpected: a replica of a street in the American Wild West complete
with trading station, livery stables, cantina and jail. How such a place
came to be built makes for interesting reading. More importantly its
presence acts as a reminder of past times, when Morningside really
was part of Edinburgh's frontierland.

The Morningside Wild West can be found in an alley down the
side of 14 Springvalley Gardens (EH10). Despite its weather-beaten
appearance it only dates back to 1995, when furniture salesman Michael Faulkner wanted some striking storage units for his company,
The Great American Indoors (his office at number 14 was previously
the Silver Slipper ballroom and before that the Springvalley Cinema,
which was forced out of business in 1938 by Morningside's new Do-

An unexpected site in Morningside is this Wild West street

minion Cinema (see no. 48)). The unit frontages were created by some set-building acquaintances, who had just returned to Edinburgh after working at Euro Disney. The wooden and adobe façades certainly look odd against a backdrop of dour Edinburgh tenements.

Unfortunately for Faulkner, the arrival of IKEA in Edinburgh just four years later brought about the demise of his business. Ever the pioneer, he returned home to Northern Ireland, where his father had briefly been Prime Minister, and settled down as an author on an uninhabited island in Strangford Lough. What had been his office was converted into apartments and it was feared that the Wild West frontages would be repurposed too. Fortunately they've been left intact, a decision in part to do with the door of the Cantina doubling as the fire exit for Morningside Library. These days though the frontages do look a little ramshackle giving the appearance of a ghost town. All that's needed is some tumbleweed…

Urbane Morningside, with its tenement-style houses and Victorian villas, might seem a strange place to find a replica Wild West but it serves as a reminder that this really was once Edinburgh's frontierland on an ancient route leading to the south west of Scotland and Carlisle. The so-called Bore Stane embedded in the perimeter wall of the former Morningside Parish Church opposite 122 Morningside Road (EH10) is a survivor from those far-off days. It is said to mark approximately where in 1513 Scottish forces mustered under James IV (1488–1513) before marching south to the Battle of Flodden – and defeat at the hands of the English. A 'bore stane' is a stone with a hole bored in it to support a flag. This one lacks a hole but it is located at the highest point of the Burgh Muir, where Scottish kings traditionally trained their troops before battle.

Several street names in Morningside also speak of former times. Streets such as Eden Lane, Canaan Lane, Nile Grove and Jordan Lane all have Biblical associations, as does the Jordan Burn, which runs eastwards from Craighouse Hill – between Jordan Lane and Nile Grove – to join the Braid Burn at Peffermill (see no. 103). Explanations for these names range from Jews having settled in the area to Cromwell's troops inventing place names while exploring unfamiliar territory. A more likely explanation is that they indicate the presence of gypsies on the Burgh Muir in the 16th century. The former existence of an Egypt Farm at the junction of what is now Nile Grove and Woodbourn Terrace supports the theory, the word 'gypsy' being derived from 'Egypt', whence the travellers were once thought to have come.

Other locations nearby: 91

91 Coffee from a Police Box

EH10 4QQ (South & East Suburbs), a café tour including
The Counter at 216a Morningside Road
Bus 5, 11, 16, 23, 36 to Spring Valley Gardens

Cafés in Edinburgh come in all shapes and sizes. There are grand ones serving tea in elegant surroundings such as the Signet Library Colonnades in Parliament Square (EH1), the Royal Overseas League at 100 Princes Street (EH2), and the Dome's Georgian Tea Room at 14 George Street (EH2) (see no. 14). The first floor café in Debenhams at 109 Princes Street (EH2) is surprising in that it was once part of the Scottish Liberal and Conservative Clubs, which explains the unexpected bust of Gladstone and a stained glass triptych installed by his opponent Disraeli. Others are more modest and with a different purpose, such as the Serenity Café at 8 Jackson's Entry (EH8), Scotland's first café run by and for people in recovery,

A former Morningside police box converted into a café

and Anteaques at 17 Clerk Street (EH8), where tea and scones can be enjoyed against a backdrop of antiques for sale. Falko Konditormeister at 185 Bruntsfield Place (EH10) is different again, selling handmade bread and cakes to exacting German artisan standards, with conversational German language classes each Wednesday morning.

There are others with a literary twist, such as the Elephant House (EH1) at 21 George IV Bridge, where a young J. K. Rowling wrote several of her *Harry Potter* books (see no. 37). Of particular interest is Deacon's House Café in Brodie's Close at 304 Lawnmarket (EH1). It is housed in the former cabinet workshop of the infamous William Brodie (1741–1788), a respected trade guild deacon and city councillor, who was hanged at the Old Tolbooth jail after it was revealed he led a secret double life as a burglar. His case inspired Robert Louis Stevenson to pen his *Strange Case of Dr. Jekyll and Mr. Hyde* a century later.

A unique take on café premises in Edinburgh is its former police call boxes. One hundred and forty of these indestructible cast iron kiosks in the form of miniature Greek temples were erected across the city in the 1930s. They were designed by City Architect Ebenezer MacRae (1881–1951), who is also remembered for his tram shelters. Rendered obsolete by the arrival of mobile phones, the remaining 85 have gradually been auctioned off for use mainly as coffee and fast food stands.

A fine example of a converted police box is The Counter at 216a Morningside Road (EH10). Through quaint hinged windows, a friendly barista purveys own-brand locally-roasted coffee, as well as a selection of cookies. An immediate success with locals, the owners have now commandeered further police boxes outside Usher Hall on Lothian Road (EH1) and on High Riggs in Toll Cross (EH3), as well as a converted narrow boat in Lochrin Basin (EH3) on the Union Canal (see no. 49).

Other examples of successful police box conversions include Bollywood the Coffee Box at 99a Bruntsfield Place (EH10), Over Langshaw Farmhouse Ice Cream at the junction of the Grassmarket and West Bow (EH1), and Souped Up at 22a St. Patrick Square (EH8). Tupiniquim on Lauriston Place (EH1) is particularly ambitious in that it is not only used to sell Brazilian crepes but also doubles as Edinburgh's smallest cinema, concert hall and puppet theatre! Elsewhere police boxes are being used as florists and pop-up art venues, and in 2015 even spawned an annual Edinburgh Police Box Festival.

Most non-natives will be unaware that the University of Edinburgh in Southside contains several cafés open to the public. They include the DHT Café in the David Hulme Tower in George Square, the Absorb Café in the Appleton Tower at 11 Crichton Street, and the Exchange Café in the Business School at 29 Buccleugh Place (all EH8).

Other locations nearby: 90

92 The Art Deco Petrol Station

EH9 1QF (South & East Suburbs), the former Southern
Motors Garage at 39 Causewayside
Bus 42, 67 to Summerhall; 29 to Newington Road

The Modernist architect Sir Basil
Unwin Spence (1907–1976) was born
in Bombay, where his father worked
for the Royal Mint. He is most famously associated with the radical
rebuilding of Coventry Cathedral in
England and the Beehive, the New
Zealand Parliament's Executive Wing
in Wellington. It is therefore easy to
overlook the fact that he was educated and spent much of his working
life in Edinburgh, where several less
well known buildings bear witness to
his talents.

Aged twelve, Spence was sent to
Edinburgh by his Scottish father to be
educated at George Watson's College
for Boys in Lauriston. Then in 1925
he enrolled at the Edinburgh College
of Art on Lady Lawson Street (EH3),
where his peers described his work
as showing "unusual brilliance". During this time he also spent a year in
the London office of respected architect Sir Edwin Lutyens (1869–1944),
where he worked as an assistant with
fellow Scottish architect William Kininmonth (1904–1988).

The Southside Garage was an early commission for
architect Basil Spence

After graduating in 1931, Spence
returned to Edinburgh and worked with Kininmonth in the office of
Rowand Anderson & Paul in Rutland Square (EH1). From here they
pursued several residential commissions, including Lismhor House at
11 Easter Belmont Road (EH12). Still contemporary today, this Modernist dwelling incorporates many potent elements of 1930s architecture:
rooms formed by a series of inter-connected white-rendered cubes, a

semi-circular lounge bay window like the prow of a ship, and large metal-framed windows admitting the maximum amount of light.

Another of Spence's commissions from this period is the former Southern Motors Garage at 39 Causewayside (EH9). Built in 1933, this magnificent piece of *Art Deco* architecture reflects an age when driving was every bit as glamorous as cruising. Now used as a wine warehouse, the listed building retains its wide windows, red signage and dropped kerbstones, where vehicles once came and went. An information board illustrates how the place looked in its prime. Those appreciative of such faded glamour should also check out the Maybury at 1–5 South Maybury (EH12) and the White House at 70 Niddrie Mains Road (EH16), both former 1930's roadhouses designed by William Innes Thomson (1910–1990) in the same streamlined style as Spence's garage.

Spence's international career only really flourished after the Second World War, when he established his own London practice. He was knighted in 1960 for his work at Coventry and followed it up with the British Embassy in Rome and the Hyde Park Cavalry Barracks. Spence never forgot Edinburgh though and continued to design buildings for the city. They include the quirky Brown's Close apartments at 79–121 Canongate (EH8), the Brutalist University of Edinburgh Main Library at 30 George Square (EH8), and the massive John Lewis Department Store on Leith Street (EH1). Best of all is the unique Mortenhall Crematorium on Howden Hall Road (EH16), the main chapel of which uses the same angled rooflines used by Spence at Coventry and on the Canongate.

Not far from Causewayside on Grange Road (EH9) is Grange Cemetery. Laid out in 1847, this rectilinear burial ground was designed by the Edinburgh architect David Bryce (1803-1876) and includes the grave of world-renowned mapmaker John Bartholomew (1805-1861). Of particular interest along the north wall is the spectacular 'Egyptian Portal to the Land of the Dead'. Replete with a magnificent stone palm tree and two broken obelisks, it forms a unique headstone for the family of Scotland's foremost fishing net manufacturer, William Stuart (1820–1888). It is the antithesis of Basil Spence's Modernism and yet every bit as fashionable at the time it was erected.

Other locations nearby: 45, 46, 47, 93

93 The Story of Edinburgh's Jews

EH9 1NW (South & East Suburbs), the Jewish cemetery in
Sciennes House Place
Bus 42, 67 to Summerhall; 29 to Newington Road

One aspect of Edinburgh life that rarely makes the pages of conventional guidebooks concerns the city's Jews. With roots stretching back to the 17th century, this ancient community remains a living one. Home to an imposing synagogue and several of Scotland's rare Jewish cemeteries, Jewish Edinburgh is well worth exploring.

The story of Edinburgh's Jews begins in 1691, when one David Brown, a professing Jew, applied to Edinburgh Town Council to reside and trade in the city. By 1780 a small Jewish community was in place but it was not until a decade later that the first Jew asked to be buried there. He was Herman Lyon, a dentist and chiropodist, who had arrived from Prussia in 1788. He petitioned the Council to purchase a burial plot on Calton Hill for himself and his family although little trace remains of it today.

This tiny Jewish cemetery can be found in Sciennes House Place

Scotland's first official Jewish cemetery was opened in Sciennes in 1816 by the Edinburgh Hebrew Congregation (EHC), which at the time consisted of 20 families. Used until 1867, its weathered headstones inscribed in Hebrew can be seen through railings in Sciennes House Place (EH9). Scotland's first Jewish immigrants, who came from Germany and the Low Countries to trade in clothing, furs and jewellery, are buried here.

The first synagogue in Scotland was established in 1817 in a rented room on North Richmond Street (EH8). It was used until 1868, when the community relocated to a larger building between Charles Street Lane and Teviot Row House, now part of the University of Edinburgh. Having grown to around 500 members, the community moved again in 1898 to a former church on Graham Street (EH6). By this time its dead were being buried in an enclosed area along the east wall of Newington Cemetery on Dalkeith Road (EH9). When this was filled to capacity a new burial ground was opened in Piershill Cemetery on Portobello Road (EH8), which is still used today. It includes a memorial commemorating Jewish soldiers who died fighting in various regiments of the British Army during the First World War.

The founding in 1890 of the New Hebrew Congregation unfortunately created a rift in Edinburgh's Jewish community. Based in a synagogue in Richmond Court (EH8), the New Hebrew Congregation attracted poor, recently-arrived immigrants and Jews working in the Caledonian Rubber Works, who had been evicted from their synagogue in Dalry. The EHC meanwhile catered for the city's already well-established middle class Jews.

Calls to unite the two congregations were made in 1907 during a visit to Edinburgh by the Chief Rabbi. In 1927 after much effort by Edinburgh's Rabbi Salis Daiches they were heeded and in 1932 Edinburgh's first purpose-built synagogue opened at 4a Salisbury Road (EH16). Edinburgh's only synagogue today, it was built to accommodate a thousand worshippers and features a striking collection of stained glass windows. Its location in Edinburgh's South Side away from the old Jewish quarters signalled the improved social standing of its members.

Although membership of the synagogue is much smaller now – the prayer hall has been halved to accommodate a reduced congregation of just 150 – the community remains upbeat. In addition to weekly services (Friday, Saturday and Sunday), all Jewish festivals are celebrated and there is a weekly Yiddish class. The ritual bath *(Mikveh)* is still in use, the longstanding Jewish Literary Society still meets, and the German bakery Falko Konditormeister in Bruntsfield produces kosher unleavened *Challah* each Friday. Tours of the synagogue can be arranged by appointment (www.ehcong.com).

Other locations nearby: 45, 46, 47, 92

94 Saved from a Stag

EH8 8DX (South & East Suburbs), the ruins of Holyrood
Abbey at the bottom of the Canongate
Bus 6, 35 to Holyrood Parliament

Legend relates how in 1127, whilst hunting in the Forest of Drumsheugh, David I (1124–1153) was thrown from his horse after it was startled by a stag. Realising he might be gored and knowing he had been hunting on a holy day (the Feast of the Holy Cross or Rood), when sport was banned, the king knelt and prayed. Upon so doing the sun's rays formed a golden cross between the stag's antlers and the king's life was spared. In gratitude he founded Holyrood Abbey, which despite lying in ruins remains Scotland's finest example of medieval church architecture.

David also had practical reasons for founding an abbey. Eager to improve the lot of the Scots, he knew that abbeys were not only powerhouses of

The ruins of Holyrood Abbey, with the Palace of Holyroodhouse in the background

prayer but also facilitated improved farming techniques, literacy and medicine. Holyrood Abbey was served by a chapter of Augustinian Canons then resident at Edinburgh Castle and its original layout probably resembled that of the Canons' mother church, Merton Priory, in Surrey. Reconstructed between 1195 and 1230, the current layout consists of an aisled choir with transepts and a central tower (now little more than footings in the grass) and an eight-bay aisled nave (still standing), with twin towers at the west front (one of which remains). The possession of a fragment of the True Cross known as the Black Rood made the abbey one of the most powerful in Scotland.

Many important events have occurred in the abbey. The Parliament of Scotland convened here numerous times, kings and queens were married within its walls, and in 1328 the Treaty of Edinburgh-Northampton, which recognised the Kingdom of Scotland as independent, was signed here by Robert the Bruce (1306–1329).

The abbey's proximity to Edinburgh Castle meant that it was often visited by Scottish royalty, who lodged in a guesthouse alongside the cloister. By the mid-15th century, with the emergence of Edinburgh as the main seat of the royal court, the guesthouse was being used increasingly for secular purposes. As a result James IV (1488–1513) began transforming it into the royal residence known as the Palace of Holyroodhouse (see no. 95).

Unfortunately in the 1540s during the War of the Rough Wooing, the invading English damaged the abbey, with further damage inflicted a decade later during the Scottish Reformation. Monastic services ended and the east end was demolished leaving only the nave, which by then was serving as a parish church for the *burgh* of the Canongate. When in 1686 James VII/II (1685–1688) established a Jesuit college within the palace, the abbey became a Royal Chapel for the Order of the Thistle, and the Protestant congregation relocated to the Canongate Kirk (see no. 26). Two years later, the chapel was damaged during the Glorious Revolution and re-roofed in stone. Despite this in 1768 a violent storm left it the roofless albeit romantic ruin seen today.

David I also gave the area surrounding the Holyrood Abbey to the Augustinians. He permitted them to establish a *burgh*, one quite distinct from Edinburgh, which became known as the Canongate after the Canons' Way running through it (today the lower half of the Royal Mile). This explains why the arms of the Canongate incorporating a stag's head with a cross between its antlers can still be seen in the area despite it having been amalgamated with Edinburgh in 1856. Examples include the apex of the Canongate Kirk, the Canongate Tolbooth and the Mercat Cross (see nos. 13, 15 & 26).

Other locations nearby: 28, 29, 95, 96

95 A Refined Royal Residence

EH8 8DX (South & East Suburbs), the Palace
of Holyroodhouse at the bottom of the Canongate
Bus 6, 35 to Holyrood Parliament

Holyrood Abbey, which today lies in ruins at the foot of the Canongate, was established in 1128 by David I (1124–1153) (see no. 94). As a royal foundation close to Edinburgh Castle it inevitably became an important administrative centre. Early Scottish parliaments were convened here and several kings were born, married and buried within its walls. Visiting royalty lodged in a guesthouse, which stood alongside the abbey cloister.

By the mid-15th century, with the emergence of Edinburgh as the main seat of the royal court, the guesthouse was being used increasingly for secular purposes. This prompted James IV (1488–1513) to erect a Gothic palace on the site in the early 1500s. Built as a series of ranges around a quadrangle, with

The Palace of Holyroodhouse stands at the foot of the Canongate

an entrance on the west side, this first Palace of Holyroodhouse contained a great hall, royal apartments, a chapel and menagerie.

Between 1528 and 1536, James V (1513–1542) added to the palace. The ranges were reworked in Renaissance style, an armoury, mint and forge were installed, and the north-west tower was built to provide new royal apartments. Only the tower remains from this period and it can be visited today as part of the official tour. Famously occupied by Mary, Queen of Scots (1542–1567) from her return to Scotland in 1561 until her forced abdication in 1567, this is where she witnessed the brutal murder of her private secretary, David Rizzio (1533–1566), at the hands of her jealous second husband, Lord Darnley (1565–1567). Some swear they can still see the bloodstains on the floorboards. Of Mary's privy garden north of the palace only a small pavilion known erroneously as Queen Mary's Bath House survives on Abbeyhill.

When James VI/I (1567–1625) became King of England in 1603 and moved to London, the palace no longer served as the seat of a permanent royal court. Only with the Restoration of Charles II (1660–1685) and the return of the Privy Council to Holyrood did work on the palace continue. New plans drawn up by the gentleman-architect Sir William Bruce (1630–1710) called for refined new royal apartments: the Queen's in the west range and the King's in the south and east, the two connected by a gallery to the north. Also dating from this time is the south-west tower built to match the one already standing.

The work was completed in 1679 in time for the arrival of the future James VII/II (1685–1688) and it is this general layout encased in a neo-Classical shell that visitors see today. Especially noteworthy is the original plaster ceiling in the King's Bedchamber, the French tapestries in the Morning Drawing Room, and the 110 portraits of Scottish monarchs in the Great Gallery, beginning with the legendary Fergus I, who supposedly ruled Scotland from 330BC.

Although the palace lost its principal functions following the Union of England and Scotland in 1707, it was still used by nobles: Bonnie Prince Charlie held court here in 1745 and the exiled French King Charles X later took advantage of the abbey's right of sanctuary (the letter 'S' in the road at the start of Abbey Strand once marked the limit of sanctuary for aristocratic debtors known as the Abbey Lairds). Renovated following George IV's visit to Scotland in 1822, the Palace of Holyroodhouse has served since the 1920s as the British monarch's official residence in Scotland.

Works of art from the Royal Collection are displayed in the Queen's Gallery, a former church in front of the palace, opened by Queen Elizabeth II in 2002.

Other locations nearby: 28, 29, 94, 96

96 Volcanoes and Crags

EH8 8HG (South & East Suburbs), a walk around Holyrood
Park starting from the car park on Queen's Drive near the
Palace of Holyroodhouse
Bus 6, 35 to Holyrood Parliament

The geological forces that dictated the distinctive layout of Edinburgh's
Old Town also shaped Hollyrood Park. During the Carboniferous period
350 million years ago volcanic flues pushed up through the sedimentary rocks here. When these cooled they formed hard dolerite plugs,
which not only resisted the scouring effects of subsequent glacial erosion but also shielded tapering, steep-sided ramps of softer sedimentary rocks, creating what geographers call crag-and-tail formations. In
the Old Town, Edinburgh Castle was built on the crag: the Royal Mile
along the tail (see no. 6 & 11). By contrast the lack of building in Holyrood Park means the crag-and-tail can be seen in its elemental glory. A
circular walk starting from the car park at the Palace of Holyroodhouse
allows visitors to get up close to the geology and provides a history
lesson along the way.

From the car park climb the steps to reach the Radical Road, a track
paved by unemployed weavers in the aftermath of the Radical War of
1820. During the 12th century David I (1124–1153) probably came this

Salisbury Crags rearing up behind the Canongate, with Arthur's Seat beyond

way to hunt and according to legend was inspired to build Holyrood Abbey after being saved from a stag (see no. 94). By the early 1500s Scotland's monarchs were occupying a palace alongside the abbey and in 1541 James V (1513–1542) enclosed the hunting estate as a Royal Park, which it remains today albeit one open to the public under the auspices of Historic Environment Scotland.

The first geological feature is Salisbury Crags. These 150 feet-high dolerite outcrops are the weathered remains of lava streams that seeped sideways from the volcanic flue. The geologist James Hutton (1726–1797) could see them from his house on St. John's Hill (EH8) – the site is today marked by a small geological garden – and cited them in his book *Theory of the Earth* as evidence that volcanic activity rather than the sea shaped the landscape. His belief that the Earth's crust is in a continual state of melting and eroding was controversial at the time but is now taken for granted.

Beyond where the Radical Road joins Queen's Drive are Samson's Ribs, a formation of columnar basalt created the same way as Salisbury Crags. Both formations have attracted climbers, including local man Harold Raeburn (1865–1926), who in the 1890s became a leading light of the Scottish Mountaineering Club. Climbing today is restricted to the South Quarry area of Salisbury Crags.

A track leads from Queen's Drive up to Arthur's Seat, which at 823 feet above sea level is the highest point in Edinburgh. This is what remains of the volcanic flue itself and like the Castle Rock has re-sisted glacial erosion. Evidence has been found here of an Iron Age hill fort built 2,000 years ago by the Votadini tribe. The magnificent view prompted French novelist Jules Verne (1828–1905) to exclaim that "No pen can do justice to this breathtaking scene".

Now follow the track northwards between more crags to reach the ruins of St. Anthony's Chapel. Sitting picturesquely above St. Marga-ret's Loch, it is connected to Holyrood Abbey by a well-worn track and possibly served as a religious beacon to sailors on the Forth. From here it is a short walk back to the car park.

The importance of Holyrood Park and James Hutton in the development of geological science is celebrated in Our Dynamic Earth on Holyrood Road (EH8), an interactive science centre for all the family. Serious geologists can by appointment visit the Cockburn Geological Museum in the Grant Institute of the King's Buildings Campus of the University of Edinburgh on West Mains Road (EH9).

Other locations nearby: 28, 29, 94, 95

97 Dr. Neil's Lochside Eden

EH15 3PX (South & East Suburbs), Dr. Neil's Garden on Old Church Lane
Bus 42, 44, 104, 113 to Duddingston Village

The village of Duddingston nestles peacefully beneath Arthur's Seat, on the banks of Duddingston Loch. Born out of a Celtic crannog settlement called Treverlen, Duddingston is first recorded in lands granted to Kelso Abbey by David I (1124–1153). The abbey leased the land to an Anglo-Norman knight called Dodin de Berwic, whence the name Duddingston is derived.

In subsequent centuries Duddingston became a centre for weaving linen and formed part of an estate acquired in 1745 by the Earl of Alcorn. His Palladian home, Duddingston House, stands on what is now the local golf course. In 1745 Bonnie Prince Charlie rested his cavalry on the estate before the Battle of Prestonpans and held a council of war in a house on The Causeway. Another claim to fame is that Dr. James Tytler (1745–1804), Britain's first balloonist (1784) and editor of the *Encyclopaedia Britannica*, lived in Duddingston before fleeing to Berwick on account of bigamy.

Pleasure-seekers of old gravitated to Duddingston to enjoy ice-skating and curling on the frozen loch. These days the ice is rarely

Dr. Neil's Garden on the banks of Duddingston Loch

thick enough so they use Murrayfield Ice Rink instead. Walkers and cyclists still come though, descending from Arthur's Seat or else along the abandoned Innocent Railway (see no. 46). Upon arrival they can drink at one of Scotland's oldest pubs, the Sheep Heid Inn at 43–45 The Causeway. Said to date back to 1360, it boasts Scotland's oldest wooden skittles' alley installed in 1870.

Visitors also come to visit Dr. Neil's Garden. This tranquil Eden can be found on Old Church Lane (EH15) between the 12th century Duddingston Kirk and the loch. It stands as a testimony to the interests, imagination and sheer hard work of two Meadowbank GPs, Andrew and Nancy Neil. Well-travelled and energetic, the Neils began creating their garden in 1965 on a piece of church land used previously for grazing. They were assisted in the task by various patients, who benefitted from the fresh air and peaceful setting. The planting consists mostly of conifers, heathers and alpines, with more exotic magnolias, azaleas, and rhododendrons. The trio of towering Californian Redwoods and the Monkey Puzzle tree were given to the Neils as gifts.

Initially the garden was only open to visitors on certain weekends although the Neils always welcomed villagers. By the time the Neils died in 2005 a charitable trust had been established to safeguard the garden for future generations. The public now have unrestricted access and are encouraged by the garden's volunteers to seek peace, inspiration and friendship here. A daisy-shaped physic garden planted in memory of the Neils reflects their particular medical interests.

In one corner is the octagonal Thomson's Tower, which is open in July and August. Designed by William Henry Playfair (1790–1857), it was built in 1825 for the Duddingston Curling Society, a group of Edinburgh gentlemen that relocated here after the draining of the Nor' Loch (see no. 61). It's worth noting that their rules of 1803 still form the basis of international curling today. Since being restored in 2009, the tower's lower floor, where the stones were once stored, has contained a museum of curling. The upper room served originally as a meeting place for curlers and an artist's studio for Rev. John Thomson (1778–1840), minister of Duddingston Kirk. Thomson entertained many friends here and in the neighbouring manse, including fellow artist Henry Raeburn (1756–1823), whose famous painting *The Skating Minister* depicts the loch (see no. 57). The room is used today as an interpretation centre for the village and the loch, which is now a bird sanctuary.

98 Hotels with History

EH16 5UT (South & East Suburbs), a tour of historic
and unusual hotels including Prestonfield House
on Priestfield Road
Bus 2, 14, 30, 33 to Queen's Crescent then walk along
Kilmaurs Terrace, turn right onto Kilmaurs Road and walk
along Kirkhill Drive to reach the hotel entrance

More than 12 million nights are spent annually by visitors to Edinburgh. Accordingly the city offers a wide range of paid accommodation from five star *Grande Dame* hotels to modest guesthouses. What follows is a selection that caught this author's eye.

For those with deep pockets and a penchant for history there is plenty to please. Take the boutique hotel No. 11 Brunswick Street (EH7) opened in 1991. This former private townhouse completed in 1822 was one of the last to be built in the Georgian New Town. From the 1930s onwards it was the club house of the Black Watch, the oldest kilted regiment in the British Army, which explains the ruts in the lobby floor where the soldiers once rolled beer barrels into the bar! Other former townhouses converted to hotels include the George at 19–21 George Street (EH2) and the Bonham at 35 Drumsheugh Gardens (EH3).

Edinburgh's first large purpose-built hotel was the Waterloo on

Prestonfield House is
a hotel with plenty of
history

Waterloo Place (EH1), which opened in 1819. Charles Dickens stayed here and in 1834 a magnificent breakfast was staged to celebrate the abolition of slavery. The Georgian building reopened as the Apex Waterloo Place in 2009.

Not far away at the east end of Princes Street is the Balmoral, formerly the North British Station Hotel, which opened in 1902 for passengers using Waverley. The clock here is deliberately set three minutes fast to ensure people don't miss their trains. Its counterpart, the Waldorf Astoria Caledonian at the west end of Princes Street, opened a year later, as part of the Caledonian Railway's Princes Street station. Closed in 1965, the station's gates now lead to a car park on Rutland Street and the station clock adorns the hotel bar.

Some grand hotels are interesting conversions, including the Scotsman on North Bridge, formerly the offices of the newspaper of the same name, and the Malmaison in Leith in a former Seamen's Mission. Another conversion is Prestonfield House on Priestfield Road (EH16). Completed in 1687 as a country home for Edinburgh's Lord Provost, Sir James Dick (1643–1728), the house was used to entertain guests such as the American polymath and statesman Benjamin Franklin (1706–1790) and dictionary compiler Dr. Samuel Johnson (1709–1784). The public rooms are still hung with 17th century leather from Córdoba and Mortlake tapestries, which were popular in the Stuart Court.

At the other end of the spectrum are Edinburgh's guesthouses. Noteworthy is Stevenson House at 17 Heriot Row (EH3), the childhood home of author Robert Louis Stevenson (1850–1894) (see no. 7 & 89). His statue adorns the entrance hall, the master bedroom was once occupied by Stevenson's parents, and the original enamelled bath is still in use. Another is B + B Edinburgh at 3 Rothesay Terrace (EH3), the former Victorian home of John Ritchie Findlay (1824–1898), owner of *The Scotsman* newspaper. The building's wood-panelled interiors and fireplaces remain intact, with a first floor view of Well Court in Dean Village, which was commissioned as a philanthropic project by Findlay to provide housing for local tanners (see no. 51).

Definitely quirky is the Victorian two-room guesthouse at 2 Cambridge Street (EH1). Theatrically appointed, it features the owner's own inventions, including a row of wall-hung cinema seats playing film clips and the so-called 'Dream-A-Tron' to help guests to sleep.

For something really unusual why not stay in Liberton Tower, a late 15th century tower house on Liberton Tower Lane (EH16) in the Braid Hills. The third floor accommodation with its four poster bed is reached by an external wooden staircase and there are superb views from the roof.

99 Of Connery and Kilns

EH15 1TQ (South & East Suburbs), the Portobello pottery
kilns outside 19 Bridge Street
Bus 21, 26, 42, 45, 49, 69 to Bridge Street

For over 200 years a trip to Portobello has meant sea, sand and amusements. These amenities are still available but there are also several less well-known locations that bear witness to Portobello's bygone history.

Those interested should alight the bus at Bridge Street. Beyond some nearby iron railings can be seen the Figgate Burn flowing into the Firth of Forth. Its name is a reminder that until the mid-1700s Portobello was an area of barren moorland known as the Figgate Muir. Crossed by the Edinburgh-Musselburgh road, its emptiness despite being only three miles from central Edinburgh made it popular with smugglers.

In 1742 a retired sailor called George Hamilton built himself a cottage and harness-maker's shop on the moor to service passing coaches. Whilst serving in the Royal Navy in 1739 he had participated in the capture of Portobelo in Panama from the Spanish. The event triggered a wave of patriotism in Britain during which an area of London was named Portobello and George Hamilton named his cottage Portobello Hut. By the 1750s a small settlement had developed around the cottage and took the same name.

These old kilns are a reminder that Portobello was once renowned for its ceramic industry

Walk down Bridge Street noticing the single-storey house with red pantiles on the left. This is where Portobello's most famous son, the entertainer Sir Harry Lauder (1870–1950), was born. In his day he sold as many records as Enrico Caruso and the Portobello stretch of the A1 Edinburgh bypass is named in his honour.

Harry's father was a potter and this should be borne in mind at the bottom of Bridge Street, where a pair of 12 metre-high pottery kilns can be found. Built in the early 1900s, they are the last surviving bottle kilns in Scotland (so-called because of their shape) and are all that remains of the factory of A. W. Buchan & Co. Until the company relocated in 1972, they were used to fire utilitarian objects, such as ginger beer bottles, whisky flagons and hot water bottles, as well as decorative tableware (a potter's wheel from the factory is preserved in the Museum of Edinburgh on the Canongate). The iron bands around the kilns acted as strengthening during firing. The clay beds of the Figgate Burn explain why the industry was established here, and were first exploited during the 1760s to provide bricks for Edinburgh's New Town.

Now walk down Pipe Lane and onto The Promenade. Of Portobello's harbour built in the 1780s at the mouth of the Figgate Burn nothing remains, although the storms that destroyed it sometimes reveal its foundations. It was used to export brick, tile and earthenware goods until 1846, when the arrival of the railway provided easier access to markets and raw materials.

From 1795 onwards, when the first bathing machines appeared, Portobello also developed as a holiday resort. Additionally military drills and reviews were staged on the mile-long golden sands and in 1871 a pier was built at the bottom of Marlborough Street. The Marine Gardens and a funfair helped keep the punters happy, as did the indoor baths opened on The Promenade in 1901, which are still enjoyed today (see no. 52).

Portobello's heyday as a resort was not to last though and the pier was demolished in 1917. A huge open air swimming pool built in 1936, where a young Sean Connery served as life guard, was demolished in the 1970s. The Marine Gardens and funfair were cleared too, transforming Portobello into the quiet seaside suburb it is today.

At the far end of The Promenade are Joppa Rocks, ancient fossil-filled limestones that fascinated local geologist Hugh Miller (1802–1856) and which for centuries were used to pan salt.

100 A Noble Seat and Royal Retreat

EH16 4SY (South & East Suburbs), Craigmillar Castle on
Craigmillar Castle Road
Bus 21, 24, 33, 38, 49 to Little France Crescent then follow
the gravel path on the left passing the Royal Infirmary of
Edinburgh until it joins Craigmillar Castle Road and turn
left to reach the visitor centre (note: last entry to the
castle is 30 minutes before closing time)

Craigmillar Castle is one of the best preserved medieval castles in Scotland. A noble's handsome country seat, it was close enough to the political life of Edinburgh yet far enough away. As such it became a favoured royal retreat and never moreso than for Mary, Queen of Scots (1542–1567).

The oldest part of Craigmillar is the four-storey fortified tower house with its vaulted great hall on the first floor. This was built around 1400 by members of the Preston family, whose ancestor Simon de Preston, Sheriff of Midlothian, had been granted the land in 1374 by Robert II (1371–1390). During the 1440s Sir William Preston added the distinctive machicolated curtain wall creating the inner courtyard. Another Simon Preston added another curtain wall in 1510 forming the outer court and the east and west gardens.

The well-preserved ruins of Craigmillar Castle

During the English invasion of 1544 led by the Earl of Hertford, Craigmillar and its laird were captured and the castle slighted. Craigmillar's enviable position, however, and its suitability for hunting meant it was quickly rebuilt. Notably a new accommodation range was installed along the east side of the inner courtyard. It was most likely here that Mary, Queen of Scots resided when she visited Craigmillar in September 1563. Her French retinue gave their name to Little France on nearby Old Dalkeith Road.

During Mary's second visit in December 1566, whilst recovering from illness and the murder of her Italian secretary, David Rizzio (1533–1566), her noblemen suggested the removal of her unpopular husband, Henry Stuart, Lord Darnley (1565–1567). An agreement, the Craigmillar Bond, was duly drawn up and signed by Mary's secretary although it is unlikely the queen realised Darnley would be murdered.

In 1572 following Mary's flight into England, the regent of Scotland, John Erskine, used Craigmillar as a base during his siege of Edinburgh Castle, which was being held by supporters of the exiled queen. The last monarch to visit Craigmillar was Mary's son, James VI (1567–1625), in 1589, when he was the guest of Sir David Preston.

In 1660 the Prestons sold Craigmillar to Sir John Gilmour. It was at this time that the castle entered its final building phase, with the construction of the inner courtyard's west range. By the early 1700s, however, the Gilmours decided it would be easier to build a new home rather than continuously upgrade a medieval castle. Accordingly Craigmillar was abandoned and the Gilmours built Inch House in Gilmerton.

The excellent preservation of Craigmillar's fabric means that visitors today can experience the entire building from the gloomy basement to the top of the tower house, including a chapel and a dovecote. The view from the roof reveals a P-shaped garden pond built by the Prestons. Equally boastful is a carved *rebus* depicting a cheese press and a barrel (or tun), a visual pun for the name Preston.

A visit to Craigmillar can be extended by exiting north onto Niddrie Mains Road then heading east for half a mile to the Thistle Foundation on Craigmillar Castle Avenue. This community for disabled war veterans was founded in 1944 by Sir Frances and Lady Tudsbery and at its heart is the Arts and Crafts-inspired Robin Chapel commemorating their only son killed a year later (Choral Evensong on Sundays at 4pm). Farther on in the back garden of 36 Niddrie House is the Wauchope Mausoleum. It is all that remains of the 17th century Niddrie Marischal House, which was financed by local coal seams and demolished in the 1960s. It can be visited during Edinburgh Doors Open Day (www.doorsopendays.org.uk).

101 The Secret of Gilmerton Cove

EH17 8QH (South & East Suburbs), Gilmerton Cove
beneath 16 Drum Street
Bus 3, 29 to Gilmerton (note: guided tours
by appointment only)

The suburb of Gilmerton lies four miles south east of the centre of Edinburgh and is named after the Gilmour family, the 17th century lairds of Craigmillar Castle. Originally a separate village, it grew from medieval origins to accommodate local coal miners and quarrymen. They are long gone now and few would make a special journey here were it not for Gilmerton Cove, an extraordinary subterranean complex beneath a former miner's cottage at 16 Drum Street (EH17).

The Cove consists of a 40 foot long tunnel off which branch seven chambers, all hand-carved from the sandstone bedrock on which this part of the village stands. The chambers contain what appear to be rock-hewn benches and tables. What makes the place really mysterious is that no-one really knows when, by whom or for what purpose. Since 2003 visitors have been able to don a hard hat and explore this mysterious place for themselves courtesy of the Gilmerton Heritage Trust.

No-one really knows
who excavated
Gilmerton Cove

An early explanation for the Cove is that in 1719 a local blacksmith called George Paterson began excavating it as an underground dwelling and workshop. It is said to have taken him five years although it seems unlikely that one man could have done such work alone. The features traditionally identified as his forge and fireplace show no signs of burning and the only record relating to Paterson is a church summons for allowing alcohol to be consumed in the Cove on the Sabbath. It therefore seems more likely that Paterson took a pre-existing underground complex and adapted it for use as a secret drinking den. The benches and tables are certainly grouped like those in a pub and the well-like feature in the floor could have been a sump to soak up spilt drinks.

If this theory is correct then what was the original function of the Cove? Considering the longstanding connection of Gilmerton with mining, it seems more likely that the chambers were trial bores to see whether coal or other minerals were present. The chisel marks on the walls suggest a possible date in the first half of the 17th century after which the chambers were presumably abandoned because nothing was found.

Such a prosaic explanation has not prevented many other functions being attributed to the Cove. After Paterson's death it allegedly became a place of illicit activity, as really happened with Edinburgh's South Bridge Vaults (see no. 33). These range from an illegal whisky distillery and smugglers' hideout to a meeting place for the Hellfire Club, an association of wealthy young men notorious for their orgies and candlelit pagan rituals. Others have suggested that the word 'Cove' points to its use as a coven during the time when witches were persecuted or as a refuge for the Covenanters, who were hunted down for opposing the meddling of the Stewart kings in the affairs of the Scottish Church. This abundance of theories, however, only really serves to highlight the fact that the Cove contains no real archaeological evidence making accurate dating impossible.

Undoubtedly the most far-fetched theory concerns a Freemasons' compass symbol carved on one of the stone tables. Fans of *The Da Vinci Code* have excitedly conjectured that it supports the possibility that a blocked tunnel in the Cove connects with Rosslyn Chapel to the south, where more symbols pertaining to the Knights Templar have been found. But as the tunnel points north, Craigmillar Castle is a more likely though still extremely far-fetched candidate (see no. 100). Either way since the tunnel cannot be unblocked for fear the road above it will collapse, this is another secret the Cove will keep to itself.

102 From a Tick to a Giant Turtle

EH9 3JT (South & East Suburbs), the Natural History Collections of the University of Edinburgh in the Ashworth Laboratories of the King's Buildings Campus on Charlotte Auerbach Road
Bus 24, 42 to King's Buildings; 41 to Royal Observatory; 3, 8, 29, 31, 37 to Lady Road then walk along Esslemont Road (note: visits by appointment only)

East of Blackford Hill on West Mains Road (EH9) is the King's Buildings Campus of the University of Edinburgh. Here in the Ashworth Laboratories on Charlotte Auerbach Road can be found the Natural History Collections of the University of Edinburgh, one of the city's least known museums.

One of Phyllis Bone's zoological roundels depicting a bison

The Ashworth Laboratories are easy to identify because the façade is adorned with 17 zoological roundels by Phyllis Bone (1894–1972), the first female sculptor admitted to the Royal Scottish Academy. Three roundels – a dung beetle, an octopus and a crab – represent invertebrates, whilst all the other 14 are vertebrates and represent the principal zoogeographical regions (Palaearctic: reindeer, golden eagle, polar bear; Nearctic: beaver, bison; Ethiopian (Afrotropical): aardvark, chimpanzee, lion; Oriental (Indomalaya): Indian elephant, rhinoceros, tiger; and Australia, New Zealand and South America: kangaroo, sphenodon lizards, and nine-banded armadillo respectively). The same taxonomic framework was used to arrange the extraordinary collection inside the building, which includes everything from a tick to the shell of a giant turtle.

The story of the collection begins in 1692, when Robert Sibbald (1641–1722), Edinburgh's first professor of Medicine, presented a collection of natural history specimens to the University. Displayed in what is known today as the Old College on South Bridge (EH8), it was one of Britain's first museums and predated the founding of the British

Museum by 60 years. Successive professors then chopped and changed the collection until 1812, when Robert Jameson (1774–1854) moved it into what is now the Talbot Rice Gallery.

By the time Jameson died the collection numbered 74,000 specimens and it was decided to install it in a new custom-built museum, which is today the National Museum of Scotland on Chambers Street (EH1) (see no. 35). Disagreements between the museum and university authorities, however, saw the the museum appoint its own curator and the university begin assembling a new collection from scratch.

By the early 20th centrury the Old College was deemed inadequate not only for this new collection but also for teaching and research. This prompted one of the professors, J. Harley Ashworth, to make an appeal to the John D. Rockefeller International Education Board in America. The resulting funds permitted the construction of a new Department of Zoology, which opened as the Ashworth Laboratories in 1929. Considered as having the most advanced facilities at the time, the building featured a teaching museum alongside the main teaching laboratory, with large north-facing windows ideal for microscopy and a special ceiling to reduce harmful ultraviolet light. The need to increase laboratory space in the 1950s, however, saw the museum relocated to other parts of the building and the larger vertebrate specimens discarded. Fortunately hundreds of fascinating specimens remained, including a world class coral collection amassed during an expedition to the Great Barrier Reef in 1928.

Over the last 30 years, with the emphasis of biological teaching shifting to the cellular and molecular level, the collection has been reappraised. In 1987 the invertebrate collection was reorganised to demonstrate the evolution and diversity of such organisms and the part they play in the planet's ecology. A decade later the vertebrate collection was redisplayed and named in honour of Aubrey Manning, Professor of Natural History (1973–1997). The entire collection has also been digitised so that those unable to visit can now view the museum virtually.

The Natural History Collections of the University of Edinburgh remain an active teaching and research collection so visits are normally by appointment only (www.nhc.ed.ac.uk). They are, however, open on University Open Days and during Edinburgh Doors Open Day, when buildings not normally accessible to the public are opened (www.doorsopendays.org.uk).

Other locations nearby: 103

103 High on Blackford Hill

EH9 3HJ (South & East Suburbs), the Royal Observatory
Edinburgh Visitor Centre on Observatory Road
Bus 24 to Blackford Avenue or 41 to Royal Observatory
then walk up Observatory Road; 3, 8, 29, 31, 37 to Lady
Road then walk along Esslemont Road/West Mains Road
(note: Public Astronomy Evenings by appointment only)

High on Blackford Hill between Morningside and Liberton are the remains of an ancient hillfort. It is not too fanciful to think that prehistoric people clambered up here to gaze at the stars. Certainly professional astronomers have been doing so since 1896, when the Royal Observatory Edinburgh (ROE) relocated here from Calton Hill. With the added interest of panoramic views, geological formations and a nature reserve, an ascent of Blackford Hill is well worth the effort.

A combination of chronic underfunding and encroaching light pollution prompted the ROE to relocate to Blackford Hill (see no. 64). Instrumental in the move was James Lindsay, 26th Earl of Crawford (1847–1913), a former president of the Royal Astonomical Society, who offered to donate his own astronomical instruments and library on condition a new observatory be built.

The Royal Observatory Edinburgh on Blackford Hill

The new building comprised two copper-roofed observatories, one containing a refractor telescope and the other a reflector. As in the old observatory, a highly accurate clock was used to control the time ball at the top of the Nelson Monument on Calton Hill, to which it was connected by a telegraph wire, as was the One O'Clock Gun at Edinburgh Castle. Both are now triggered manually.

During the 20th century, the ROE increasingly outsourced its observational activities and concentrated instead on stellar photography, teaching and telescope construction. The original Victorian observatories remain though and the one containing a 36-inch reflector installed in 1930 forms part of the official tour. The observatory staff are keen to engage public interest in their activities and offer popular astronomy evenings throughout the year by appointment and lectures during the winter months (www.roe.ac.uk).

The stars aside, Blackford Hill is criss-crossed by footpaths offering panoramas not only of the city but also the Pentland Hills and the Firth of Forth. Geologically speaking, together with the Braid Hills to the south, Blackford Hill is formed from the oldest rocks in Edinburgh, namely Lower Devonian lavas quite different to the Carboniferous volcanic plugs that form Edinburgh's other hills (see no. 96). Of particular interest is Agassiz Rock towards Blackford Glen Road. This is named after a Swiss geologist, Louis Agassiz (1807–1873), who came here in 1840 and identified the first physical evidence for glacial action in Scotland. The visibly-scoured rock is today used for bouldering.

On the southern flank of Blackford Hill is the Hermitage of Braid and Blackford Hill Local Nature Reserve. It encompasses 60 hectares of diverse protected habitat from high open grassland down to the ancient wooded gorge of the Braid Burn, which rises in the Pentland Hills and joins the Figgate Burn at Duddingston (see no. 99). Some of Edinburgh's oldest trees are here, attracting woodpeckers, kestrels and tawny owls, the riverbanks home to kingfishers, herons and otters.

The area is steeped in history beginning in the 12th century, when the Braid estate was acquired by the de Brad family. Henri de Brad was Sheriff of Edinburgh and hunted deer and wild boar here. In the 18th century the estate was purchased by Charles Gordon of Cluny (1738–1814), who famously refused to get out of bed because he couldn't afford to! Despite this in 1775 he commissioned the architect Robert Burn (1752–1815) to design the castellated Hermitage House, which was completed in 1788. The building was presented to the City in 1937 and serves today as a visitor centre. Its walled garden, dovecote, ice house and water pump are all still intact.

Other locations nearby: 102

*   *   *

"Reikie, fareweel! I ne'er cou'd part
Wi' thee but wi' a dowy heart."
(Robert Fergusson, 1750–74, from *Auld Reikie, a Poem*)

Opening Times

Correct at time of going to press but may be subject to change.

Several of the places listed below can be visited during Edinburgh Doors Open Day, when buildings not normally accessible to the public are opened by the Cockburn Association, Edinburgh's Civic Trust (www.doorsopendays.org.uk).

21st century Kilts (EH2), 48 Thistle Street, Tue–Sat 10am–6pm (appointments recommended)

Abbotsford (EH2), 3–5 Rose Street, Mon–Thu & Sun 11am–11pm, Fri & Sat 11am–12pm

Amarone (EH2), 13 St. Andrew Square, Mon–Fri 8am–10.30pm, Sat & Sun 10am–10.30pm

Anteaques (EH8), 17 Clerk Street, Fri, Sat & Sun 11am–7pm

Apprentice Training Restaurant (EH5), Edinburgh College Granton Campus, 350 West Granton Road, lunch Tue–Fri and dinner Wed & Thu by appointment www.Edinburghcollege.ac.uk

Archivists' Garden (EH1), see Scotland's People Centre

Armchair Books (EH1), 72–74 West Port, daily 10am–6.30pm (later in Aug)

Armstrongs (EH1), 81–83 Grassmarket, Mon–Thu 10am–5.30pm, Fri & Sat 10am–6pm, Sun 12am–6pm

Assembly Rooms (EH2), 54 George Street, during advertised events & Edinburgh Doors Open Day; Jamie's Italian Mon–Thu 12am–10.30pm, Fri & Sat 12am–11pm, Sun 12am–10pm

Avizandum (EH1), 56a Candlemaker Row, Mon–Fri 9.30am–6pm, Sat 10am – 1pm (except Jun–Aug when closed on Sats)

Bagpipes Galore (EH12), 20 Haymarket Terrace, Mon–Fri 10am–5pm, Sat 10am–4pm

Beehive Inn (EH1), 18–20 Grassmarket, Mon–Sat 9am–1am, Sun 12.30am–1am

Bollywood the Coffee Box (EH10), 99a Bruntsfield Place, summer daily 11am–8pm

Borland's (EH7), 7 Croall Place, Mon, Tue, Thu & Fri 10am–5.30pm, Wed 10am–1pm, Sat 10am–4.30pm

Boundary Bar (EH6), 379 Leith Walk, Mon–Thu 12am–11pm, Fri & Sat 12am–1am, Sun 12am–11pm

Bow Bar (EH1), 80 West Bow, Mon–Sat 12am–12pm, Sun 12am–11.30pm

Cadenhead's (EH8), 172 Canongate, Mon–Sat 10.30am–5.30pm

Cadies & Witchery Tours (EH1), 84 West Bow, daily 10.30am–7pm

Café Hub (EH1), Castlehill, Mon–Sat 9.30am–5pm, Sun 10am–5pm

Café Royal (EH2), 19 West Register Street, Sun–Wed 11am–11pm, Thu 11am–12pm, Fri & Sat 11am–1am

Camera Obscura (EH1), Castlehill (Royal Mile), Jul & Aug 9am–9pm, Sep & Oct 9.30am–7pm, Nov–Mar 10am–6pm, Apr–Jun 9. 30am–7pm (last Camera Obscura presentation begins one hour before closing and sometimes earlier in winter)

Canderson's (EH6), 102 Leith Walk, Mon–Sat 10am–5.30pm

Canongate Kirk (EH8), 153 Canongate, May–Sep Mon–Sat usually 11am–4pm, Sun 2–5pm; Kirkyard always open

Central Bar (EH7), 7–9 Leith Walk, daily 11.30am–11pm

Central Library (EH1), George IV Bridge, Mon–Wed 10am–8pm, Thu–Sat 10am–5pm

Chancery of the Order of St. John Scotland (EH8), St. John's House, 21 St. John Street, visits by appointment only tel. 0131 556 8711

Chapel of St. Albert the Great (EH8), 23 George Square, daily 8am–6pm

Church of St. John the Evangelist (EH2), Princes Street, Mon–Fri 9am–4.45pm, Sat Easter–Sep 8am–4pm, Oct–Easter 8–12.30am, Sun Easter–Sep 8am–7pm, Oct–Easter 8am–2pm, 5–7pm

City Art Centre (EH1), 2 Market Street, Mon–Sat 10am–5pm, Sun 12am–5pm

City Dome (EH7), Calton Hill, Apr–Jul & Sep Tue–Sun 10am–5pm, Aug daily 10am–6pm, Oct–Mar Tue–Sun 10am—4pm

City of Edinburgh Methodist Church (EH8), 25 Nicolson Square, Mass Sun 11am & 6.30pm

Cockburn Geological Museum (EH9), Grant Institute, King's Buildings, West Mains Road, visits by appointment only www.ed.ac.uk/geosciences/about/history/museum

Colinton Parish Church (EH13), Dell Road, Mon–Fri 9am–4pm

Conan Doyle (EH1), 71–73 York Place, Sun – Thu 12am–11pm, Fri & Sat 12am–12pm

Contini Cannonball Restaurant (EH1), 356 Castlehill, Tue–Fri 5–10pm, Sat 12am–10pm

Contini Ristorante (EH2), 103 George Street, Mon–Fri 7.30am–11pm, Sat 9am–12pm, Sun 9am–11pm

Corstorphine Heritage Centre (EH12), Dower House, St. Margaret's Park, Wed & Sat 10–12am

Corstorphine Hill Tower (EH12), off Clermiston Road, May–Sep Sun 2–4pm

Corstorphine Hill Walled Garden (EH12), off Clermiston Road, daily 11am–4pm

Corstorphine Old Parish Church (EH12), Kirk Loan, Wed (except Dec & Jan) 10.30–12am

Counter (EH1), Usher Hall, Lothian Road, Mon–Fri 7.30am–3pm, summer Sat 9.30am–3pm

Counter (EH3), Toll Cross, High Riggs, Mon–Fri 7.30am–3pm

Counter (EH3), Lochrin Basin, Union Canal, Tue–Sun 7.30am–3pm

Counter (EH10), 216a Morningside Road, Mon–Fri 7.30am–3pm, Sat 9.30am–3pm

Craigmillar Castle (EH16), Craigmillar Castle Road, Apr–Sep daily 9.30am–5.30pm, Oct–Mar Mon–Wed, Sat & Sun 10am–4pm

Cramond Heritage Trust (EH4), The Maltings, 2 Riverside, Apr–Sep Sat & Sun 2–5pm

Cramond Kirk (EH4), 14 Cramond Glebe Road, summer Thu–Tue 12am–5pm, winter Thu–Sun 12am–5pm

Cranachan and Crowdie (EH8), 263 Canongate, daily 11am–6pm

Crombie (EH2), 63 George Street, Mon–Sat 9.30am–6pm

Deacon's House Café (EH1), 304 Lawnmarket, Brodie's Close, daily 8am–5.30pm

Deadhead Comics (EH1), 47 West Nicolson Street, Tue–Sat 10am–6pm, Sun & Mon half days

Debenhams (EH2), 109 Princes Street, Mon–Wed 9.30am–6pm, Thu 9.30am–8pm, Fri 9.30am–6.30pm, Sat 9am–6.30pm, Sun 11am–6pm

Devil's Advocate (EH1), 9 Advocate's Close, daily 12am–1am, lunch 12am–4pm, dinner 5–10pm

Dig-In (EH10), 119 Bruntsfield Place, Mon–Fri 10am–7pm, Sat 9.30am–5pm

Dome (EH2), 14 George Street, Grill Room daily 12am–12pm, Club Room Mon–Thu 10am–4pm, Fri & Sat 10am–12pm, Georgian Tea Room daily 11am–5pm

Dovecot Studios (EH1), 10 Infirmary Street, Gallery Mon–Sat 10.30am–5.30pm, Tapestry Studio Viewing Balcony Thu & Fri 12am–3pm, Sat 10.30am–5.30pm

Dr. Neil's Garden (EH15), Old Church Lane, daily 10am to dusk; Thomson's Tower Jul & Aug Sun 2–4pm

Drumsheugh Baths Club (EH4), 5 Belford Road, members only Mon–Fri 6.30am–9pm, Sat & Sun 8am–8pm, non-members by appointment only www.drumsheughbaths.com

Edinburgh Books (EH1), 145–147 West Port, Mon–Sat 10am–6pm

Edinburgh Bookshop (EH10), 219 Bruntsfield Place, Mon–Fri 10am–6pm, Sat 9am–6pm, Sun 11am–4pm

Edinburgh Cast Collection (EH3), Edinburgh College of Art, 74 Lauriston Place, daily 9am–5pm (report to reception on arrival)

Edinburgh Castle (EH1), Castlehill, Apr–Sep 9.30am–6pm (last entry 5pm), Oct – Mar 9.30am – 5pm (last entry 4pm)

Edinburgh Central Mosque (EH8), 50 Potterow, daily 9am–7pm guided tours by appointment only www.edmosque.org; Original Mosque Kitchen daily 11.30am–8pm

Edinburgh Centre for Carbon Innovation (EH1), High School Yards, guided tours by appointment only www.Edinburghcentre.org

Edinburgh Farmers' Market (EH1), Castle Terrace, Sat 9am–2pm

Edinburgh Gin Distillery (EH1), 1a Rutland Place, guided tours by appointment only 10am, 12am & 2pm, connoisseurs tour 11am, 1pm & 3pm, gin making 12.15am www.Edinburghgindistillery.co.uk

Edinburgh Hebrew Congregation Synagogue (EH15), 4 Salisbury Road, visits by appointment only www.ehcong.com

Edinburgh Royal Botanic Garden (EH3), Inverleith Row/Arboretum Place, Nov–Feb 10am–4pm, Mar & Oct 10am–6pm, Apr–Sep 10am–7pm (glasshouses close one hour earlier); herbarium & library Mon–Fri 10am–4pm

Edinburgh Sculpture Workshop (EH6), 21 Hawthornvale, exhibitions and tours www.Edinburghsculpture.org

Edinburgh Trades (EH3), Ashfield, 61 Melville Street, by appointment only www.Edinburghtrades.org

EH15 Training Restaurant (EH15), Edinburgh College Milton Road Campus, 24 Milton Road East, lunch Tue–Fri, dinner Tue, Wed & Thu by appointment only www.Edinburghcollege.ac.uk

Elephant House (EH1), 21 George IV Bridge, Mon–Thu 8am–10pm Fri 8am–11pm, Sat 9am–11pm, Sun 9am–10pm

Elvis Shakespeare (EH6), 347 Leith Walk, Mon–Sat 10am–6pm, Sun summer only

Fabhatrix (EH1), 13 Cowgatehead, Mon–Fri 10.30am–6pm, Sat 10.30am–5.30pm, Sun 12am–5pm

Falko Konditormeister (EH10), 185 Bruntsfield Place, Wed–Sat 9am–6pm, Sun 9.30am–6pm

Fruitmarket Gallery (EH1), 45 Market Street, Mon–Sat 11am–6pm, Sun 12am–5pm

Gardener's Cottage (EH7), 1 Royal Terrace Gardens, London Road, Mon, Wed–Fri 5–10pm, Sat & Sun 10am–2.30pm, 5–10pm

George Hughes Fishmongers (EH10), 197 Bruntsfield Place, Tue–Fri 8am–5.30pm, Sat 8am–3pm

Georgian Antiques (EH6), 10 Pattison Street, Mon–Fri 8.30am–5.30pm, Sat 10am–2pm

Georgian House (EH2), 7 Charlotte Square, 1–23 Mar & Nov daily 11am–4pm, 24 Mar–Jun, Sep & Oct daily 10am–5pm, Jul & Aug daily 10am–6pm, 1–18 Dec Thu–Sun 11am–4pm (last admission 45 minutes before closing)

Gilmerton Cove (EH17), 16 Drum Street, guided tours daily 10am–4pm by appointment only www.gilmertoncove.org.uk

Gladstone's Land (EH1), 477b Lawnmarket, end Mar –Oct, 10am–5pm (last entry 4.30pm)

Glenogle Baths (EH3), Glenogle Road, Mon–Fri 7am–10pm, Sat & Sun 8am–6pm

Golden Hare Books (EH3), 68 St. Stephen's Street, daily 10am–6pm

Golf Tavern (EH10), 30–31 Wright's Houses, Mon–Fri 11am–1am, Sat & Sun 9.30am–1am

Grand Lodge of Scotland and Freemasons' Hall (EH2), 96 George Street, guided tours by appointment only Mon – Fri 10am & 2pm www.grandlodgescotland.com

Grassmarket Weekly Market (EH1), Grassmarket, Sat 10am–5pm

Halfway House (EH1), 24 Fleshmarket Close, daily 11am–11pm

Greyfriars Kirk, Kirkyard & Museum (EH1), Greyfriars Place, Apr–Oct Mon–Fri 10.30am–4.30pm, Sat 11am–2pm, Mass Sun

Hermitage House Visitor Centre (EH10), Braid Road, Mon–Fri 9am–4pm, Sun 12am–4pm

Easter Road Stadium (EH7), Albion Place, tours by appointment only www.hibernianfc.co.uk

Hindu Mandir (EH6), St. Andrew Place, Mon–Sat 9.30–11.30am, 6–8pm, Sun 11am–2pm

History of Education Centre (EH7), Leith Walk Primary School, 9 Brunswick Road, Mon, Tue, Wed & Thu by appointment only www.histedcentre.org.uk

Holyrood Abbey (EH8), see Palace of Holyroodhouse

I. J. Mellis Cheesemonger (EH1), 30a Victoria Street, Mon–Wed 9.30am–6pm, Thu–Sat 9.30am–7pm, Sun 11am–5pm

James Clerk Maxwell Foundation (EH3), 14 India Street, tours Mon–Fri 10–12.30am, 2–5pm by appointment only www.clerkmaxwellfoundation.org

Jenners (EH2), 48 Princes Street, Mon–Wed 9.30am–6.30pm, Thu 9.30am–8pm, Fri 9.30am–7pm, Sat 9am–7pm, Sun 11am–6pm

Jinglin' Geordie (EH1), 22 Fleshmarket, Mon & Tue 11am–10pm, Wed 11am–11pm, Thu–Sat 11am–1am, Sun 12.30am–8pm

John Knox House and Scottish Storytelling Centre (EH1), 43–45 High Street, Mon–Sat 10am–6pm, Sun (Jul & Aug only) 12am–6pm

John Morrison Kiltmakers (EH1), 63 High Street, Mon – Sat 9am–5.30pm

Kagyu Samye Dzong Tibetan Buddhist Meditation Centre (EH6), 25 Bernard Street www.Edinburgh.samye.org

Kay's Bar (EH3), 39 Jamaica Street, Mon–Thu 11am–12pm, Fri & Sat 11am–1am, Sun 12.30am–11pm

Kinloch Anderson (EH6), 4 Dock Street, Leith, Mon – Sat 9am–5.30pm

Kleen Cleaners (EH1), 10 St. Mary's Street, Mon–Fri 8.30am–5.30pm, Sat 10am–4pm

Lady Haig's Poppy Factory (EH7), 9 Warriston Road, guided tours Mon–Fri from 10am by appointment only www.ladyhaigspoppyfactory.org.uk

Lauriston Castle (EH4), 2a Cramond Road South, guided tours of the interior only Apr–Oct Mon–Thu 2pm, Sat & Sun 2pm, Nov–Mar Sat & Sun 2pm; gardens Apr–Sep 8am–8pm, Oct–Mar 8am–5pm

Leith Athletics (EH6), 208–210 Leith Walk, Mon–Sat 9am–5pm

Leith Barbers (EH6), 1 Great Junction Street, Mon–Fri 8am–5pm, Sat 8am–4pm

Leith Dockers Club (EH6), 17 Academy Street, Mon–Thu 11am–12pm, Fri & Sat 11am–1am, Sun 10am–12pm

Leith Market (EH6), Dock Place, Sun 10am–5pm

Library of Mistakes (EH4), 4a Wemyss Place Mews, visits and dinner parties by appointment only www.libraryofmistakes.com

Lickety Splits (EH1), 6 Jeffrey Street, Mon–Sat 10am–6pm, Sun 12am–5pm

Magdalen Chapel (EH1), 41 Cowgate, Tue, Thu & Fri 10.30am–2.30pm

Mansfield Traquair Centre (EH3), 15 Mansfield Place, 2nd Sun each month 1–4pm

McNaughtan's (EH7), 3a Haddington Place, Tue–Sat 11am–5pm

Meadowbank Stadium Antique & Collectors Fair (EH7), 139–143 London Road, first Sun each month 10am–4pm

Mermaid (EH6), 43–45 Leith Walk, Mon–Fri 11.30am–1.30pm, 4.30–11.55pm, Sat 3.30–11.55pm, Sun 4.30–11.55pm

Milne's Bar (EH2), 35 Hanover Street, Mon–Thu & Sun 11am–11pm, Fri & Sat 11am–1am

Mosque Kitchen (EH8), 31–33 Nicolson Square, daily 11.30am–10pm

Mousetrap (EH6), 180 Leith Walk, daily 2pm–1am

Mr. Wood's Fossils (EH1), 5 Cowgatehead, Mon–Sat 10am–5.30pm (Sun 10am–5.30pm Jul, Aug & Dec only)

Murrayfield Stadium (EH12), Roseburn Street, tours by appointment only www.scottishrugby.org

Museums Collection Centre (EH3), 10 Broughton Market, guided tours first Tue of the month at 2pm

Museum of Boxing (EH6), Leith Victoria Athletic Club, 28 Academy Street, visits by appointment www. leithvictoriaaac.com

Museum of Childhood (EH1), 42 High Street (Royal Mile), Mon–Sat 10am–5pm, Sun 12am–5pm

Museum of Edinburgh (EH8), Huntly House, 142 Canongate, Mon–Sat 10am–5pm, Sun 12am–5pm (Aug only)

Museum of Fire (EH3), 76–78 Lauriston Place, Mon–Fri 10am–4pm, tours by appointment only tel. 0131 228 2401

Museum on the Mound (EH1), North Bank Street, Tue–Fri 10am–5pm, Sat & Sun 1–5pm

Napiers the Herbalists (EH1), 18 Bristo Place, Mon 10am–6pm, Tue–Fri 9.30am–6pm, Sat 9.30am–5.30pm, Sun 12am–5pm

National Library of Scotland (EH1), George IV Bridge, Mon, Tue, Thu & Fri 9.30am–8.30pm, Wed 10am–8.30pm, Sat 9.30am–1pm

National Museum of Scotland (EH1), Chambers Street, daily 10am–5pm; Tower Restaurant daily 10am–11pm

National Museums Collection Centre (EH5), 242 West Granton Road, visits by appointment only www.nms.ac.uk

Natural History Collections of the University of Edinburgh (EH9), King's Buildings Campus, Ashworth Laboratories, Charlotte Auerbach Road, visits by appointment only www. nhc.ed.ac.uk

Nelson Monument (EH7), Calton Hill, Apr–Sep Mon–Sat 10am–7pm, Sun 12am–5pm, Oct–Mar Mon–Sat 10am–3pm

Newington Cemetery (EH9), Dalkeith Road, daily all hours

Nobles (EH6), 44a Constitution Street, Mon–Fri 12am–1am, Sat & Sun 10am–1am

Old Calton Burial Ground (EH1), 27 Waterloo Place, daily all hours

Old Children's Bookshelf (EH1), 175 Canongate, Mon–Fri 10.30am–5pm, Sat 10am–5pm, Sun 11am–4.30pm

Old St. Paul's Church Scottish Episcopal Church (EH1), Carruber's Close off High Street/63 Jeffrey Street, Mon–Fri 9am–5pm

Old Town Bookshop (EH1), 8 Victoria Street, Mon–Sat 10.30am–5.30pm

Our Dynamic Earth (EH8), Holyrood Road, 23 Mar–Oct daily 10am–5.30pm, Jul & Aug 10am–6pm, Nov–22 Mar, Wed–Sun 10am–5.30pm

Out of the Blue Flea Market (EH6), Dalmeny Street Drill Hall, last Sat each month 10am–3pm

Over Langshaw Farmhouse Ice Cream (EH1), junction of Grassmarket and West Bow, summer Easter–Sep 9am–5pm

Oxford Bar (EH2), 8 Young Street, daily 11am–1am

Palace of Holyroodhouse (EH8), Canongate, 26 Mar–31 Oct daily 9.30am–6pm (last admission 4.30pm), 1 Nov–25 Mar daily 9.30am–4.30pm (last admission 3.15pm); Holyrood Abbey Apr–Oct; Queen's Gallery 26 Mar–31 Oct daily 9.30am–6pm (last admission 5pm), 1 Nov–25 Mar daily 9.30am–4.30pm (last admission 3.30pm)

Parliament Hall (EH1), Parliament House, 11 Parliament Square, Mon–Fri 10am–4pm

Patrick Geddes Centre (EH1), Riddle's Court, 322 Lawnmarket, opening summer 2017, www. patrickgeddescentre.org.uk

People's Story Museum (EH8), 163 Canongate, Mon–Sat 10am–5pm, Sun (only during the Edinburgh Festival) 12am–5pm

Peter Bell Books (EH1), 68 West Port, Tue–Fri 2–5pm, Sat 11.30am–5pm

Piershill Cemetery (EH8), Portobello Road, daily all hours

Polwarth Parish Church (EH11), 36–38 Polwarth Terrace, Mar–Nov Wed 11am–3pm

Port O'Leith (EH6), 58 Constitution Street, Mon–Fri 11am–1am, Sat 9am–1am, Sun 12am–1am

Portobello Swim Centre (EH15), 57 The Promenade, Mon–Fri 7am–10pm, Sat 9am–4pm, Sun 9am–6pm; Turkish Bath Mon 12am–9.15pm, Tue–Fri 8am–9.15pm, Sat 9.30am–3.30 pm, Sun 9.30am–5pm

Ramsay Cornish Vintage Lane Sale (EH6), 15–17 Jane Street, Thu 11am (viewing 9.30–11am); weekly General Furnishings & Collectibles auction, bi-monthly specialist Antiques auction, quarterly Silver & Jewellery auction all Sat 11am (viewing Fri 9.30am–5pm & Sat 9.30–11am)

Real Mary King's Close (EH1), 2 High Street, guided tours only Mar 25–Oct 1 daily 10am–9pm, Nov 1–Mar 24 Sun–Thu 10am–5pm, Fri & Sat 10am–9pm

Redhall Walled Garden (EH14), 97 Lanark Road, Mon–Fri 9am–4pm

Robin Chapel (EH16), Craigmillar Castle Avenue, Choral Evensong Sun 4pm

Rosebank Cemetery (EH6), 104 Pilrig Street, open all hours

Royal Bank of Scotland (EH2), Dundas House, 36 St. Andrew Square, Mon, Tue, Thu & Fri 8.30am–5.30pm, Wed 9.30am–5.30pm, Sat 9am–4pm

Royal College of Physicians of Edinburgh (EH2), 9 Queen Street, New Library Mon–Fri 9.30am–5pm by appointment only tel. 0131 225 7324

Royal Commonwealth Pool (EH16), Dalkeith Road, Mon–Fri 5.30am–10pm, Sat 5.30am–8pm, Sun 7.30am–8pm

Royal Dick (EH9), 1 Summerhall, Mon – Sat 12am–1am, Sun 12.30am–12pm

Royal Edinburgh Community Gardens (EH10), Morningside Terrace, Tue, Wed & Fri 10am–4pm

Royal Oak (EH1), 1 Infirmary Street, Mon–Sat 11.30am–2am, Sun 12.30am–2am; Rebus Tours depart Sat 12am

Royal Observatory Edinburgh Visitor Centre (EH9), Blackford Hill View, Public Astronomy Evenings May–Sep one Fri each month 7.30–9pm, Oct–Apr each Fri 6.30–7.30pm & 8–9pm by appointment only www.roe.ac.uk; Winter Talks Oct–Mar Mon 7.30–8.30pm

Royal Overseas League (EH2), 100 Princes Street, Afternoon Tea daily 2–4pm by appointment only www.rosl. org.uk

Royal Scottish Academy (EH2), The Mound, Mon–Sat 10am–5pm, Sun 12am–5pm

Royal Yacht Britannia (EH6), Leith Docks, Ocean Drive, Ocean Terminal, Jan–20 Mar 10am–3.30pm, 21 Mar–31 Mar 9.30am–4pm, Apr–Sep 9.30am–4.30pm, Oct 9.30am–4pm, Nov & Dec 10am–3.30pm

RZSS Edinburgh Zoo (EH12), 134 Corstorphine Road, Apr–Sep 9am–6pm, Oct & Mar 9am–5pm, Nov–Feb 9am–4.30pm

S. Luca (EH10), 16 Morningside Road, daily 9am–10pm

Scotch Whisky Experience (EH1), 354 Castlehill, Jan–Mar & Sep–Dec 10am–5pm, Apr – Aug 10am – 6pm

Scotlands People Centre (EH1), General Register House at 2 Princes Street and New Register House at 3 West Register Street, Mon–Fri 9am–4.30pm

Scott Monument (EH2), East Princes Street Gardens, Apr–Sep daily 10am–7pm, Oct–Mar daily 10am–4pm (last entry 3.30pm)

Scottish Geneaology Centre (EH1), 15 Victoria Terrace, Mon, Tue, Thu & Fri 10.30am–5.30pm, Wed 10.30am–7.30pm, Sat 10am–5pm

Scottish Mineral and Lapidary Club (EH6), 16–20 Maritime Lane, www. lapidary.org.uk

Scottish National Gallery (EH2), The Mound, daily 10am–5pm (Thu 7pm); Scottish Café & Restaurant Mon–Sat 9am–5pm (Thu 7pm), Sun 10am–5pm

Scottish National Gallery of Modern Art (EH4), 75 Belford Road, daily 10am–5pm (extended hours in Aug)

Scottish National Portrait Gallery (EH2), 1 Queen Street, daily 10am–5pm (Thu 7pm)

Scottish Parliament (EH99), Horse Wynd at the foot of the Canongate, Mon, Fri & Sat 10am–5pm (last entry 4.30pm), Tue, Wed & Thu 9am–6.30pm (last entry 6pm); when Parliament is in recess (excluding Feb recess & Christmas, when the building is closed to the public) open Tue, Wed & Thu 10am–5pm (last entry 4.30pm)

Scottish Pictures (EH1), 64 West Port, Wed–Sat 10am–5pm

Scottish Poetry Library (EH8), 5 Crichton's Close, Tue–Fri 10am–5pm (Thu 7pm), Sat 10am–4pm

Scottish Storytelling Centre (EH1), 43–45 High Street, Mon–Sat 10am–6pm, Sun (Jul & Aug only) 12am–6pm

Serenity Café (EH8), 8 Jackson's Entry, daily 9am–7pm

Sheep Heid Inn (EH15), 43–45 The Causeway, Mon–Thu 11am–11pm, Fri & Sat 11am–12pm, Sun 12.30am–11pm

Sheila Fleet (EH3), 18 St. Stephen Street, Mon–Sat 10am–5.30pm

Signet Library Colonnades (EH1), Parliament Square, lunch Mon–Fri 11am–1.30pm Afternoon Tea Mon–Fri 1–7pm, Sun 11am–7pm (last booking 5pm) by appointment only www.signetlibrary.co.uk

Sir Arthur Conan Doyle Centre (EH12), 25 Palmerston Place, Mon–Thu 10am–9pm

Songkran Thai Restaurant (EH3), 8 Gloucester Street, daily 5.45–12pm

Souped Up (EH8), 22a St. Patrick Square, daily 8.45am–5.15pm

South Bridge Vaults (EH1), Mercat Tours, 28 Blair Street, self-guided tours by appointment only Apr–Oct daily 10.30 & 11.30am, Nov–Mar Sat & Sun 10.30 & 11.30am www.mercattours.com

South Leith Parish Church (EH6), Kirkgate, Mass Sun 11am, Thu 1pm

Spoon (EH8), 6a Nicolson Street (EH8), Mon–Sat 10am–11pm, Sun 12am–5pm

St. Andrew's & St. George's West Church (EH2), 13 George Street, Mon–Fri 10am–3pm, Sat 11am–2pm, Sun Mass 9, 9.45 & 11am

St. Cecilia's Hall (EH1), Niddry Street, www.ed.ac.uk

St. Cuthbert's Episcopal Church (EH13), Westgarth Avenue, Mass Sun 10.30am

St. Cuthbert's Parish Church (EH1), 5 Lothian Road, Tue–Thu 10am–3pm, (Easter–Sep usually Fri–Mon)

St. Giles' Cathedral (EH1), High Street (Royal Mile), May–Sep Mon–Fri 9am–7pm, Sat 9am–5pm, Sun 1–5pm, Oct–Apr Mon–Sat 9am–5pm, Sun 1–5pm; Thistle Chapel Mon–Sat 10am–4pm, Sun 1–5pm; rooftop tours by appointment from 10am stgilestower@gmail.com

St. Mary's Metropolitan Cathedral (EH1), Picardy Place, Mon–Fri 8.30am–6.30pm, Sat 8.30am–7pm, Sun 8.30am–8.30pm

St. Triduana's Chapel & St. Margaret's Parish Church (EH7), 176 Restalrig Road South, Mon & Fri 9am–5pm, Sun 11.30–12am by appointment only www.stmargarets-restalrig.com; Church of St. Margaret's Restalrig, Mass Sun 10.30am

St. Vincent's Chapel (EH3), St. Vincent Street, Mass Sun 10.30am

Stills: Centre for Photography (EH1), 23 Cockburn Street, Mon–Thu 11am–9pm, Fri & Sat 11am–6pm

Stockbridge Market (EH3), Kerr Street, Sun 10am–5pm

Storries (EH6), 279 Leith Walk, all hours

Summerhall Distillery and Pickering's Gin (EH9), 1 Summerhall, guided tours by appointment only Mon–Fri 2pm, 4pm & 6pm, Sat & Sun 2.30pm, 4pm & 6pm www.pickeringsgin.com

Surgeons' Hall Museums (EH8), Nicolson Street, daily 10am–5pm (last admission 4.30pm)

Talbot Rice Gallery (EH8), University of Edinburgh, Old College, South Bridge, open during exhibitions only www.ed.ac.uk/talbot-rice

Tartan Weaving Mill & Exhibition (EH1), 555 Castlehill, daily 9am–5.30pm

Those Were the Days (EH3), 26 St. Stephen Street, Mon–Wed, Fri & Sat 11am–6pm, Thu 11am–7.30pm, Sun 12am–5pm

Tram Stop Market (EH1), Picardy Place, Sat 11am–6pm

Transreal Fiction (EH1), 46 Candlemaker Row, Mon–Fri 11am–6pm, Sat 10am–6pm

Trinity Apse (EH1), Chalmers Close off High Street, by appointment only www.Edinburghmuseums.org.uk

Trinity House Maritime Museum (EH6), 99 Kirkgate, Mon–Fri tours by appointment only www.trinityhouse-leith.org.uk

Tupiniquim (EH1), Lauriston Place, Mon–Sat 10am–6pm

Tynecastle Stadium (EH11), McLeod Street, tours by appointment only www.heartsfc.co.uk

University of Edinburgh Anatomical Museum (EH8), Edinburgh Medical School, Teviot Place, Doorway 3, last Sat each month 10am–4pm (closed Jun, Jul & Dec)

University of Edinburgh Main Library (EH8), 30 George Square, daily 7.30am–2.30am

Valvona & Crolla Delicatessen (EH7), 19 Elm Row, Mon–Thu 8.30am–6pm, Fri & Sat 8am–6.30pm, Sun 10am–5pm

Vine Trust Barge (EH6), Prince of Wales Dock, visits by appointment only www.vinetrust.org

War Poets Collection (EH14), Craiglockhart Campus, Edinburgh Napier University, 219 Colinton Road, Trimester 1 & 2 (Sep–Apr) Mon–Thu 8.45am–9pm, Fri 8.45am–8pm, Sat & Sun 10am–4pm, Trimester 3 (May–Aug) Mon–Thu 8.45 am–7pm, Fri 8.45am–5pm, Sat 10am–4pm

Warrender Baths (EH9), 55 Thirlestane Road, Mon–Fri 7am–10pm, Sat 8.30am–6pm, Sun 9am–6pm

Waverley Market (EH1), Edinburgh Waverley railway station, Calton Road, Fri 11am–7pm

Wedgwood (EH8), 267 Canongate, lunch Mon–Sat 12am–3pm, Sun 12.30am–3pm, dinner daily 6–12pm

West Port Garden (EH1), Grassmarket, Sun 2–4pm

Whiski Rooms (EH1), 4–7 North Bank Street, visits by appointment www.whiskirooms.co.uk

White Hart Inn (EH1), 34 Grassmarket, Mon–Fri 11am–11pm, Sat & Sun 11am–12pm

White Horse Inn (EH8), 266 Canongate, Mon–Sat 11am until late, Sun 12.30am until late

Wm. Christie (EH10), 186 Bruntsfield Place, Mon–Fri 8am–5pm, Sat 8am–3.30pm

Word Power Books (EH8), 43–45 West Nicolson Street, Mon–Sat 10am–6pm, Sun 12am–5pm

Writers' Museum (EH1), Lady Stair's Close off the Lawnmarket, Mon–Sat 10am–5pm, Sun (Aug only) 12am–5pm

Bibliography

GUIDEBOOKS

The Literary Traveller in Edinburgh (Allan Foster), Mainstream Publishing, 2005

Edinburgh on Foot (Richard Hallewell), Hallewell Pocket Walks, 2016

The Filthy Guide to the Edinburgh Fringe (Paul Levy), CreateSpace Independent Publishing Platform, 2015

Arthur's Seat: Journeys and Evocations (Stuart McHardy & Donald Smith), Luath Press, 2012

Calton Hill: Journeys and Evocations (Stuart McHardy), Luath Press, 2013

Edinburgh & Leith Pub Guide (Stuart McHardy), Luath Press, 2008

Scotland's Democracy Trail (Stuart McHardy & Donald Smith), Luath Press, 2014

A Walk Down Edinburgh's Royal Mile (Eric Melvin), CreateSpace Independent Publishing Platform, 2014

A Walk Through Edinburgh's New Town (Eric Melvin), CreateSpace Independent Publishing Platform, 2014

Locals' Guide to Edinburgh (Owen O'Leary), Oh Really Creative t/a Word of Mouth Travels, 2013

Rough Guide Directions: Edinburgh (Donald Reid), Rough Guides, 2008

The Civilized Shopper's Guide To Edinburgh And Glasgow (June Skinner Sawyers), Little Bookroom, 2008

CAMRA's Edinburgh Pub Walks (Bob Steel), CAMRA Books, 2010

The Edinburgh Castle Guide (C. J. Tabraham), Historic Scotland, 2003

Edinburgh Graveyard Guide (Michael Turnbull), Scottish Cultural Press, 2006

Eyewitness Edinburgh Pocket Map & Guide (Various), Dorling Kindersley, 2015

Time Out Edinburgh (Various), Time Out, 2015

Wallpaper City Guide (Various), Wallpaper, 2014

Lonely Planet Pocket Guide Edinburgh (Neil Wilson), Lonely Planet, 2014

Companion Guide Edinburgh (A. J. Youngson), Companion Guides, 2001

SECRET AND UNUSUAL Edinburgh

Hidden Gardens of the Royal Mile (Jean Bareham), Green Yonder Tours, 2011

Secret Edinburgh (Jack Gillon), Amberley Publishing, 2015

Edinburgh: City of the Dead (Jan-Andrew Henderson), Black and White Publishing, 2010

Black Markers: Edinburgh's Dark History Told Through its Cemeteries (Jan-Andrew Henderson), Amberley Publishing, 2015

An Edinburgh Companion (Herb Lester Associates), 2014

Haunted Edinburgh (Alan Murdy), The History Press, 2007

Secret Edinburgh: An Unusual Guide (Hannah Robinson), Jonglez, 2016

Curious Edinburgh (Michael T. R. B. Turnbull), The History Press, 2005

Edinburgh Curiosities (James U. Thomson), John Donald, 2004

SUBTERRANEAN Edinburgh

Edinburgh Rock: The Geology of Lothian (Euan Clarkson & Brian Upton), Dunedin Academic Press, 2013

The Town Below The Ground: Edinburgh's Legendary Underground City (Jan-Andrew Henderson), Mainstream, 1999

ART AND ARCHITECTURE

Edinburgh Street Furniture (David Brandon), Amberley Publishing, 2011

Edinburgh New Town: A Model City (Michael Carley, Robert Dalziel, Pat Dargan & Simon Laird, Amberley Publishing, 2015)

Lost Edinburgh: Edinburgh's Lost Architectural Heritage (Hamish Coghill), Birlinn, 2008

The Buildings of Scotland: Edinburgh (John Gifford et al), Yale University Press, 1984

Vanishing Edinburgh and Leith. Being a Pictorial Record of Some of the Historical and Picturesque Buildings in the Streets, Closes and District of these Two Ancient Burghs (L Ingleby Wood), William J. Hay, 1903

Edinburgh Waverley Station Through Time (Michael Meighan), Amberley Publishing, 2014

Edinburgh: A Guide to Recent Architecture (Johnny Rogers), Batsford, 2002

Look Up Edinburgh: World Class Architectural Detail from the City of Turrets, Gables and Towers (Adrian Searle), Freight Books, 2014

Monuments and Statues of Edinburgh (Michael Turnbull), Chambers, 1989

HISTORY

Edinburgh: The Story of a City (Edwin Catford), Hutchinson, 1975

Edinburgh (David Daiches), Hamilton, 1978

Edinburgh: A History of the City (Michael Fry), Pan, 2010

The Place Names of Edinburgh (Stuart Harris), Gordon Wright, 1996

Edinburgh (Alan Massie), Sinclair-Stevenson, 1994

The Edinburgh Encyclopedia (Sandy Mullay), Mainstream, 1996

I Never Knew That About Scotland (Christopher Winn), Ebury Press, 2007

ILLUSTRATED BOOKS

Picturing Scotland: Edinburgh (Callum Cochran & Colin Nutt), Ness Publishing, 2015

Edinburgh (Mark Denton), Frances Lincoln, 2009

Edinburgh: Mapping the City (Christopher Fleet & David MacCanell), Birlinn, 2014

A Work of Beauty (Alexander McCall Smith), Royal Commission on the Ancient & Historical Monuments of Scotland, 2014

A Capital View: The Art of Edinburgh (Alyssa Popiel), Birlinn, 2014

Inside Edinburgh: Discovering the Classic Interiors of Edinburgh (David Torrance & Steven Richmond), Birlinn, 2010

Edinburgh in Old Photographs (Miles Tubb), The History Press, 2011

TRAVEL MEMOIRS

Notes on Old Edinburgh (Isabella L. Bird), CreateSpace Independent Publishing Platform, 2015

Robert Burns in Edinburgh: An Illustrated Guide to Burns' Time in Edinburgh (Jerry Brannigan & John McShane, Waverley Books, 2015

The Edinburgh Companion to Robert Burns (Gerard Carruthers), Edinburgh University Press, 2009

FICTION

The Private Memoirs and Confessions of a Justified Sinner (James Hogg), 1824

44 Scotland Street (Alexander McCall Smith), Polygon/Birlinn, 2005

Friends, Lovers, Chocolate: An Isabel Dalhousie novel (Alexander McCall Smith), Little Brown, 2005

A Good Hanging (Ian Rankin), Century, 1992

The Heart of Midlothian (Walter Scott), James Ballantyne, 1818

The Prime of Miss Jean Brodie (Muriel Spark), MacMillan, 1961

Kidnapped (Robert Louis Stevenson), Cassell and Company, 1886

Trainspotting (Irvine Welsh), Vintage, 1993

WEBSITES

www.thisisEdinburgh.com (Official guide to Edinburgh)

www.onlyinEdinburgh.com (Comprehensive online guide to Edinburgh)

www.Edinburghmuseums.org.uk (Museums and galleries administered by the council)

www.doorsopendays.org.uk (Edinburgh Doors Open Day, when buildings not normally accessible to the public are opened)

www.mercattours.com (Award-winning history walks and ghost tours)

www.greenyondertours.com (Secret Gardens and other Edinburgh walking tours)

www.Edinburghbooktour.com (Literary tour of the city)

www.Edinburghliterarypubtour.co.uk (Literary tour with tipples)

www.Edinburgharchitecture.co.uk (Architecture tours of Edinburgh)

www.secretEdinburghguideblogspot.com (Secret and hidden Edinburgh)

www.Edinburghgems.com (More hidden Edinburgh)

www.oldEdinburghclub.org.uk (Edinburgh's only local history society covering all the city)

www.visitscotland.com (National Tourism Organisation)

www.undiscoveredscotland.co.uk (Encyclopaedic survey of little-known locations)

www.travelinescotland.com (Online journey planner)

www.lothianbuses.com (Bus timetables and route maps)

White Horse Close off the Canongate (see no. 26)

Acknowledgements

For kind permission to take photographs, as well as for arranging access and the provision of information, the following people are most gratefully acknowledged:

James Baird and Liam Kane (Dr. Neil's Garden), Catherine Bromley (Festival Theatre), Jean Burke (Mercat Tours), George Burnett, Ernie Ross and Laura McVie (City Art Centre), Café Royal, Colin Campbell (Moray House School of Education), Corin Christopher (Cameo Cinema), Nicola Cole (Redhall Walled Garden), Jackie Connolly (Lady Haig's Poppy Factory), Rachel Connolly and Russell Clegg (Scottish Historic Buildings Trust), Annabel Cooper (Edinburgh Centre for Carbon Innovation), Lynn Cowan (Edinburgh Sculpture Workshop/Sutherland Hussey Harris Architects), Russell Dempster, Sarah Deters & Darryl Martin (Musical Instrument Museums Edinburgh), Margaretanne Dugan (Gilmerton Cove/Rosslyn Tours), Norman Edwards, Rosalyn Ellis (www.maproom.net), Muzo Emek (Royal Bank of Scotland), Catie Evans, David Farries, Nick Fraser (National Museums Scotland), Colin Gow and Jim McDonald (Museum of Fire), Friends of the Mansfield Traquair Centre, Rev. Neil Gardner & Imogen Gibson (Canongate Kirk), Joseph Gartin & Andrew Johnson (Camera Obscura and World of Illusions), Caroline Gerard (Friends of Warriston Cemetery), Mike Gerrard, Karen Glen and Thomas Kirk (Scottish Courts), Rachel Goddard and Gavrielle Kirk-Cohen (RZSS Edinburgh Zoo), Stephen Graham and Dominique Cottee, Annie Greiffenberg (Royal Edinburgh Community Gardens), James Hamilton (Wilfred Owen in Edinburgh Project), Robert Hamilton (www.onlyinedinburgh.com), Gemma Henderson, Victoria Garrington and Katy Allison (City of Edinburgh Council Museums and Galleries Service), Wendy Henderson (St. Andrew's & St. George's West Church), David Hicks (Edinburgh World Heritage), Bert Hutchings & Mirella Yandoli (Greyfriars Kirk), Agnieszka Jablonska (Signet Library Colonnades/Heritage Portfolio), Jean Keltie (Old St. Paul's Scottish Episcopal Church), Tamara Key (National Galleries of Scotland), Pete Lindsell (Colinton Parish Church), Kay Leslie (St. Mary's Metropolitan Cathedral), James Linkogle, William Lytle (Edinburgh Books), Andrea Longson (Advocates Library), Doug MacBeath (Museum on the Mound), Laura MacCallum (Royal Yacht Britannia), Kim Macpherson (National Portrait Gallery), Terry Marsh, David Mcleod and Aaron Fleming (Royal College of Surgeons), Roderick McDonald, Sally and Alf McFarlane (The Counter), Alison Melton (Summerhall Distillery/Pickering's Gin), Brian Mills (People's Story Museum), Douglas Mitchell, Father Dermot Morrin (Chapel of St. Albert the Great), Joanne Morrison and Alan Whitson (City of Edinburgh Methodist Church), Cameron Pirie (The Cadies & Witchery Tours), Marek Pryjomko, Eugene Quinn, Elaine & Richard Reese, Antonia Reeve Photography, Jessica Rideout (The Real Mary King's Close), John Robertson (Faculty of Advocates), Laura Robertson (National Records of Scotland), Katy Robinson (The Georgian House), Mark Rowley (Prestonfield Hotel), Bob Sharp (Cramond), Ian Smith (Scottish Pictures), Douglas Somerset (Magdalen Chapel/Scottish Reformation Society), Suzie Stark (St. Cuthbert's Parish Church), Horst Stein, Lesley Stewart (Edinburgh Castle), Nicky Stonehill (Stonehill Salt PR Ltd.), Paul Strachan (Drumsheugh Baths Club), David Taylor (The Elephant House), Peter Taylor (Friends of Corstorphine Hill), Anna Thomson, Anne Turner (St. Triduana's Chapel and St. Margaret's Parish Church), Sam Van Kempen, Kathryn Walsh (The Hub/Edinburgh International Festival), Catherine Walker and Gillian Weller (War Poets Collection), Shane Waltener, Colin Waters (Scottish Poetry Library), Amy Wilkins (Polwarth Parish Church), Lynsey Wilson (Royal Botanic Garden Edinburgh), Maggie Wilson, Kirsten Cowie and Ailsa Deans (National Museums Scotland).

Particular thanks to Ekke Wolf for creating the layout and editing the photos, and Franz Hanns for creating the cover.

Thanks also to my mother Mary, brother Adrian and his wife Lisa Blanchflower, and great cousin James Dickinson for bringing many interesting items of Edinburgh news to my attention, to Richard Tinkler for managing my websites, and Martina Bauer for design work.

Last but definitely not least, very special thanks to Roswitha Reisinger for her tireless support of my work and her wonderful company on this adventure we call life, and to my late father Trevor for inspiring me to track down things unique, hidden and unusual in the first place.

1st Edition published by The Urban Explorer, 2016
A division of Duncan J. D. Smith
contact@duncanjdsmith.com
www.onlyinguides.com
www.duncanjdsmith.com

Graphic design: Stefan Fuhrer
Typesetting and picture editing: Ekke Wolf, www.typic.at
Cover design: Franz Hanns
Maps: Edinburgh base maps © www.maproom.net
Printed and bound by GraphyCems, Spain

ISBN 978-3-9504218-0-4